CW01648535

'In a provocative blend of Bourdieu's sociolog [illegible] contemporary theory, Hanne Tange reframes th [illegible] education. Explicitly taking practices as a categ [illegible] of international education, Tange writes with insight of the "hidden curriculum" whereby international teaching involves the transfer of practical knowledge from academic staff to students. Her emphasis on tacit as well as formalised types of knowledge is a welcome corrective to the often sterile debate concerning "intercultural competence" which too often occludes critical analysis of the concrete course activities and the socialisation processes involved in the field of international education. Read this book and profit!'

Professor Anthony Elliott, *Dean of External Engagement and Executive Director of the Jean Monnet Centre of Excellence at the University of South Australia*

'At last, a book that treats university lecturers as key thinkers and shapers of the internationalisation of higher education! Nested in a scholarly analysis of the linguistic, disciplinary, institutional and policy features of a global learning environment, this book uses rich empirical data from three major studies to give voice to the teachers engaged in curriculum and module design, classroom activities, multicultural teamwork, and assessment – the practices that have transformed international education in the last decades. An added advantage is that the study's semi-peripheral location in Europe offers a refreshingly critical perspective on the traditional US/UK nexus of "globalisation".'

Susan Wright, *Professor of Educational Anthropology, Danish School of Education, Aarhus University, Denmark*

'This book provides a substantial tool for understanding internationalisation in higher education in a larger context: its development, incentives, political and institutional backgrounds, essentially by insisting on the role of academic staff as central agents. The author's historical, social, and didactic overview together with a clear methodological approach provides a transdisciplinary analysis of concepts too often left undefined, despite their high strategic value.'

Professor Hanne Leth Andersen, *Vice-Chancellor of Roskilde University, Denmark*

Teaching Practices in a Global Learning Environment

This book examines teaching practices in international education, focusing on two significant meanings of the notion of 'practice': the concrete activities used by university lecturers and the role of education as a platform for transferring particular skills or approaches.

In addition to discussing techniques involved in programme design, curricular development, course activities, multicultural teamwork, and examination, the author explores the idea of the lecturer as an actor communicating practices, considering the role and responsibility of academic staff in the development of successful international education.

With attention to the importance of the context of internationalisation, the book draws on research from two major research projects, presenting extensive interview material with teaching staff engaged in international education and projects of internationalisation. Combining the approaches of 'pragmatism' and practice theory, as developed by Bourdieu and Schatzki, among others, *Teaching Practices in a Global Learning Environment* addresses themes including the international-ness of academic disciplines, the biographies of international educators, and language issues emerging in international education. As such, it will appeal to scholars across the social sciences and policy makers with interests in pedagogy, internationalisation, and higher education.

Hanne Tange is Associate Professor of English and Global Studies in the Department of Culture and Learning at Aalborg University, Denmark.

Global Connections

Series Editor: Robert Holton

Global Connections builds on the multi-dimensional and continuously expanding interest in globalisation, focusing on 'connectedness' and providing accessible, concrete studies across a broad range of areas such as social and cultural life, and economic, political and technological activities. Interdisciplinary in approach, the series moves beyond abstract generalities and stereotypes: 'Global' is considered in the broadest sense of the word, embracing connections between different nations, regions and localities, including activities that are trans-national, and trans-local in scope; 'connections' refers to movements of people, ideas, resources, and all forms of communication as well as the opportunities and constraints faced in making, engaging with, and sometimes resisting globalisation.

Titles in the series:

The Socio-Political Practice of Human Rights
Between the Universal and the Particular
Kiran Kaur Grewal

The Global Repositioning of Japanese Religions
An integrated approach
Ugo Dessi

Civilized Rebels
An Inside Story of the West's Retreat from Global Power
Dennis Smith

Teaching Practices in a Global Learning Environment
An Interdisciplinary Take on International Education
Hanne Tange

For more information about this series, please visit:
www.routledge.com/Global-Connections/book-series/ASHSER1306

Teaching Practices in a Global Learning Environment

An Interdisciplinary Take on International Education

Hanne Tange

Routledge
Taylor & Francis Group
LONDON AND NEW YORK

First published 2021
by Routledge
2 Park Square, Milton Park, Abingdon, Oxon OX14 4RN

and by Routledge
605 Third Avenue, New York, NY 10017

First issued in paperback 2022

Routledge is an imprint of the Taylor & Francis Group, an informa business

© 2021 Hanne Tange

The right of Hanne Tange to be identified as author of this work has been asserted by her in accordance with sections 77 and 78 of the Copyright, Designs and Patents Act 1988.

All rights reserved. No part of this book may be reprinted or reproduced or utilised in any form or by any electronic, mechanical, or other means, now known or hereafter invented, including photocopying and recording, or in any information storage or retrieval system, without permission in writing from the publishers.

Trademark notice: Product or corporate names may be trademarks or registered trademarks, and are used only for identification and explanation without intent to infringe.

Publisher's Note
The publisher has gone to great lengths to ensure the quality of this reprint but points out that some imperfections in the original copies may be apparent.

British Library Cataloguing-in-Publication Data
A catalogue record for this book is available from the British Library

Library of Congress Cataloging-in-Publication Data
Names: Tange, Hanne, 1971– author. | Routledge (Firm)
Title: Teaching practices in a global learning environment:
an interdisciplinary take on international education / Hanne Tange.
Other titles: Global connections.
Description: New York : Routledge, 2020. |
Series: Global connections |
Includes bibliographical references and index.
Identifiers: LCCN 2020021333 (print) | LCCN 2020021334 (ebook) |
ISBN 9781138225961 (Hardback) | ISBN 9781315398662 (eBook)
Subjects: LCSH: International education. | Global method of teaching.
Classification: LCC LC1090 .T26 2020 (print) |
LCC LC1090 (ebook) | DDC 370.116–dc23
LC record available at https://lccn.loc.gov/2020021333
LC ebook record available at https://lccn.loc.gov/2020021334

ISBN 13: 978-0-367-56904-4 (pbk)
ISBN 13: 978-1-138-22596-1 (hbk)
ISBN 13: 978-1-315-39866-2 (ebk)

DOI: 10.4324/9781315398662

Typeset in Times New Roman
by Newgen Publishing UK

Contents

Figures

Tables

Acknowledgements

The book builds on research conducted over an extended period of time, from my first appointment as English teacher at a Danish engineering college in 2002 to the present where as lecturer in an English-medium program, I find myself caught up in the politics of 'de-internationalisation'. It is impossible to name all individuals who have helped the project along through contributions as collaborators, informants, critical readers, and colleagues at the universities of Aarhus and Aalborg. But without your feedback and support this book would have been impossible to write.

A special thanks to my partner in crime, Lisanne Wilken, who was present at Klitgaarden, Skagen, when in February 2016 I made the decision to write this book. Thanks are also due to my co-author Sharon Millar, who helped transform my loose ideas of knowledge geographies into the method used for contextual mapping, to members of my project team – Margrethe Petersen, Tanja Kanne Wadsholt, Peter Kastberg, and Mette Ginnerskov Dahlberg, and to my colleague Kirsten Jæger for the conversations inspiring my theory-building.

Jesper Oehlenschläger helped transform rough sketches into the three beautiful drawings that are used to illustrate my build-up of the global practice-scape – thank you very much for this. I should also like to acknowledge the contributions of Neil Jordan and Astrid Salt, Routledge. You have made my task as an author so much more manageable.

Finally, I want to mention family and friends. When I decided to write a monograph I was aware that this would steal a lot of time. And yes – I have dedicated weekends and holidays to the project that could have been spent with you. Thank you for your support and understanding throughout the years – without you I would never have made it.

Part I

Introduction

Teaching Practices in a Global Learning Environment is a book about the practice of international education. The book comes out of a period characterised by a dramatic growth in student and staff mobility, the rapid expansion of international degree programmes within and beyond the English-speaking world, and educational policies and reforms catering for the provision of 'global' education. This has inspired an ever-growing body of literature dedicated to international higher education, which may prompt the critical reader to ask: What more is there to add? Departing from the position of a practice researcher, the author retorts that this is the moment where one can truly begin to grasp what more precisely processes of 'internationalisation' have been doing to teaching and learning in higher education. In other words, we have reached the point where it becomes possible to reflect on the nature of the changes that have occurred over the past 20 to 25 years. Key actors in the transformation have been the university lecturers, who might originally have volunteered or been pushed into the international classroom, and who subsequently have had to develop skills enabling them to reach out to a student cohort composed of individuals from diverse socio-cultural, educational, and linguistic backgrounds. The literature has stressed the necessity of training international educators, and more often than not, the task has been given to cross-cultural consultants and university Learning Labs, who do not always possess the practical insights accumulated by teachers working in an international learning environment. As a result, pedagogic advice becomes detached from the actual teaching of international courses, relying on a standardised vocabulary of 'intercultural competence', 'cultural awareness', and 'open-mindedness'. This book seeks to change that, allowing university lecturers to speak about their experience of international education. Hence, the author will work in an inductive fashion, departing from the practical understandings and meanings communicated by academic staff.

As reflected in the title, this is a book about teaching practices. One meaning of *teaching practice* has been inspired by practice theorist Theodore Schatzki's notion of *Doings & Sayings*, as presented in *The Practice Turn in Contemporary Theory* (2001). This challenges the author to move beyond empty phrases such as 'intercultural competence' and 'inclusion', using lecturers' accounts of course action and interaction to explain how events unfold within the international classroom. The book will explore concrete activities such as designing a course, compiling a syllabus, lecturing to a diverse student audience, facilitating multicultural teamwork, and exam preparation, presenting the dilemmas faced by the international educators as well as solutions proposed by the teachers interviewed. A second understanding of *teaching practice* builds on the perception of study programmes as socialisation into specific disciplinary and institutional communities. Here the author draws on Pierre Bourdieu's conceptualisation of academia as a social field where actors are evaluated on their ability to master particular scientific methods, disciplinary canons, study skills, and linguistic repertoires. As the principal agents involved in assessment, the lecturers play a key role in the academic socialisation of learners, which suggests that international teaching involves the transfer of practical knowledge from academic staff to students. Successful socialisation demands an awareness of tacit as well as formalised types of knowledge, and a way to explore this 'hidden curriculum' is by engaging in conversation with university teachers. By looking at international education from the lecturer's point of view, one can thus obtain a deep understanding of the dynamics in international education, filling a gap in the current body of literature.

Finally, the book addresses the question of internationalisation through the lens of a British-educated scholar working within a Continental European context. This is important because it allows for a critical examination of basic assumptions and beliefs found in literature originating within an Anglo-American educational tradition. At the same time, research drawing on internationalisation within a Continental European university context draws readers' attention to new themes, highlighting problems caused by the current tendency to place the diverse manifestations of international education realised in the UK, Australia, US, Northern and Central Europe within the same generic category of 'Western'. The author's situatedness at a Danish provincial university inevitably influences her interpretation of the empirical data, which consists of Danish material mainly, although this will be complemented by an extensive review of literature on international education as well as material collected in other contexts, including the UK. However, the author should like to argue for Denmark as an interesting case for internationalisation, placed in a semi-peripheral position, being Western but not Anglo-American, using English rather extensively, but not with the taken-for-grantedness characteristic of countries that have English as their first language. Accordingly, an empirical investigation of international education in a country such as Denmark enlightens readers in a number of areas: First, internationalisation processes are very visible in Danish institutional settings because they request a language shift from Danish into another language (mainly English). There can be no 'business as usual' for Danish university lecturers who have to change their linguistic and communicative practice upon their entry into the international classroom. A second important factor is recruitment. Danish higher education remains free to students from EU member states, which means that international programmes tend to attract students from other EU member states rather than fee-paying overseas students. This is different to the forms of internationalisation typical of countries such as UK and Australia, prompting the author to wonder if the ideological notion of a 'Europe of Knowledge' can be realised in such a setting. Third, in terms of academic knowledge production Denmark occupies a position that is central compared to non-Western countries such as Russia, China, and Brazil, but peripheral compared to English-speaking countries such as the US and UK. Looking at the knowledge presented in international education, Danish data enable us to open the category of 'Western', asking whether the curricular frames of reference offered to students in international education favour particular geographies such as Western Europe, Anglo-America, or a generalised 'North'. A final lesson relates to language. The shift from teaching in the first language (e.g. Danish or Dutch) into 'Global English' is a significant organisational change for non-English-speaking institutions, inspiring a substantial body of literature. The concerns voiced in relation to language could be equally relevant to international educators at English-speaking institutions, but the linguistic dimension to internationalisation has only been dealt with superficially within this context, reflecting the tendency among some native speakers to take English for granted as the sole medium for teaching and learning.

To sum up, the book *Teaching Practices in a Global Learning Environment* contributes new knowledge in four key areas:

- The author assumes a position of reflexivity, acknowledging what has been happening in the research on and practice of international education within the past 20 to 25 years, but also looking ahead, asking how the field may develop in the years to come.
- The protagonists of the book are international educators, who are key actors in institutional processes of internationalisation, yet relatively silent in the literature. This gap will be filled here.
- The focal point of the research is practice, both in the form of concrete course activities and the socialisation processes involved when students seek admission into new disciplinary communities. No book has addressed lecturers' role as 'teachers of practice', which seems essential to the success or failure of international students.
- The approach is comparative, using a Danish university setting as the point of departure. This allows for a double perspective, enabling the author to compare the themes identified by scholars based within English-speaking contexts to the experiences conveyed by Continental European researchers and practitioners.

Note on the text

Interview quotations: The book incorporates a substantial number of interview excerpts. The author has attempted to reproduce the material in the manner most loyal to the informant's original style and structure, but in some cases words have been inserted to clarify the meaning. These insertions are marked by square brackets.

Translation: 53 interviews were originally performed in Danish and quotes from these have been translated into English by the author. Translated quotes are marked with (DA) in the text.

Capitalisation: The author uses capitals when referring to faculties (Humanities) and academic disciplines (Anthropology, Biology), but lower case for references to individual scientists (an anthropologist, a biologist). Geographic and socio-cultural reference points such as 'the global North' and 'Western' are capitalised except in quotations where lower case has been chosen for the original text.

1 Researching teaching practices

Why a section on methodology?

Within the last decade, several monographs have been published on teaching and learning in international education, including Simon Marginson and Erlenawati Sawir, *Ideas for Intercultural Education* (2011), Betty Leask, *Internationalizing the Curriculum* (2015), Jude Carroll, *Tools for Teaching in an Educationally Mobile World* (2015), and David Killick, *Internationalization and Diversity in Higher Education* (2017). The books share a concern with developing educational practices, foregrounding the specific needs and issues emerging within a globalised learning environment. What is also characteristic is the authors' lack of clarity about the empirical foundation underpinning authors' notions of 'good' international education. As a result, it becomes difficult to distinguish educational researchers' ideological beliefs about pedagogy from the actual work carried out by academic practitioners acting and interacting in the international classroom.

Transparency about research design and methodology matters if readers are to accept a text as a piece of research, as this enables them to evaluate the quality of the work involved. Transparency seems particularly important when writing about the field of higher education where authors may simultaneously be positioned as participants in and observers of teaching practice. Accordingly, the present writer finds it necessary to provide an account of her methodological reflections, departing from three questions:

1. What is the researcher's position in relation to the field of international higher education?
2. What empirical material has informed the author's account of educational practices?
3. How were the empirical insights produced through research transformed into a book on international teaching practices?

Positioning the researcher

In *Homo Academicus* (1988), Pierre Bourdieu foregrounds the dilemma of the educational sociologist, who may pretend that she can occupy a position of objective detachment from her object of study and yet, as participant in the academic field, is inevitably biased from past experiences with and present stakes in field battles over disciplinary authority, power, and prestige. According to Wacquant, Bourdieu resolves his dilemma by insisting on *reflexivity*, resting on a 'self-analysis of the sociologist as cultural producer and a reflection on the sociohistorical conditions of possibility of a science of society' (Bourdieu/Wacquant 1992, 36). To avoid colouring his scientific gaze by preconceived theories and ideologies, Bourdieu claims to be working from the position of a *sociological practitioner*, insisting that pictures of social reality such as those presented in publications such as *Homo Academic* and *The State Nobility* be grounded in empirical research (Hammerslev/Hansen 2009, 11).

The present author's approach has been influenced by Pierre Bourdieu's reflexive sociology in three ways: First, *empirical work* has been central to the identification and development of the teaching practices highlighted in subsequent chapters of the book. Inevitably, the research was in its initial stage shaped by the researcher's disciplinary interests and knowledge, but these, as Charmaz (2006, 17) notes, 'provide a place to *start*, not to *end*'. Any preconceived notions and theories have been examined carefully in relation to themes emerging from the empirical analyses, and, where necessary, modified or abandoned. A second guiding principle is the condition of *ontological and epistemological openness*. Levin and Greenwood (2011, 28) recommend that openness be realised through 'multiperspective research', 'methodological diversity', and 'inclusiveness of stakeholders', granting to researchers the freedom to choose whatever conceptual and methodological tools they deem suitable for investigating action and interaction within their chosen field of study. Grounded Theorists present openness as a state of *not knowing*, emphasising that social scientists' conceptualisation be based on analyses of the empirical material and not predetermined by preconceived ideas about constructs such as race, class, and nationality (Glaser/Strauss 2008, Charmaz 2006). A final element is the conscious choice of a *qualitative research design* and *methodology*. Such a decision has implications for the researcher's position, placing her firmly within rather than outside the field of study. Denzin and Lincoln (2011, 3) observe:

> *Qualitative research* is a situated activity that locates the observer in the world. Qualitative research consists of a set of interpretive, material practices that make the world visible. These practices transform the world. They turn the world into a series of representations, including fieldnotes, interviews, conversations, photographs, recordings and memos to the self.

Denzin and Lincoln's characterisation of qualitative research as a situated activity highlights the researcher's dilemma as a social scientist who seeks detachment from, and yet, by virtue of her function as ethnographer and interviewer, cannot avoid being present in the field of study. This paradox becomes particularly visible in higher education research which, Clegg and Stevenson (2013, 7) note, is produced by scholars who, 'by virtue of their position [in academia] have insider knowledge of the systems they are researching'.

The question of *positionality* may be approached through a reflection on the roles that the researcher performs as part of her endeavour to produce, interpret, and represent teaching practices. Denzin and Lincoln (2011, 4) have compared the pursuit of the qualitative researcher to that of a *bricoleur* or *quilt-maker*, who brings together a diversity of theoretical perspectives and empirical sources with the ambition of constructing a specific account of social reality. Yet the task of quilt-making can only be undertaken at the point where all pieces have been created, and involves the transformation of the material into some form of representation, in this case a monograph. This stage is preceded by knowledge production where the present author found herself performing two roles in particular, namely those of a *participant observer* and *sociological practitioner*. As regards the *participant observer,* the author acknowledges that she has continuously been present in the field of international higher education since commencing her research in 2007, which has undoubtedly shaped her understanding of teaching and learning practices. Particularly at the early stage of the research, observations and interviews were conducted at institutions where the author was employed, and this research is best characterised as 'self-ethnography', with all the challenges that such a methodology presents (Alvesson 2003). The second role of *sociological practitioner* partly reflects a conscious decision to obtain knowledge from empirical sources, partly the author's lack of sociological training, which meant that she had to develop practical knowledge about interviewing and documentary analysis while actually using such methods to conduct the research. Hence, the researcher's methodology is best described as a process of *Learning by Doing*, in the pragmatic tradition of John Dewey (Corbin/Strauss 2008, 1–5). Two additional roles emerged from the educational scholar's position as insider within the field of higher education. First, the author found herself acting in the capacity of an educational consultant, whom informants might enlist to discuss, support, or evaluate a particular teaching practice. As noted by Clegg and Stevenson (2013), informants respond to the identity of the researcher as an academic insider, treating the research interview as an opportunity to seek confirmation, voice their criticism, or obtain an expert opinion on international education. Second, the author would occasionally perform the role of a critical researcher, contributing as a specialist to the political discussion of English-medium education in Denmark. While justifiable as action research (Levin/Greenwood 2013), such engagement becomes problematic when undertaken simultaneously with interview research. Informants conscious of the author's media appearances may have been inspired to raise specific concerns, which means that the empirical material will have to be read with a critical eye. Accordingly, the unique experiences conveyed by a single informant must be assessed in relation to the general picture emerging from the systematic examination of a large collection of interviews and documents.

Collecting teaching practices

In the ideal world, research projects depart from either a theoretical conceptualisation or the assumption that a close study of a particular practice will yield new knowledge to the empirical scholar. According to Bernard (2006, 70) reality is more chaotic, with the ethnographer's work shaped by factors such as personal interest, disciplinary training, resources, access opportunities, and the promise that an inquiry offers in terms of scientific discovery. Since commencing her work in 2007, the author's journey has progressed from an initial piece of convenience research to a large-scale project, involving qualitative research interviews in multiple sites, documentary analysis of material collected from informants, and comprehensive desk research of literature published on international higher education. The original motivation came from the author's involvement with staff development at a Danish engineering college, which between 2002 and 2004 saw a dramatic growth in the number of international exchange students. The participant observations made at this institution were later published in the form of a self-ethnographic account, which used critical incidents to reflect on how a process of internationalisation was experienced by academic and administrative staff (Tange 2008). Self-ethnography carries a high risk of subjectivity so in order to continue her work in the field of international education the author found it necessary to complement this early research with an empirical investigation that allowed for greater distance between the researcher and her object of study. The principal research method has been qualitative research interviews, supplemented by documentary analysis and desk research.

The book *Teaching Practices in a Global Learning Environment* builds on 68 semi-structured qualitative interviews, amounting to approximately 65 hours of recorded conversations, excluding any small-talk preceding and following the interviews. The interview research consists of three separate inquiries:

- 2007–9: Danish university lecturers' experiences with English-medium teaching (36 interviews)
- 2010: British university lecturers' experiences with international education (7 interviews)
- 2012–14: Pedagogic practices in four international MA programmes (25 interviews).

The first investigation focuses on a comparison between Danish- and English-medium teaching, asking informants about any difference that they experience between education performed in their native language of Danish and addressing a group of domestic students, and an international course taught in English to a mixed class of Danish and international students. The sample counted 36 informants who were located at five institutions and represented the subject areas of Engineering, Business, Life Science, Social Science, and Humanities. The language theme meant that only academic staff with teaching ability in Danish were able to participate, which, in hindsight, seems problematic given that this excludes the significant number of international staff teaching in English. An additional concern is the interviewer's request that informants compare 'Danish' to 'international' classes. Arguably, this may have prompted informants to exaggerate the importance of linguistic and cultural diversity, leading to a representation of international students as an exotic 'Other', defined by deviation from the 'normality' embodied by domestic learners. The British interview study is best described as a continuation of the first Danish inquiry. The author wanted to test if the same picture of international education would emerge in an educational setting that took for granted the use of English as a teaching medium and used the opportunity of a research visit to the UK to conduct interviews with seven British-employed lecturers from Natural Science, Business, and Humanities. The findings were compared to the Danish results, enabling an identification of similarities and differences in the way British and Danish-employed academics describe international education. The third interview study shifts the focus away from cultural and linguistic difference to the practices actors engage in when performing the activity of teaching. Following the analysis of interview data produced in the first Danish and British inquiries, the author became aware of the possibility that she may have constructed a specific picture of reality by asking informants about the difference between actors and situations labelled as 'local' and 'international', respectively. To avoid this problem she decided to rethink the themes brought up in the third study, removing from her interview guide all references to international education and students. The third interview inquiry was undertaken as part of a collective project on internationalisation as social practice at one Danish case university (see Wilken/Tange 2011). The project involved four MA programmes, which had been designed as international, interdisciplinary courses, bringing together disciplines from Humanities, Natural Science, Social Science, and Business. Twenty-five academics were involved in the research and the sample includes international as well as local staff. In the interviews, informants were asked to describe their teaching practices, departing from themes such as *classroom teaching*, *teamwork*, *project work*, and *exams*. In addition, interviewees were probed about their academic discipline and contextual framing.

Documentary analyses is a broad category of investigation, which ranges from the close reading of policy documents to the identification of practices based on sources such as institutional strategy papers, study regulations, course curricula, and academic literature (Tight 2013, 145–6). The author became aware of documents as a possible empirical source on teaching practices in the course of the third interview study where several informants referred to texts they had produced in order to clarify a specific course assignment or exam format. Picking up on such cues, the researcher asked for any material relating to teaching and learning, which led to a systematic collection of course descriptions, syllabi, and lecturer CVs. In addition to materials requisitioned directly from academic staff, the text corpus includes a range of institution-specific documents such as course curricula, programme descriptions, departmental and institutional web pages, university policy papers, and leaflets produced to recruit students from other institutions, disciplines, and countries. A third type of empirical data was documents published by governmental institutions, national/international media, intergovernmental organisations, and think tanks. These texts include regulatory frameworks (national and European), intergovernmental agreements (e.g. the Bologna Declaration), databases on academic migration (e.g. UNESCO, EUROSTAT), and media stories addressing topics such as international education, student mobility, and language politics. The external documents are important because they provide a foundation for the examination of structural conditions in international higher education, enabling a general discussion of migration flows, Englishisation, and the ongoing internationalisation of the academic disciplines.

A final method for collecting lecturers' practical knowledge is desk research. Glaser and Strauss (2008) suggest that library material be considered a source of empirical data in Social Science because it carries the advantage of accessibility in situations where: 1) 'the researcher is separated from his data by spatial obstacles' (176); and 2) the researcher has reached the stage of an investigation where 'he may already have left the field, and cannot fill the gaps in his data' (177). Both reasons are relevant in relation to the present work. First, the book *Teaching Practices* aims to provide an account of the general changes that academic staff associate with the globalisation of teaching and learning practices, which, ideally, demands empirical research conducted in multiple socio-cultural and linguistic contexts. Second, the teaching practices identified in empirical data were not always sufficiently detailed, which meant that the researcher required additional knowledge in these areas. To answer these challenges, a comprehensive review of academic literature was conducted in relation to each of the nine themes used to structure this book. Arguably, this has resulted in an extended context, allowing the author to compare the first-hand accounts derived from the Danish and British data with other educational scholars' studies of teaching practice in English-speaking countries, Continental Europe, and South East Asia.

Representing 'international education'

The term *representation* describes the process of transforming the empirical material into analytical or conceptual themes that can subsequently be disseminated through writing or speech. Within a discipline such as Anthropology the researcher sets out with the ambition of writing an *ethnography*, which brings together all the practices and relationships observed within a particular community or 'culture' (see Spradley 1979). In comparison, Grounded Theory, in the format proposed by Kathy Charmaz (2006), presupposes that writing occurs simultaneously with data production and analysis and is treated as a *draft*, which can be presented, revised, and extended in response to new empirical discoveries, literature research, and conversations with informants, colleagues, or stakeholders within the field of study. The author's approach has been characterised by draft writing, of the kind described by Charmaz (2006, 151ff.). Between 2007 and 2019, papers were produced continuously, enabling the author to test key themes and conceptualisations through a variety of formats, including journal articles, conference papers, debriefings with informants, and seminars with university managers, International Office personnel, academic staff, and students. The assemblage of the pieces into a book on *Teaching Practices* marks the end of the journey, weaving together the themes and reflections that have emerged from the empirical work.

As explained in the previous section, the production of the empirical material was separated into several stages, which has affected the development of the analytical framework. To explain the analytical process leading to the identification of the practices explored in the present volume the author will therefore distinguish between the original comparative study, which comprised the first 36 Danish interviews and seven British; and the second, practice-oriented inquiry, which involved 25 interviews as well as a text corpus. The general approach used to process the empirical data may be described as a form of *taxonomic analysis* (Spradley 1979, 132ff.) where a limited number of domains are established on the basis of an initial reading of the transcribed interviews. Domains are subsequently explored through the identification and ordering of themes and sub-themes into a hierarchical tree diagram, which displays both the density of particular (sub-)themes and any relationships between them. Table 1.1 provides an example of a tree diagram from interview study 1, listing sub-themes relating to the theme *affects teaching* within the domain of language.

Table 1.1 Analytical themes and sub-themes

Theme	*Sub-theme*	*Sub-theme*
Affects teaching	Comprehension	
	Information	Access to knowledge
		Literature
		Terminology
	Interaction	No difference
		More interaction
		Less interaction
	Language problems	Translation clusters
		Resource persons
		Written English
		Questions
		Openness about

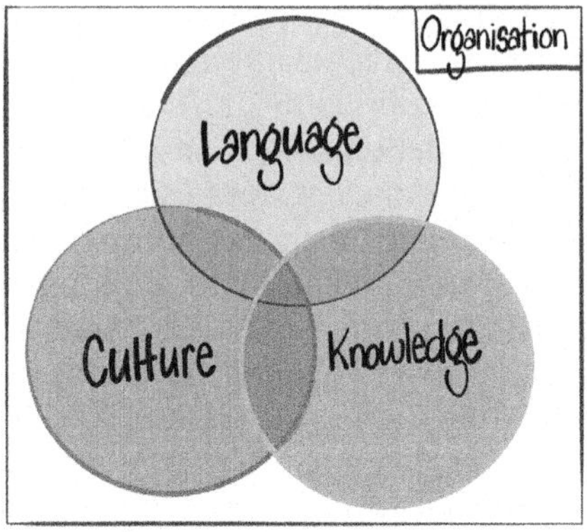

Figure 1.1 Domains

The first inquiry asked informants to compare international and domestic classes, which may explain why two key domains, *language* and *culture*, feature prominently in the empirical analysis. To these were added the domains of *knowledge* and *organisation*, which foreground the importance of disciplinary, educational, and institutional environments to the way informants experience international education. The relationship between the four domains has been visualised in Figure 1.1, which shows language, culture, and knowledge as interconnected elements within the frame constituted by *organisation*, which is here used as a broad category involving all functions within the academic system that possess the power to define, regulate, and evaluate teachers' practice. Examples are study boards, departmental councils, faculty management, and institutional policy-makers.

The second interview study departed from an understanding of academic practice inspired by the reflexive sociology employed by Pierre Bourdieu in publications such as *Homo Academicus* (1988). Instead of building on preconceived notions such as 'domestic' or 'international', the analytical framework was developed from informants' description of teaching and learning practices, which produced a different picture of the social reality that is international education. Six domains were used to structure the thematic analysis: *Field*, *Epistemologies*, *Practical knowledge*, *Asymmetries*, *Power*, and *Reproduction*. The naming of the domains reflects the influence of Bourdieu, but the concepts are here used as *thinking tools*, suggesting possible interpretations of, rather than fixing the meanings derived from, the empirical material. In addition to descriptions of informants' practical work, the analysis contains a global dimension, highlighting to what extent informants treat academia as multi-sited and multi-scalar, connecting to diverse socio-cultural, educational, and scientific contexts through their choice of literature, participation in disciplinary communities, and migration experiences. By examining documents such as lecturer CVs and course syllabi, the researcher was able to expand on the analytical themes of contextual framing and academic mobility, highlighting how staff located at a specific university in Denmark engage through teaching and research with a range of local, national, and international geographies.

Simultaneous with the process of data production and analysis the author published a series of articles, which address themes such as 'difference' between Danish- and English-medium education (Tange 2010, 2012a, 2012b), intercultural encounters between Danish lecturers and international students (Tange/Jensen 2012, Tange/Kastberg 2013), academic norms (Tange 2016), curricular contexts (Tange/Millar 2016), and socialisation processes (Tange 2019). Yet the article format proved limiting in terms of the number of themes and educational settings that could be addressed in a single piece of writing. The author therefore sought to produce an extended text that might account in a more satisfying way for the complex relationships between structural conditions at the institutional, national, supernational, and global levels and the actual teaching practices performed and developed by academics acting in the capacity of international educators. To accomplish this, the book *Teaching Practices in a Global Learning Environment* has been divided into four main sections:

- Part I contains chapters on research design, methodology, conceptual and theoretical influences. Ideally, the theoretical inspiration could have been left out because of the author's claim to develop themes suggested by the empirical material. Yet the concepts of field, practice, and change are fundamental thinking tools and useful background knowledge for readers new to this way of studying higher education.
- Part II examines four structural conditions that have shaped the way actors perceive and engage with internationalisation processes. They are: *globalisation* (Chapter 3), *academic disciplines* (Chapter 4), *mobility* (Chapter 5), and *the English language* (Chapter 6). Arguably, the combined effect of the four has transformed academia from a national to a global field, persuading actors of their need to perform in the role of 'international' scholars and educators.
- Part III zooms in on specific teaching practices, examining action and interaction relating to the *design* of international programmes (Chapter 7), academic *rules and routines* (Chapter 8), *curricular contexts* (Chapter 9), *multicultural teamwork* (Chapter 10), and *assessment* (Chapter 11). Themes were selected because of their density in the empirical material, and the author does not seek to claim these as the only teaching practices relevant to the performance of international education.

- The concluding section brings the structural conditions and teaching practices together, foregrounding relationships within the field of international education. Based on such *quilt-making* the author addresses the question of internationalisation as social change, asking if lecturing staff rather than managers and policy-writers should be considered the principal agents transforming teaching and learning.

2 Theories and practices

Teaching practices in globalised world

I have already defined *teaching practices* as a phenomenon involving both concrete actions taken by teachers in order to enhance learning and a process of socialisation facilitating students' internalisation of the practical knowledge necessary to perform successfully within a given programme. This conceptualisation is influenced by Gert Biesta (2009), who defines as the functions of education: 1) *qualification,* i.e. 'providing [learners] with the knowledge skills and understanding … that allow them to "do something"' (39); 2) *socialisation*, i.e. 'the many ways in which, through education, we become members of and part of particular social, cultural and political "orders"' (40); and 3) *subjectification*, i.e. the 'process of individualisation' that enables individuals to become aware of themselves as agents acting within, against or independent from social, cultural, and political orders (40). Underpinning such an understanding is the perception of education as multi-formed and multi-sited. An inquiry into the teaching practices of international education will therefore need a theoretical framework that can simultaneously embrace the *actual activities* undertaken by teachers and students in the classroom, the process of *teaching* the explicit or tacit knowledge required to succeed within a discipline or programme, and the various *contexts* within which teachers' performance of higher education is situated. The present chapter seeks to establish such a foundation, building on the theories proposed by Pierre Bourdieu, Theodore Schatzki, and John Dewey.

Nicolini (2012) has provided a useful introduction to practice theory, identifying as common traits to the sociologists and philosophers referred to as 'practice theorists' a concern with *activity and agency,* the *habitual (re)production of practice*, the *material dimension* to social life, and an acceptance that *knowledge is embedded* within specific sites and situations. Nicolini draws on Reckwitz (2002), who lists as key elements: 'Body, mind, things, knowledge, discourse, structure/process, the agent and the shifted status of these' (250). Nicolini and Reckwitz agree on a broad conceptualisation of practice theory, bringing together a diverse group of social and cultural theorists, including Michel Foucault, Pierre Bourdieu, Judith Butler, Anthony Giddens, Bruno

Latour, Harold Garfinkel, Theodore Schatzki, and Ludwig Wittgenstein. Similarly, Bain and Mueller (2016) insist that practice theory be regarded as a unity-in-diversity, describing the tradition as a 'broad polysemic field' (33). The pluralist nature of practice theory has resulted in a 'programmatic form of eclecticism', in the words of Nicolini (2012, 215), encouraging researchers to compile their own packages of theoretical concepts and methods. Shared by all is the emphasis on *empirical inquiry*, which means that any theoretical understanding should be derived from research on the agents performing action and interaction within a particular setting (Bain/Mueller 2016, 33). This reflects a concern that practice, not theory, be prioritised in Social Science (see Schatzki et al. 2001). In addition, practice theorists generally insist that three aspects should to be addressed: 1) concrete activities and performances; 2) the location of action in space and time, and 3) the relationship between the individual and 'the social' (Reckwitz 2002, Halkier/Jensen 2008, Bain/Mueller 2016).

To support theory-building, the present inquiry starts from two key issues in practice theory, namely the *location of action* and *agents' performance of action and interaction*. To these is added the third, complementary theme of *practice change* within a globalised teaching and learning environment. This builds on the argument put forth by Richard Edwards and Robin Usher (2008, 2), who characterise globalisation as a force of large-scale transformation, and possible disruption, in higher education:

> The reconfiguration of pedagogical practices around the globe has taken on a momentum that an earlier generation might well have considered startling and disorienting. Indeed, many still working in the education and training arenas do experience a high degree of disorientation and dislocation.

Writing in 2008, Edwards and Usher point to a dramatic change driven by new technology and altered perceptions of time/space and involving the remaking of pedagogy, learning sites, and systems of representation. Ten years later, it has become possible to document such a transition empirically by inviting actors to reflect on the ways their teaching practices have been transformed in response to macro-level processes of globalisation. The educational philosopher John Dewey offers a theoretical perspective on practice change. Dewey's theory of experiential learning assumes that an initial state of perplexity will facilitate a reflection on and subsequent adjustment of practice (Dewey 2011, Buch/Elkjær 2015), which suggests that agents are capable of altering their ways of acting in situations where old habits no longer seem to work. The implication is that teachers should be recognised as change agents who are located within and actively contribute to the reconfiguration of a global learning environment.

Locating action

Characteristic of practice theory is the insistence that actions be situated within particular physical and social contexts. Schatzki (2005) describes his approach to social reality as a *site ontology*, while Kemmis (2009) uses the concept of *practice architecture* to contextualise practices in education. Anticipating these recent adoptions of a spatial terminology is the field theory developed by Pierre Bourdieu. A much-cited definition is offered by Bourdieu in conversation with Loïc Wacquant:

> [A] field may be defined as network, or configuration, of objective relations between positions. These positions are objectively defined, in their existence and in the determinations they impose upon their occupants, agents or institutions, by their present and potential situation (*situs*) in the structure of the distribution of species of power (or capital) whose possession commands access to the specific profits that are at stake in the field, as well as by their objective relation to other positions (domination, subordination, homology etc.).
>
> (Bourdieu/Wacquant 1992, 97)

As noted by Wilken (2011, 51), Bourdieu treats field as an analytical concept that can explain the social relations emerging in his empirical studies of class (1986a), academic systems (1988), cultural production (1993), arts (1996a), and elite schools (1996b). Bourdieu defines the notion of fields in a variety of ways, which may have added to the confusion that some readers experience as the result of a writing style which to Jenkins (2002, 163–4) is unnecessarily elevated, technical, and idiosyncratic. Two analogies are commonly employed to clarify Bourdieu's field concept. First, fields have been compared to a market where customers have different abilities to buy objects or services. In *Language and Symbolic Power* (1991) Bourdieu employs the market metaphor in relation to language, using this to explain why some speech acts carry political authority, while others do not: 'Utterances receive their value (and their sense) only in their relation to a market, characterized by a particular law of price formation' (67). A second popular analogy is the football pitch, which Thomson (2008, 68) employs to explain how Bourdieu's field theory works in practice:

> A football field is a boundaried site where a game is played. In order to play the game, players have set positions – when the football field is represented in visual form, it is as a square with internal divisions and an external boundary, with the set positions marked in predetermined places. The game has specific rules which novice players must learn, together with basic skills, as they begin to play.

Together the market and football pitch metaphors foreground four key elements in Bourdieu's theory: First, a field is *bounded*, which implies that it cannot be extended indefinitely in space and time. Two, a field is organised *relationally*, which means that each actor's position and possibility for action is determined by her relationship with other players in the field. Third, a field is a *regulated* site because there are particular laws that decide how an agent should and probably will act. Finally, *resources*, or Bourdieu's *capital* (1986b), are important, since they determine to what extent individuals are capable of claiming a position of power or prestige within a field.

Of particular interest is Bourdieu's analysis of the academic field in *Homo Academicus* (1988). The focal point is the French academic system prior to and during the 'critical moment' of 1968, but Bourdieu identifies institutional structures, positions, resources, and struggles that are characteristic of university settings more generally. First, *Homo Academicus* presents academia as a series of *bounded sites*, ranging from the local department via the faculty and single university to a national system composed of all institutions involved in the provision of higher education and research. At the national level, the educational field connects with the field of power, which means that the status of institutions depends on their involvement in the training of political, economic, and bureaucratic elites (Swartz 1997). Second, one finds at each level within the academic system a *relationship* between actors placed in dominant and dominated positions. Within the department, the professor represents power vis-à-vis junior scholars and students, and such authority can be extended or limited, depending on the status of the department and faculty. Hence, social scientists generally speak with less authority than academics positioned within Medicine and Law, who benefit from a professional association with political and economic fields of power (Bourdieu 1988, 38). Third, Bourdieu's *homo academicus* enacts her authority through the *regulation of action*, rewarding desirable practices and dissuading what is considered deviant behaviour. Novice players have to learn the rules of the game, but frequently norms and routines are not explicated in the academic system, but consist of tacit knowledge that actors gradually acquire as they move from their initial position as first-year student towards the disciplinary mastery of a postgraduate student or junior scholar (Gerholm 1990). Newcomers' introduction to the academic system can be smoothed considerably if they possess *capital* in the form of elaborate language, canonical knowledge, or the disposition of someone naturally 'fit' to succeed in academia. Bourdieu (1986b) refers to such resources as *symbolic* or *cultural capital*, which can assume three forms: 1) a particular mind-set or *habitus*, 2) objects such as machines and books, and 3) educational qualifications (106). According to Bourdieu (1988, 43–7), indicators of acquired cultural capital are place of birth, parents' professional background, previous education, studies overseas, committee memberships, and publications.

Bourdieu's field theory and the site ontology proposed by Theodore Schatzki (2002, 2005) are comparable in a number of ways. First, Bourdieu and Schatzki agree that human action will always be situated within a particular context. Schatzki (2002) stresses in his definition of social sites 'human co-existence' (146), thus sharing with Bourdieu a preoccupation with the relationships established between actors, who 'find themselves simultaneously in the same setting' (148). A second common point is the acceptance that a form of practical understanding regulates the performance of practices within a particular setting. According to Schatzki (2002, 2005), practical knowledge defines what is acceptable to the actors partaking in a specific practice, which means that action is controlled in a manner comparable to the rules governing performance in Bourdieu's field. A final commonality is the perception of social sites as nested, ranging from specific, localised spheres of action to practices arranged at the organisational and national levels. To Bourdieu this multi-layered system is ordered hierarchically, while Schatzki (2002, 154–5) prefers the image of a network which can be expanded where nodes interconnect with practices located in other national or international sites. Schatzki's network metaphor is interesting because it suggests that the system can be extended indefinitely, which enables the transcendence of spatial and temporal boundaries that is associated with globalisation (see Edwards and Usher 2008). An important difference is Schatzki's reluctance to accept Bourdieu's proposition that agents are predisposed towards certain types of action. Instead, Schatzki (2005, 481) insists that actors will perform in the way that makes most sense within a given site and practice, which means that any converging patterns should be ascribed to human coexistence within a shared site rather than underlying structures of power and domination.

Agents, action, practices

Practices are 'what people do' (Bain and Mueller 2016, 30), involving a *doer*, a *doing,* and something *done*. According to Grootenboer et al. (2017, 2–3) the concept of practice has been used common-sensically in the literature, '[pointing] to both broader *and* particular acts, actors, actions and activities encountered in the practical social world'. Yet theorists agree that an adequate analysis of social practice will require a description of the actual activity performed as well as a demonstration of how such action is embedded within a social context. Grootenboer et al. (2017, 4) offer this example:

> [A] teacher will engage in teaching practices that are idiosyncratic and specific for her particular classroom, but at the same time she is part of the particular community of teachers at her school; these practices are nuanced and unique on the one hand, yet are also nested within a broad profession of educators. In this, her individual teaching practices are simultaneously shaped by the 'traditions' of the broader practice, but at the same time the traditions of the broader practice are also made and remade by the practices of individuals[.]

In any given situation one can identify an *agent*, who is capable of *acting* in the way that she sees most fit, but who tends to act in a manner that reflects her embeddedness within a specific *practice*, which comes with its own set of traditions, norms about appropriate ways of doing things, collegial relations, and institutional policies. Hence, practice theorists distinguish between *action*, which is a single activity such as giving an instruction or forming a group, and *practice*, which combines all activities involved, for instance, in lecturing or multicultural teamwork.

The understanding of practice as a bundle of activities builds on the theory proposed by Schatzki (1996, 2002). Schatzki (2001, 48) defines practices as 'organized nexuses of activity', involving one or several agents, the performance of activity, material artefacts, and the setting where action unfolds. Central to Schatzki's conceptualisation of practice are *Doings & Sayings*, which are defined as 'actions that people directly perform' and 'things people do with their bodies' (2002, 72). To these Stephen Kemmis adds the third element of *Relatings*, which he describes as 'ways of relating to people and the world' (Kemmis/Mahon 2017, 109). According to Schatzki, four components are involved in the social organisation of practices. The first element is *practical understanding*, which Schatzki (2002, 77) explains as: 'knowing how to X, knowing how to identify X-ings, and knowing how to prompt as well as respond to X-ings'. Practical understanding is to be treated as skills or know-how, distinguishing the competent agent from a novice, and here Schatzki (2002, 78–9) sees a key difference between his theory and Bourdieu, who ascribes the 'logic of practice' to actor disposition or *habitus*. A second component is *rules*, which are explained as 'explicit formulations, principles, precepts, and instructions that enjoin, direct, or remonstrate people to perform specific actions' (Schatzki 2002, 79). This resembles the argument of Collins (2001), who problematises the notion of tacit knowledge, insisting that the lack of articulation could imply mastery of a practice, which makes it unnecessary for practitioners to formulate rules. The third element of *teleoaffective structures* consists of 'a range of normativized and hierarchically ordered ends, projects, tasks, to varying degrees allied with normativized emotions and even moods' (Schatzki 2002, 80). Actions can be more or less acceptable, in other words, which suggests a social organisation similar to Bourdieu's field where actors' performances are recognised as more or less legitimate, depending on an agent's role and resources. The final ordering principle is the *general understandings* of the project in which agents are involved. In relation to this, Nicolini (2012, 167) foregrounds reflexivity, suggesting that this is where a project gains 'its identity, both discursively and practically'. Hence, one can establish a connection between educators' general understanding of the function(s) of education (Biesta 2009) and the practical knowledge utilised in the act of teaching. If she believes *qualification* to be the principal objective, a teacher will favour tasks that enable knowledge transfer, seeking to train learners to master specific techniques. In comparison, teachers building on a perception of education as *subjectification* are likely to privilege actions that encourage an exploration of learner identities, selecting classroom activities that focus on reflection rather than training.

A key element in Schatzki's theory is his foregrounding of *Doings & Sayings*, which provides a starting point for an inquiry into teaching and learning practices. In comparison, Bourdieu offers only limited guidance as to how the study of social practice can be approached, requesting that readers deduct this from the empirical analyses provided. What seems more problematic is Schatzki's insistence that his theory be treated as separate from the work of Bourdieu. Schatzki (2002, 78–9) is critical of Bourdieu's concept of *habitus*, which he dismisses as intuitive and determinist, demanding from agents a normative 'sense of the game' instead of the actual performance of activities. Yet Schatzki acknowledges the regulatory influence of teleoaffective structures, emphasising that feelings of 'oughtness' and 'acceptability' normalise action within a social site (2002, 80). Arguably, Schatzki here accepts that action may be habituated, which indicates that he could be exaggerating his difference to Bourdieu. Such an argument can be supported by a closer examination of Bourdieu's notion of *habitus*. To Bourdieu *habitus* is a key concept, enabling social scientists to overcome a problematic individual/society dualism by connecting individuals' action to structures found within the particular social field where practice is located (Swartz 1997). In *Outline of a Theory of practice*, Bourdieu offers this definition:

> The words *disposition* seems particularly suited to express what is covered by the concept of habitus (defined as a system of dispositions). It expresses first the *result of an organizing action*, with a meaning close to that of words such as structure; it also designates *a way of being, a habitual state* (especially of the body) and, in particular, *a predisposition, tendency, propensity*, or *inclination*.
>
> (Bourdieu 1977, 214, emphasis in text)

Here Bourdieu associates *habitus* with 'tendency' and 'inclination', which suggests that he sees human action as patterned rather than predetermined. This is significant as it brings his theory closer to that of Schatzki, who explains the relation between individual activity and 'the social' in the following way: 'When people heedfully interact, their actions converge, supplement, assist one another and, together with the states of affairs to which these actions give rise, form an emergent pattern' (2005, 480). The perception of human agents as individuals, who are in theory free to act as they please, but whose actions form patterns as a result of social influences within a particular site, is one that Schatzki and Bourdieu share with John Dewey. Dewey uses the term *habit* about the social dimension to human activity, defining this as: 'the mainspring of human action … formed for the most part under the influence of the customs of a group' (Dewey, as quoted in Colapietro 2004, 75). The commonalities between Bourdieu and Dewey have been noted by several scholars, who insist that the theorists' understandings of the social, habituation, and agency be treated as complementary (e.g. Colapietro 2004, Inghilleri 2014). The previous discussion shows that there are equally significant parallels between Schatzki and Bourdieu, enabling the present author to form a theoretical threesome that may inform and support the argument developed in the current book. Characteristic of all is a concern with the nature of human action, a perception of agents as simultaneously individual and socially situated, and the acceptance of practice as regulated, with converging patterns emerging from processes of habituation and socialisation.

Changing practice

Practice theory is presented as a package of diverse concepts and methods, from which the empirical researcher can pick whatever theory she sees fit for the query pursued (e.g. Reckwitz 2002, Nicolini 2012). Featuring prominently are the works of Bourdieu and Schatzki, whereas pragmatists such as Dewey have largely been ignored. Barbara Simpson (2009) attempts to redress the imbalance by highlighting the intellectual kinship between pragmaticism and the contemporary advocates of a 'practice turn'. Indeed, Simpson (2009, 1330) claims, a pragmatic perspective can be used to answer the challenges presented by recent practice theories, 'drawing together the habitual and creative aspects of practice'. The following passage from John Dewey's *Democracy and Education* (2011) provides an example of how this works (78):

> The nature of experience can be understood only by noting that it includes an active and a passive element peculiarly combined. On the active hand, experience is trying – a meaning which is made explicit in the connected term experiment. On the passive, it is undergoing. When we experience something we act upon it, we do something with it; then we suffer or undergo the consequences. We do something to the thing and then it does something to us in return: such is the peculiar combination.

What is explained here is Dewey's principle *Learning by Doing*. This, he argues, can be achieved through an experiment (the act of *doing*) which will lead to a reaction, based on which the actor decides whether to continue acting in the same way or adjust her action in response to an undesirable consequence. One could read this as *regulation* of the single actor's performance, in which case Dewey's theory complements the work of Schatzki and Bourdieu, who both insisted that chains of action and reaction support the normalisation of social practice within a specific site. However, such an interpretation neglects what is a core component in Dewey's work, namely the element of *experience*-based, *experimental* learning.

As regards the topic of *experience*, this is used by Dewey to connect the individual and the social (Buch/Elkjær 2015). According to Dewey, individuals learn by acting and subsequently reflecting on the effects of action, thereby acquiring experiential knowledge that enables them to anticipate how other, future situations might work and to adjust their practice accordingly. Over time, this means that action becomes habituated, with actors aligning their performances to the social practices and relationships favoured within their immediate environment (Dewey 1997, 2011). Yet automated practices are only possible where environmental conditions are stable, which allows agents to predict the consequences of action relatively accurately. In situations where a particular outcome cannot be taken for granted, Dewey proposes that an *experimental* method be adopted, inviting actors to engage in a process of reflective learning:

> As long as our activity glides smoothly along from one thing to another, or as long as we permit our imagination to entertain fancies at pleasure, there is no call for reflection. Difficulty or obstruction in the way of reaching a belief brings us, however, to a pause. In the suspense of uncertainty, we metaphorically climb a tree; we try to find some standpoint from which we may survey additional facts and, getting a more commanding view of the situation, may decide how the facts stand related to one another.
> (1910, 11)

Dewey proposes a model of inquiry inspired by Natural Science, where an initial state of uncertainty leads to the formulation of a preliminary theory, which is subsequently tested in an experiment. This has been criticised by educational scholars for its failure to capture the immediate practice adjustments that occur in the actual moment of teaching (van Manen 1995, Hébert 2015). However, such critique seems less relevant in relation to the present investigation where one would expect a time gap between university lecturers' initial exposure to internationalisation, e.g. in the form of institutional policy papers or a diversification of the student cohort, and their decision to adopt new teaching methods, activities, and material.

Compared to Dewey, whose approach is future-oriented, 'reaching forward towards the unknown' (Buch/Elkjær 2015, 5), Bourdieu and Schatzki seem more conservative, foregrounding the *reproduction* and *perpetuation* of practice (e.g. Bourdieu/Passeron 2000, Schatzki 2005). Yet to ignore the element of change, or 'state of becoming', would neglect a significant dimension in Schatzki and Bourdieu, misrepresenting as stable what is to them evolving. Fields change continuously, Grenfell and James (2004, 510) note with reference to Bourdieu, highlighting how relationships between actors, roles, and resources are constantly challenged, negotiated, and, where necessary, adjusted. Even more dramatic is the transformation emerging in response to situations of 'crisis', as Hardy (2008, 132) explains:

> [A]t times of crisis in particular, *habitus* must respond to abrupt, sometimes catastrophic, field changes, but that response always takes time. In such circumstances where new and stable field structures have yet to emerge, novel field opportunities, often transitory, come into being.

> *Habitus* evolves in response to these new opportunities, but in unpredictable ways where the consequences for an individual's field positioning are yet to be determined.

Such an understanding is reminiscent of Dewey, acknowledging how individual actors' sense of being 'out of touch' with their social environment inspires a process of reflection that over time can effect a change of practice. In a similar vein, Schatzki (2002, 233) argues for a state of 'endless becoming', noting how '[t]he doings and sayings that sweep the social site both maintain and alter practices' (254). Recently, Schatzki (2017) has developed his argument with reference to education, stating that a precondition for learning is an element of *indefiniteness* (31). This choice of term is interesting, with a strong reminiscence to *uncertainty* in Dewey's model. True learning, Schatzki (2017, 32) continues, involves not only the acquisition of skills (referred to as training), but a reflective engagement with the practical understanding or normativity involved in a particular practice. Only when she becomes capable of explicating the rules underpinning action can an agent contribute actively to the continuous scrutiny and evolution of social practice. Hence Schatzki (2017, 38) sees learning as central to practice change, requiring experiential knowledge of the kind proposed by Dewey. Once again, this underlines the complementarity of Dewey, Bourdieu, and Schatzki, which justifies to the present author the choice of an approach that begins with the similarities between the theorists instead of insisting on difference.

Globalising practices

The previous sections foregrounded commonalities between Pierre Bourdieu, Theodore Schatzki, and John Dewey with regard to the location of action, actors' performance of practices, and the possibility of change. What is also characteristic of these theorists is their preoccupation with social systems that are mainly national in orientation. This poses a challenge to the current research, which takes as its focal point teaching practices in a global learning environment. In consequence, this concluding section will discuss core concepts adopted from practice theory with reference to processes of globalisation and internationalisation.

The first theme of *locating action* highlighted a need to situate practice within a context. A useful concept is the perception of sites as nested, which suggests that the single action performed in a classroom is subjected to influences at the departmental, faculty, institutional, and national levels. However, to engage properly globalisation one needs to extend the range of sites, acknowledging also the supernational and global dimensions to higher education. This challenges practice researchers who will find it hard to situate action within a single location. One example is educational policies, which may be formulated by European institutions, translated by national bodies, and implemented by institutional managers, thus linking actors and activities across scales and contexts. Equally significant is Schatzki's network metaphor, which suggests that social practices interconnect across space and time, thereby transcending the boundaries of the particular site and situation. Academics, as carriers of educational and disciplinary practices, contribute to the shaping of globalisation by reaching beyond their physical location within a specific institutional environment, participating in knowledge-sharing and networking with colleagues around the world.

As regards *agents and action,* Schatzki encourages us to approach higher education through concrete Doings & Sayings performed in the classroom. Here an international dimension is manifest, for instance, in situations where actors choose to code-switch from a local language into English. Harder to document are interconnections between 'bundles of practices' such as research and education. Yet one would assume that academics partaking in international research communities will be influenced by the way their discipline is framed globally, and that such understandings have an impact on their representation of academic knowledge in the classroom. A final concern is socialisation or regulated action. Academic migration means that educational sites are co-inhabited by actors who have internalised practical knowledge in different systems and will therefore act in divergent ways. Traditionally, this would have been resolved through the regulation of action, but in situations where they possess economic as well as cultural capital, one may expect academic migrants to be less willing to accept their need to be 'normalised'. In consequence, new forms of institutional socialisation may emerge in response to globalisation, responding to and actively engaging with the movement of people, ideas, and practices.

Undoubtedly, Edwards and Usher (2008) were right when presenting globalisation as a dramatic transformation of education. At all levels one finds examples of practices transfigured, which indicates that this constitutes a 'crisis' of the kind that to Bourdieu necessitated a change in *habitus*. If so, globalisation represents a major upheaval in the life of the single lecturer, who discovers that she is required to 'globalise' research and education practices in response to new demands posed by student mobility, English-medium education, institutional internationalisation policies, and global ranking regimes. Contrasting with such an image of individuals driven by globalisation is the understanding of academics as actors actively engaged in the creation of international learning environments. Dewey's model of experiential learning acknowledges agents' capacity to manage the ambiguity emerging as the result of unpredictable environmental conditions, using this to spark a process of reflection and possible change of practice. The latter image is the more attractive one, granting to academic staff the active position of a change agent. Yet the author shall treat the two models as complementary, accepting that processes of field change and actors changing are interrelated.

Part II

Structures in a global learning environment

University teachers' action and interaction are located within specific academic environments, or *fields* to use Bourdieu's terminology. Within each site, there are rules governing actors' performance, which enable some to claim the position as successful scholars and educators, while others may lack the resources to compete in the field battle for recognition. Traditionally, the forms of capital sought by academics involved membership of disciplinary communities, appointment to top positions within a specific institutional or national system, scientific prowess demonstrated through prestigious publications, and the command of academic discourse (Bourdieu/Passeron 1994, Bourdieu 1988). However, as the consequence of globalisation one expects to see change in the conditions governing action and interaction within the academic field, predisposing some actors to internationalise their teaching and research practices. Part II foregrounds four structural conditions that currently shape the global field of higher education: Macro-level processes of globalisation and internationalisation, disciplinary orientation, academic migration, and the spread of the English language. The significance of academic disciplines and discourse was documented by Bourdieu in *Homo Academicus* (1988), although one may expect to see as the result of internationalisation an extension of such practices, motivating actors to orient their teaching and research towards a global rather than a national setting. In comparison, macro-level globalisation and student/staff mobility, in the forms realised in the 21st century, should be treated as a major transformation of the academic field, affecting both the types of *capital* sought by ambitious actors and their inclination to privilege certain activities whilst deselecting others.

The four chapters in Part II aim to balance a theoretical argument about the four structural conditions of globalisation, academic disciplines, migration, and scientific language with the concrete action and interaction described by academic staff seeking to internationalise teaching and research. In some cases, the empirical material indicates that actors' internationalisation happens in response to field conditions that reward individuals who have demonstrated their capacity to perform within a globalised environment. Chapter 4, 'Internationalising the disciplines', thus reveals how in subject areas such as Business Studies and International Relations, which are oriented towards an international environment, junior scholars planning an academic career have to accept their need to publish and teach in the global medium of English. Yet it is important not to underestimate the power of academic staff to influence and possibly create the transformation shaping global higher education. Chapter 3 suggests that international education may begin with individual lecturers' interest in opening their courses to a diverse group of learners, using the classroom presence of non-native learners to add a global dimension to their discipline. Similarly, academics increasingly consider travelling a natural part of an academic career, actively seeking opportunities to spend time in a foreign research and teaching environment. As they connect with students and colleagues from other parts of the world, actors become inclined to prefer English-medium publishing and teaching, thereby contributing to the perception of higher education as an activity undertaken in a global rather than a national field.

3 A global field of higher education

Globalisation, internationalisation, transnationalisation

Central to the practice theories of Pierre Bourdieu and Theodore Schatzki is the concept of *field* or *site* of action. Within a field, particular positions, normative understandings, and resources can be identified, enabling actors to distinguish between more or less desirable forms of action and adjust their practices accordingly. The current author interprets international education as a particular educational practice, accepting the influence of fields – the location of action within specific geographic, temporal, socio-cultural, linguistic, institutional, and disciplinary settings – on individuals' performance of teaching and learning in the classroom. The field within which international education is played out is global in scale and scope, which means that it is shaped by players and practices situated in multiple sites, at multiple levels, and with a variety of motives for engaging in processes of internationalisation. The purpose of this chapter is to present key structures and dynamics related to the *globalisation* of higher education and foreground their relationship to the *Doings & Sayings* enacted by institutions and individual academics.

To unravel the multitude of meanings associated with higher education as a *global* field it is important to establish a terminology that can embrace the diverse processes presented by educational scholars as forms of 'internationalisation'. Judging from the literature review produced by Tight (2019) this can be a daunting task. Researchers have approached the phenomena of *internationalisation* and *globalisation* from a variety of disciplinary, institutional, and geographic perspectives, inspiring conceptualisations that range from pragmatic descriptions of *how* internationalisation should be approached in an organisational context (e.g. Hudzik 2015) to ideological notions of internationalism and global citizenship (e.g. Byram 2018). The current author does not seek to reproduce an academic debate that at times seems somewhat detached from the reality conveyed by the agents performing international teaching and learning. Instead, a conceptual foundation is developed through an exploration of three dynamics commonly recognised as central to international education: *Globalisation*, *internationalisation*, and *transnationalisation*.

Globalisation places higher education in relation to a broader discussion carried out within the Social Sciences. According to Knight (2017, 15) terms such as *global citizenship*, *planetisation*, *glocalisation*, and *global rankings* have entered the vocabulary of international education research within the last decade. They reflect scholars' perception of higher education as a space interconnected through virtual/physical networks, academic mobility, global knowledge production, and supernational governance structures such as those provided by the OECD, EU, and UNESCO. Three theoretical perspectives have proved particularly useful to the conceptualisation of globalisation in higher education. First, researchers emphasising *global* higher education build on the understanding that globalisation has become social reality through time-space compression (Giddens 1990, Harvey 1989), which enables learners to access education anywhere in the world. Boden and Epstein (2011) label this condition a 'flat earth society', which, in Edwards' and Ushers' view (2008, 2), calls for a 'reconfiguration of pedagogic practices'. A second key influence is Arjun Appadurai's theory of scapes (1996). Appadurai highlights movement and interconnectivity, offering scapes as an analytical tool that has been used by educational researchers to capture the manifestation of global processes within national and institutional systems (Forstorp/Mellström 2013, Marginson/Sawir 2005). A third perspective is globalisation as discourse or social imaginary (e.g. Calhoun 2008). Arguably, globalisation becomes social reality because educational scholars keep talking and writing about it, thereby producing the idea of a shared educational culture (Geerlings/Lundberg 2018, Dale 2000). The implication is that globalisation is omnipresent, transforming individual practices, programmes, institutions, and national systems of education.

Unlike globalisation, which transcends space and time, the second concept of *internationalisation* involves a connection between actors, practices, institutions, and systems identified as national. Knight dates the idea of internationalisation as a set of institutional activities to the 1980s, at which point terms such as *international students*, *study abroad*, *institution agreements*, and *partnership projects* became common ways of describing international education (Knight 2017, 15). The terms highlight the importance attached to student mobility and the cross-border movement of resources, experts, and ideas (often from 'developed' countries in the North to the Global South). In 2000, Crowther et al. proposed a new understanding, *internationalisation at home*, which changes the focus from mobility to institution, suggesting that also students who do not travel should benefit from an international learning experience. Here internationalisation is interpreted as 'the process of integrating an international dimension into the research, teaching, and services', an '*internationalised curriculum*', and activities at the 'home' campus that bring together domestic and international students (Nilsson 2003, 31). This has prompted some scholars to propose a holistic approach, demanding change from all parts of an organisation (e.g. Leask 2015, Hudzik 2015).

Most writers build on the assumption that there is a clearly identifiable 'home' and 'abroad', accepting that institutions and actors are embedded within distinctive national systems.

Transnationalisation describes a condition where the organisation of higher education is no longer the prerogative of the nation state. While the prefix *inter-* suggested a state of being *between*, *trans-* denotes a state *beyond* a world order composed of nation states and is connected to macro-level processes of political neoliberalism, economic capitalism, massification, and commodification of higher education within an ever-expanding, borderless academic field (e.g. Caruana 2016, Kauppinen 2015). Transnational education involves universities' establishment of an international presence, e.g. through the opening of overseas campuses or strategic partnerships with local universities, and is an institutional response to the rising demand for tertiary education in countries such as China, India, Indonesia, and Vietnam (Healey/Michael 2015). A recent example is *education hubs* where countries such as Singapore and Malaysia attempt to strengthen national knowledge economies by attracting Western providers of higher education (Richards 2019). Hence, transnational implies a form of international education unbound from national systems where the Romanian student registered for a degree in Sweden will go on exchange to Malaysia to follow courses designed at the University of Nottingham, UK.

As demonstrated, the manifestation of higher education as a *global* field can be realised in various ways. The current chapter approaches internationalisation from three perspectives: 1) *Scapes, scales, and systems*, which foregrounds the spatial dimension to globalisation; 2) *Internationalising higher education*, which addresses national and institutional processes; and 3) *Policies, actors, and institutional cultures*, which examines the role of academic staff in internationalisation processes. A concluding section discusses the recent phenomenon of 'de-internationalisation', asking what implications this may have for the future of international education.

Scapes, scales, and systems

An understanding of higher education as a global field foregrounds the spatial dimension to internationalisation processes. According to Edwards and Usher (2008, 3) the discussion of globalisation and pedagogy has witnessed a 'growth of spatial metaphors', which scholars have used to explore how educational cultures are changing in response to the dynamics of space-time compression, de-territorialisation, academic migration, and the sense of simultaneity fostered by new technology and global media flows. Three metaphors serve as points of departure for the present discussion: *Scapes*, *scales*, and *systems*. Together they enable a discussion of global higher education as a social imaginary (scapes), as multi-layered and multi-sited (scales), and as a political reality shaped by policies, conventions, and developments at the local, national, and supernational levels (systems).

Researchers seeking to theorise about complex phenomena such as globalisation will often rely on the power of their imagination to construct models of social reality that can illuminate processes and structures otherwise invisible to the human eye. Kenway and Fahey (2009, 10) propose that one *globalises* the research imagination, accepting 'epistemological and geographical travel [as] the arch "wherethrough experience" is shaped'. A metaphor commonly used to explore global higher education is Appadurai's notion of scapes, which highlights the centrality of movement and flows to contemporary understandings of social reality. Forstorp and Mellström (2013) have added a sixth dimension, *eduscape*, to Appadurai's theory, which they define (336) as:

> [T]he transnational flow of ideas and people in regard to research and higher education and where nodes of knowledge centres, peripheries and positional dynamics shift over time but are connected through modern communication technologies and different epistemic, ethnic and learning communities.

Forstorp and Mellström identify several spatial constructs that may function as structural principles in education and research, including knowledge *centres* and *peripheries, positionality*, and *communities*. As will become evident in subsequent chapters, all influence the way agents understand, perform, and evaluate their identities within global academia, inspiring the movement of ideas, resources, and people. A second key metaphor is Robertson and Dale's notion of *education ensemble*, which stresses the relational and networked character of global education. Robertson and Dale (2015, 155) offer this definition:

> [T]he education ensemble represents education as also a complex collective *construction* of the social world, that is not reducible to schools, or universities, learners and teachers … Rather, education involves an array of actors and other institutions beyond the obvious or our commonsense understandings whose logics, interests and forms of authority generate tensions and contradictions within the ensemble.

As a conceptualisation of space, *ensemble* encourages researchers to foreground the importance of networks as a structure that provides the interconnectivity and reciprocity necessary to sustain the idea of higher education as a global field. At the same time, Robertson and Dale acknowledge how practices at the individual and institutional levels interact with and are changing in response to external forces, pointing to the importance of actors' embeddedness in local, national, and global systems. The awareness that internationalisation demands from agents an engagement with processes unfolding simultaneously at multiple levels has inspired the third metaphor, Marginson's and Rhoade's (2002) concept of a *glonacal agency heuristic*.

Glonacal relies on spatial terminology, combining the three levels of *global*, *national*, and *local*. *Global* here refers to processes such as neoliberalism, academic capitalism, and the commodification of education and research, which, according to Marginson and Rhoades (2002, 287) have caused researchers to neglect the alternative, *national* and *local* dimensions:

> The metaphor of academic capitalism reveals a powerful global trend but blinds us to the power of national traditions, agencies, and agents in shaping the work of higher education, as well as the local agency exercised by students, faculty, non-faculty professionals, and administrators, pursuing prestige, knowledge, social critique, and social justice.

Marginson's and Rhoades' observations have inspired their design of a three-dimensional model which shows how 1) agency can be found at three levels, and 2) 'activity and influence generally flow in more than one direction' (2002, 291). This visualisation represents an attempt to conceptualise global higher education as a multi-sited, multi-level reality, thus preparing the ground for the second theme of *scales*.

Scale is a concept adopted from human geography where it describes the units and layers organising human action, from 'the global down to the local' (Mahon/Keil 2009, 17). Howitt (2002, 305) suggests that one distinguishes between 1) *scale as site*, which refers to the geographical sense of distance created through maps and measurement; 2) *scale as level*, which implies a 'nested hierarchical ordering of space'; and 3) *scale as relation*, which highlights the interface between different levels and sites. When applied to higher education, the notion of scale foregrounds how actors and institutions contribute to the constitution of a global field through their establishment of 'cross-scale relations' (Howitt 2002, 305), interacting across sites and levels to accommodate shared interests and activities. Two examples illustrate how this works. First, international education frequently relies on linkages between units situated in different parts of the world, as seen in the case of the University of Nottingham's Ningbo campus. Without having to leave their home country, Chinese students can register for a degree authenticated within the British academic system, which makes their education multi-sited, based on a connection between two nodes, Nottingham and Ningbo, within a global academic space. A second example is the multi-layered policy-landscape governing international education in Denmark, Sweden, and Finland. Within the same institution, 'international' MA courses accredited within the national educational system run parallel to 'Nordic' Masters sponsored by the Nordic Council of Ministers, and *Erasmus Mundus* programmes approved by the European Union. All types of international education require institutions to interact with units located at different levels within the scalar hierarchy. However, rather than follow a hierarchical logic, progressing from local to national and international, institutions will skip the national level where this has limited policy-making power in relation to a specific form of education,

Figure 3.1 A multi-scalar system

engaging directly with agencies at the Nordic or European levels. A popular way to depict scalar hierarchies, or *contexts* as multi-layered spaces are sometimes named in educational research (e.g. Leask 2015), is to make use of concentric circles. The author should like to propose a visualisation of global higher education that includes six scales:

Organisation refers to the university as institution and incorporates sub-organisational units such as faculty, department, research, and teaching groups. The *local* or *community* level is the city or district in which an institution is located, while the *subnational* level can be found in federal systems where higher education is organised by single states (US) or Bundesländer (Germany). The *supernational* scale is enacted by intergovernmental, regional organisations such as the European Union, whereas the *global* level is all-inclusive, incorporating all flows, discourses, actors, and policies in a manner that sustains the idea of a globalised academic space.

Theories of scapes and scales tend to represent internationalisation as an opening of higher education that enables individual actors, research groups, and institutions to perceive academia as one borderless field. In contrast, the third concept of *systems* foregrounds questions of policy-making and implementation, accepting that international education, as an institutional and individual practice, is affected by decisions made at multiple levels within the global system. When approaching global higher education from a systems perspective, it becomes clear that the vision of a borderless field is an ideological construct with few supporting structures. As Hazelkorn (2018) observes, no form of quality assurance has yet been accepted worldwide, which makes it difficult to compare academic performance and knowledge production.

Instead, actors rely on ranking lists produced by private agencies and professional associations, which is problematic, given that these use different criteria as their benchmark for assessing quality teaching and research (Jöns/Hoyler 2013). In comparison, the power of supernational systems as a force shaping higher education has been established in several review articles assessing the changes following from the *Europeanisation* policies initiated by the Bologna Declaration 1999 (e.g. Bergan/Deca 2018, Dobbins/Kwiek 2017). First, the Bologna process demanded structural changes such as the introduction of a common accreditation system (ECTS) and a three-cycle structure (BA-MA-PhD), but to these have been added a value-based approach, emphasising 'freedom of expression, academic freedom and institutional autonomy, independent students' unions, and free movement for students and staff' (Gallagher 2018). Despite efforts to establish a supernational system, great divergence remains within the European Area of Higher Education, which testifies to the power of national policy-makers who are ultimately responsible for the interpretation and implementation of internationalisation in their countries. A country's willingness to embrace global higher education will depend on a variety of factors, including welfare provision, labour market situation, immigration policies, native language, voter preferences, and a country's position as a net receiver or sender of student migrants. In times of rising nationalism, this can create a backlash within the national systems, motivating politicians to dismiss international education as an elitist project 'jeopardizing universities' national mission and relevancy in the societies that give them life and purpose' (Douglas 2016, as quoted in van der Wende 2017, 14).

Internationalising higher education

The verb *internationalise* suggests a process that transforms a unit from an inward-looking, national condition to an externally oriented, international focus. Internationalisation processes can affect entire national systems, as has been the case in Australia where a decrease in public funding for higher education led to a dramatic growth in the number of fee-paying, international students and consequent change in the demographics of the student population (Schapper/Mayson 2005). However, many researchers choose to present internationalisation as an institutional change process, identifying stages that mark universities' transition from a predominantly national organisation towards a 'global' presence as provider of education in multiple sites around the world. One example is David Killick, whose *continuum* model represents change in the form of a progression from an initial *regional/national* phase via the *post-national* and *international* stages to the *global* university (2017, 26). Killick's typology encourages educational scholars to treat internationalisation as an evolution that resembles the expansion of businesses from local to multinational. Yet the model seems to overlook the divergence found within national and regional systems, which makes it impossible to reduce universities' development to a single path leading from national to global. Two examples may illustrate this point. First, research by literary historians such as Robert Crawford (1992, 1998) suggests that the idea of a *national*, British university only came into existence in the 18th and 19th centuries, when the disciplines of English Literature and Rhetoric were developed at Scottish universities in response to a demand from Scots seeking to pursue a career within the legal and political institutions governing the United Kingdom. This implies that there could be a stage preceding Killick's regional/national type. Second, Killick ignores the impact of scientific language, which may have been nationalised in areas with a hegemonic, imperial tradition (e.g. Britain, France, Germany, China), but which in other parts of the world demanded from the scientists seeking to partake in intellectual debates skills in 'global' languages such as Latin, French, German, or Mandarin (Mortensen/Haberland 2012). The implication is that researchers should not attempt to reduce internationalisation to a standard narrative, but take into consideration the variety of motives and environmental factors that influence the process at the national and institutional levels.

Internationalisation, as a strategic initiative to strengthen national knowledge economies, has become accepted in most countries around the world. The arguments used by policy-makers include human capital development, access to 'global' skills, research capability, talent recruitment, innovation, and entrepreneurship, which are discourses found in national systems as diverse as Britain, Sweden, Poland, Pakistan, China, and Japan (Caruana/Montgomery 2015, Dobbins/Kwiek 2017, Hammond 2016). How internationalisation is realised will depend on a country's position in the world, with some regions currently functioning as net providers of education and research (typically, Western Europe and English-speaking countries), while other national systems rely on an import of knowledge in order to meet demands in areas such as science and technology (e.g. South East Asia, Africa). This difference shows in the case study by Forstorp and Mellström (2013) where, in an attempt to build capacity, the Government of Pakistan enters into a partnership with the Swedish Royal Institute of Technology, leading to the foundation of a joint Pakistani-Swedish University financed by Pakistan, but dependent on expertise from Sweden. To unravel the divergent motives that inspire national governments to pursue strategies of internationalisation, Qiang (2003) proposes a typology that distinguishes between four rationales: *Political*, *academic*, *cultural/social*, and *economic*. Hammond (2016) summarises the four types as follows:

- *Political*: 'Related to issues of national security, stability and peace' (558)
- *Academic*: 'Linked to the goal of achieving international standards for teaching and research' (558)
- *Cultural/Social*: 'Emphasis on preservation of national culture, understanding foreign languages and cultures, and respect for diversity' (558)
- *Economic*: 'Direct response to market forces associated with economic globalization. Emphasis on developing human resources for the nation to stay internationally competitive.' (558)

When applied to Forstorp's and Mellström's (2013) example of a strategic partnership between the Pakistani and Swedish governments, one expects to see differences with regard to the rationales motivating policy-makers. The Government of Pakistan has as its key objectives academic and economic development, aiming to engage in collaborative activities to improve the quality of teaching and research in science and technology and thereby contribute to Pakistan's transition from an agricultural to a knowledge economy. In comparison, the Swedes are more likely to enter the partnership for political reasons, using higher education as the means to promote peace and economic development in what they may perceive to be an unstable region. Another possible motive is economic, since a joint Pakistani-Swedish university can be used to spot talented Pakistani researchers, who can be offered postgraduate education or employment in Sweden. Different rationales result in divergence with regard to the realisation of international education. In 2015 (110), Knight identified a *classic* model of internationalisation, where universities seek cross-border partnerships in research and education, but where the principal locus of activities remains a campus in the home country. This approach has been the predominant one in Western Europe, North America, and Australia since the 1990s and presupposes the mobility of exchange and fee-paying international students. As a contrast, Knight (2015, 110) suggests the *satellite* model where universities meet the global demand for education by establishing an overseas presence through satellite campuses or alliances with international partners. Particularly in South East Asia and the Gulf Region, Western universities' willingness to relocate programmes and staff has motivated national policy-makers to develop education hubs, allowing countries such as Singapore, Malaysia, and Dubai to 'position themselves as centers for student recruitment, education and training' (Knight 2011, 222). An emergent form of internationalisation is *online education*. American universities such as Stanford, Illinois, Duke, and Johns Hopkins offer free courses through internet portals such as Coursera, which enables students to access education independent of their geographical position (Pedersen 2015). In the light of current technological developments, one may expect such an approach to gain importance in future as this offers policy-makers a way of evening out the present knowledge gap between developed and developing countries.

At the institutional level, internationalisation approaches are shaped by factors such as the volume of international research and education, the values advocated by university managers, and the position allocated to non-natives within an organisation. As regards the scope and scale of international activities, Burnett and Huisman (2010, 122) have identified four institutional types:

1 *Ad hoc and marginal*: Universities have few international activities and no strategy for internationalisation
2 *Systematic and marginal*: Universities have few activities, but regard internationalisation as a strategic priority

3 *Ad hoc and central*: Universities have a high activity level, but no clearly defined strategy
4 *Systematic and central*: Many international activities, reinforced through a strategic commitment to internationalisation.

Within type one institutions, internationalisation can be realised through exchange agreements negotiated and managed by individual members of staff, with only limited involvement by university managers. Judging from interview statements made by experienced international lecturers, such an approach was fairly common in the 1980s and early 1990s, but has given way to more strategic responses where academic and administrative leaders assume responsibility for the control and coordination of international activities. Once internationalisation becomes a strategic commitment, institutional policy-makers tend to adopt a more value-based perspective. Based on a literature review Qiang (2003) distinguishes between four 'stances' characteristic of universities' international missions:

- *Activity*, focusing on 'activities such as curriculum [and] student/faculty exchange' (250)
- *Competency*, with an emphasis on 'skills, knowledge, attitudes and values' (250)
- *Ethos*, 'which emphasizes creating a culture or climate that values and supports international/intercultural perspectives' (251)
- *Process*, aiming to '[integrate] an international/intercultural dimension into teaching, research and service' (251)

Interestingly, neither approach acknowledges a purely economic take on internationalisation, as realised when institutions prioritise the recruitment of fee-paying, international students or market educational programmes to buyers in Singapore and China. Yet critical researchers argue that *transnational academic capitalism* is currently the dominant paradigm in global higher education, privileging 'market-like activities that integrate universities, departments and scholars to the knowledge-based economy' (Kauppinen 2015, 337). This raises concerns about the possible roles assigned to international students. Ideally, internationalisation demands a combination of the *ethos*, *competency*, and *process* approaches where an international and intercultural dimension becomes central to education, enabling non-native and domestic students to claim a 'common international or global identity, positionality and interest' (Tannock 2018, 173). Yet, Tannock observes, British experience shows that international students are frequently placed in one of two disadvantageous positions. First, many universities take an ethnocentric approach to international education, perceiving non-natives as deficit learners who have moved to the UK to take advantage of a superior British academic system (Tannock 2018, 163). A second, internationalisation-at-home perspective treats international students as a resource for domestic learners, who can acquire 'global' skills within an international learning environment. To Tannock this stance is equally problematic, given that institutions often collect higher fees from students originating outside the home country (2018, 171). The literature on strategic internationalisation offers few solutions to the challenges posed by Tannock, which suggest that one needs to approach the theme of *internationalising* differently. Hence, the third section highlights the role of academic staff in institutional processes of internationalisation.

Policies, actors, and institutional cultures

Since 2000, internationalisation has increasingly been presented as an organisational change process involving all units, functions, and actors within a university. In the literature, this is manifest in contributions from educational consultants, who advocate a holistic approach, insisting that universities need to design *all* educational programmes, curricula, disciplinary groupings, and extra-curricular activities with internationalisation in mind. Examples are European researchers' promotion of an 'internationalisation-at-home' agenda (Nilsson 2003, Crowther et al. 2000), Leask's effort to 'internationalise' curricula in Australian Higher Education (2015), and the American John Hudzik's strategy for 'comprehensive internationalization' (2015). To *internationalise*, Hudzik observes, 'is to focus on how abstract visions for the internationalization of teaching/learning/research/scholarship, and service/engagement play out' (2015, 1). Hudzik foregrounds the formulation and implementation of an organisational internationalisation strategy, identifying as principal actors institutional leaders (e.g. the president, deans), administrative functions (International Office, campus services), and '[h]ighly regarded individual faculty [who may] exert leadership and influence simply by being involved internationally' (2015, 68). Hudzik acknowledges that 'leadership is not necessarily hierarchical' and 'comes from many sources' (2015, 67), which suggests that he is aware of the dangers in focusing exclusively on the managerial and bureaucratic functions within an academic institution. Yet he shares with other proponents of holistic internationalisation a top-down perspective, largely ignoring how projects undertaken by individual academics to pursue a specific research or educational interest may initiate a bottom-up transformation of institutional cultures. A more balanced view is provided by Trondal (2010), who identifies 'two worlds of change' where strategic attempts to internationalise 'by hierarchy and design' are contrasted with 'internationalisation by "choice" and discipline', defined by Trondal as follows:

> Universities are traditionally seen as meritocratic communities of fellow peers that enjoy large degrees of scholarly autonomy from state, society and markets. This conception views universities as republics of scholars where scholarly freedom is the *raison d'être*. According to this vision, the

> internationalisation of research should chiefly be understood as cross-border contact patterns and mobility between individual faculty members.
> (Trondal 2010, 356)

Trondal is supported by Primeri and Reale (2012), whose empirical research demonstrates how, within one Italian university, the impact of EU policy frameworks differs between academic disciplines and departments as the result of individual research leaders' varying willingness to shape practices according to European guidelines. Similarly, Harrison (2015) challenges the internationalisation-at-home approach to education, stressing how at the end of the day the successful integration of an international/intercultural dimension depends on the attitudes of lecturers and home students. The implication is that academic staff should be regarded as key actors in the processes transforming university cultures into an inclusive, international environment.

Interview study one asked 36 academics from five Danish institutions: *How did you become involved in international education?* Based on the answers the author was able to construct a picture of internationalisation processes, as experienced by academic staff located within a variety of institutional, faculty, and disciplinary settings. Two key distinctions were adopted from the literature to support the analysis: 1) *ad hoc* and *systematic* (Burnett/Huisman 2010), which describe the organisation of activities; and 2) *bottom-up* and *top-down* (Trondal 2010), which highlight where in an institutional hierarchy an internationalisation initiative originates. The interview statements suggest a general movement from an early ad hoc and bottom-up phase towards the adoption of a systematic approach managed by university leaders and key administrators. This trajectory contains four stages:

- *Loose organisation*: Primarily involves single modules or electives in English which are run by enthusiasts among academic staff; little involvement of faculty or central management.
- *Parallel organisation*: Departments or faculties translate existing programmes into English to accommodate a growing number of non-natives (within the EU often exchange students); in some institutions this happens on the initiative of university leaders.
- *Spread of internationalisation*: New international programmes launched to recruit globally oriented domestic and non-native students; frequently, the drivers are enthusiasts among academic staff who may use a managerial awareness of internationalisation to further a particular research and educational agenda.
- *Strategic internationalisation*: All programmes at a certain level (mainly MA), within specific departments or disciplines are internationalised; typically, this happens as the result of a strategic prioritisation by university

leaders who, for instance, can attempt to make internationalisation compulsory by implementing a policy of teaching in English only.

The four phases show how internationalisation may transform institutional cultures that are traditionally non-English speaking. Within such a setting, the gradual spread of international teaching becomes very visible because it demands from academic staff and domestic students an acceptance of English as the medium of instruction. However, informants' reflections relate to processes of a more general nature, offering an insight into academics' perception of internationalisation as organisational change.

Arguably, most universities begin with a *loose organisation* of international activities. Within the chronology suggested by Knight (2017) an ad hoc approach characterises the early development of mobility programmes in the 1980s and 1990s, which explains why it is sometimes overlooked by educational scholars writing in the 2010s. Yet experienced international lecturers tend to describe internationalisation as a process initiated by named individuals, who engage in such effort to further an internationalist agenda within their department or discipline. One example is this lecturer from Nordic Studies:

> [W]e were two … recently completed PhD students, who started some new courses and said: We want to try our luck with international students. We have a disciplinary specialisation that is not only relevant to local students, but which … attracts attention in many parts of the world. So we wanted to start teaching in English, and we wanted to offer summer schools and semester programmes. (DA)

Parallel languages is a form of organisation found predominantly in environments that are traditionally non-English speaking, but where the recruitment of non-native exchange students has created a demand for teaching in English. The decision to run courses in both English and the native language is often pragmatic, responding perhaps to resistance from domestic students and staff to English-medium education (Tange 2012a), although disciplines such as Business Studies or Communications have introduced English versions of existing courses in order to attract globally minded students (Lueg/Lueg 2015). Even if the pressure to increase the number of English-medium courses may originate with academics acting in the capacity of international coordinators, university management becomes more involved at this stage, supporting the process by establishing administrative functions such as an International Office.

The third phase is characterised by an expansion in international activities. New, international programmes are launched, which, unlike courses translated from the national language into English, have been designed with a mixed native and non-native student cohort in mind. In the interviews, this type of internationalisation is foregrounded by academics from disciplines such as Development Studies, Anthropology, and International Relations, who generally present their stance as more 'globalised' than the departmental culture in general. An associate professor (European Studies) observes:

> [I suppose] more things happen here because we are a group who constantly draw attention to it. Now you have to remember that this is in English and we also have other types of students. And now we have two English-medium programmes within the department, right, and we have other ones, [in] Area Studies, that have a language dimension. So it is not completely strange. (DA)

Other informants relate how they were recruited as part of an institutional effort to develop international education. In such cases, the initiative lies with institutional leaders who may attempt to internationalise an organisational culture that is predominantly local or national, by allocating resources and staff to subject areas expected to promote an internationalist agenda.

The fourth phase is best described as a process of systematic, top-down internationalisation controlled by university leaders. Such a development resembles Hudzik's strategy of comprehensive internationalisation and is presented by academic staff as a managerial decision made by actors positioned outside the lecturers' department, discipline, and programme. The interview data provide two examples of institutions that have promoted comprehensive internationalisation by implementing an English Only policy for MA education. In addition to teaching in a foreign language, such organisational change demands from lecturers a rethinking of course reading, curricular contexts, and classroom pedagogies, which can be time-consuming. Even informants supportive of international education express ambivalence about such a strategy, pointing to the lack of dialogue between top management and sub-organisational units such as programme committees and teaching groups. An agricultural scientist observes:

> I feel a bit uncomfortable about the very dogmatic approach that at least our management has taken [that] everything has to be in English at MA level. And that it has almost appeared as if we, as heads of studies, have been tapped in our heads with [the policy] that from 2008 all our postgraduate programmes have to be in English, and it is not up for discussion. Or rather – [managers] are happy to discuss it, but will not be shaken. (DA)

Not surprisingly, academic staff are most enthusiastic about internationalisation in institutional cultures where they are involved as key drivers in the process of internationalising research and education. In comparison, even experienced international educators express scepticism about the strategic approaches to internationalisation initiated by university leaders, highlighting the difficulties that this can create for students and staff.

De-internationalising higher education?

The section on scapes, scales, and systems ended with the warning that in times of rising nationalism voters and politicians may denounce internationalisation as an elitist project that moves resources from areas of local or national interest to international activities that can be used to strengthen universities' global brand (Altbach/de Wit 2015, van der Wende 2017). Recent events in relatively open educational systems such as Australia, Britain, and Denmark provide examples of this, with academic leaders now requested to defend institutions' international mission against welfare nationalist accusations that state-funded institutions should prioritise local and national interests. In Australia, political scientist Greg Melleuish fuelled the debate by insisting that 'the country's universities had "failed in their national responsibilities to the Australian people"' (Ross 2019), and his point was reinforced in an editorial, published in *The Australian*, October 2019: 'Australian universities should prioritise the teaching of the nation's culture, literature, art, politics and history'. In the UK, post-Brexit negotiations have left academic leaders and staff uncertain about the future position of British universities within the educational and research frameworks sponsored by the European Union, while British withdrawal from the EU is also expected to cause a drop in applications from EU students (Ziguras 2016). In Denmark, politicians' concern over the rising number of EU citizens claiming free higher education and student grants motivated the formulation of a new policy in August 2018, which requested that universities reduce their English-language places by up to 1,200. Danish universities responded by announcing in November 2018 that some international programmes would close, while others were 'de-internationalised' (Bothwell 2018). In this context, 'de-internationalisation' means that formerly English-medium programmes have been requested to introduce an entrance requirement of Danish equivalent to High School level A and change the teaching language for at least 50% of all modules into Danish. Effectively, this blocks international students from entering the programmes and represents a profound change of study environments as well as institutional culture.

De-internationalisation is a recent phenomenon and no research has yet established its impact on academic environments. What follows is therefore speculation only. The author anticipates effects in three key areas. First, de-internationalised programmes will see the make-up of the student cohort change from a mixed group to one that consists mainly of natives. Arguably, this has consequences for learners' ability to access a global pool of knowledge, develop intercultural competences, engage in multicultural teamwork, build international networks, and practise their English with peers from a variety of linguistic backgrounds. Second, the demand that 50% of all modules be taught in Danish challenges international staff since this limits their teaching options considerably. A final concern is the impact on institutions' international profile. In terms of global ranking, the proportion of international students is used as a benchmark by the THE-QS list, which means that a reduction in their number will influence Danish universities' position negatively (Jöns/Hoyler 2013). Together with the likely impact of de-internationalisation on Denmark's reputation as a destination country for mobile academics, this places Danish universities at a disadvantage in the competition for talent and resources unfolding within the global field of higher education.

4 Internationalising the disciplines

Disciplines in the academic system

Scientific disciplines represent one of the principal structures used to explain academics' perception and performance of higher education and research. Through disciplinary labels connections are established between individuals scholars' particular activities and the enterprises undertaken jointly within a research group, school, department, and faculty, and this installs in academics a sense of distinction – the understanding that 'our' way of doing science is fundamentally different to the practices found among colleagues working in other subject areas. Bourdieu observes on such differentiation in *Homo Academicus* (1988, 58):

> [B]etween the clinical practitioners and the mathematicians, or even between the jurists and the sociologists, lies all the distance that separates two different modes of production and reproduction of knowledge and, more generally, two systems of values and two lifestyles or, in other words, between two ways of envisaging the successful man.

Educational sociologists have conceptualised disciplines in a variety of ways, including *tribes and territories* (Becher 1989), *narratives* (Gilbert/Mulkay 1984) *disciplinary containers* (Johnston 1996), *communities of practice* (Tight 2008), *networks* (Fenwick/Edwards 2014), and *oceans of knowledge* (Manathunga/Brew 2014). This changing terminology reflects an epistemological debate where researchers have increasingly distanced themselves from the essentialism associated with the notion of academic *tribes and territories*, produced by Becher (1989) to support the claim that scientists' perceptions of knowledge could be ascribed to their membership of a particular discipline (see Trowler 2014b, Clegg 2012). Instead, one needs to engage with the *Doings & Sayings* found within scientific communities, asking whether practices reflect actors' affiliation with specific subject areas or should be explained by alternative factors such as personality, institutional position, social status, relationships, or power.

A central concern is agency, defined here as the possibility for single actors to act independently within or between disciplines. Approaching the question from an organisational perspective, Carmichael (2012, 38) proposes that one distinguishes between an understanding of disciplines as 'techno-managerial spaces', used by university managers to provide structure to scholarly and educational activities, and disciplines as 'conceptual territories', realised by academic staff when engaging in teaching and research. In relation to this one may speculate whether universities' tendency to rely on a disciplinary organisation of academic work has produced an arbitrary sense of difference among academic staff, encouraging scientists to think and act within separate, disciplinary containers rather than develop the interdisciplinary relationships that have become increasingly important to contemporary knowledge production (Brew 2008). Abandoning the preconceived notion of disciplinary categories altogether, Fenwick and Edwards (2014, 38–9) suggest that academic work be examined through actor-network theory, foregrounding connections between actors, activities, discourses, rituals, and artefacts. Similarly, Trowler (2014a, 34) argues that one begins from a study of actors' practical knowledge, performances, and concrete action:

> Disciplines are enacted as social practices are performed and as micropolitics are played out: teaching; research; conference attendance; departmental meetings; collaborative writing; mixed-disciplinary meetings of a political nature – for example where resource allocation is at stake; funding applications, etc.

The current discussion builds on an understanding of academic disciplines as a practice involving both a process of socialisation (into a discipline, department, and institution) and a set of *Doings & Sayings* that successful academic performers need to master in order to be recognised by peers. Examples of disciplinary practices can be found in research as well as education, which seems natural, given that most academics work in the dual capacity of scholar and teacher.

A final consideration is the question *if* and *how* disciplines are internationalising. Interestingly enough, the topic of internationalisation is largely missing from the sociological debate on academic disciplines, which suggests either that 1) the theme is irrelevant to a discussion of disciplinary practices, or 2) the authors engaging in such debates are situated in environments that have not experienced any great change. As regards the first point, internationalisation may appear irrelevant to researchers who perceive academic disciplines as *global* in orientation and outreach. Such claims have been supported by historic references to European medieval universities and wandering scholars, causing some authors to argue that contemporary internationalisation has changed very little (e.g. Welch 1997). An alternative perspective is provided by researchers who claim scientific knowledge to be *universal*, produced, in Rata's words, through 'scientific disciplinary procedures: the processes of review and criticism that occur over time and that allow for the separation of the ideas from their original socio-historical location' (2012, 106). In contrast to *social* knowledge, which is tied to particular groups and places, *universal* knowledge is presented as generally applicable, which means that it can be taught in the same way around the world. A second explanation for the scarcity of articles on *internationalising the disciplines* could be that authors partaking in such debates are frequently writing from a position at English-speaking institutions ranked high in Marginson's global hierarchy (2008, 306). These scholars are likely to have been among the beneficiaries of internationalisation within their subject area, producing the 'global' models and journals that serve as benchmarks for academics located in other parts of the world. In contrast, Chinese scientists will have to struggle to achieve international recognition, adopting English as a publication medium and accepting their need to 'produce and disseminate what the Anglophone community values as knowledge' (Feng et al. 2013, 266).

Murray Saunders (2014) names internationalisation as one of five *catalysts of change* transforming disciplinary practices. The present chapter will explore this claim, suggesting that disciplines change in response to the demand that academics *internationalise* research and teaching practices. The first section addresses the question of academic socialisation, asking whether global action and interaction have become normative practices in Science. The second examines research practices, demonstrating how academic status has become attached to an idea of 'international' scholarship and networking. The final section focuses on how disciplinary affiliation impacts academics' attitude to international education, arguing that divergent perceptions of knowledge cause academics to experience internationalisation as more or less challenging.

What comes naturally

In *Homo Academicus* (1988) Bourdieu presents academic disciplines as autonomous fields within which scientists compete for peer recognition, social status, and influence. In order to succeed scholars must demonstrate mastery of the rules that determine how the scientific 'game' is played within their discipline, and novice scholars undergo a process of disciplinary socialisation, gradually acquiring the practical knowledge that distinguishes experts within their field. Building on Bourdieu's work, Gerholm (1990) suggests that disciplinary rules and routines are tacit, which means that they are rarely explicated to the students seeking recognition as competent members of their scientific community. The implication is that academics are not necessarily aware of the norms governing action, including the close relationship between their subject area and a specific way of performing research and education. A similar point is made by Mills and Huber (2005), who insist that anthropologists internalise discipline-specific ways of teaching and learning as part of their subject specialisation, which motivates the authors to question the current trend at universities to allocate responsibility for teacher development to separate pedagogic units. An alternative approach focuses on the social learning processes that occur within disciplinary *communities of practice*. According to Tight (2008, 596) communities of practice are structured more loosely than Becher's disciplinary tribes, which allows academics to belong to multiple groupings that reflect their simultaneous involvement in discipline-based research, academic development, teaching, and departmental politics. Focusing on academic discourse, Hyland (2012) shows how teachers' comments on student writing provide an example of social learning, introducing the learner to norms that she will be expected to internalise in order to master academic discourse within her subject area. Hyland (2012, 4) observes on this process: 'Behind the feedback comments is an assumption that the student is learning to identify with the community and that this is aided through interactions of this kind with experienced members.'

The literature on academic disciplines supports the argument that subject specialisation involves a high degree of habituated action and tacit knowledge, which novice scholars must acquire in order to demonstrate competence within their field of study. Only the most talented are encouraged to pursue an academic career, which leads one to expect a high degree of compliance with disciplinary norms within scientific communities of practice. What remains to be established is to what extent internationalisation has become normative within the academic disciplines. Writing in 1999, Bourdieu expressed scepticism about 'scientific internationalism' (220), stressing how the image of ideas travelling seamlessly around the world was a myth, and that texts adopted from other intellectual traditions were generally mistranslated and misread. According to Bourdieu (1988) the problem was context, or 'field of production' (221), for in order to engage with the meanings originally intended one would have to know what intellectual, institutional, and disciplinary conditions shaped the author's choice of scientific models, theorists, and discourse. Bourdieu's claim that texts are situated within particular social spaces provides a contrast to Rata (2012, 106), who regards scientific knowledge as universal and therefore separable from authors' geographical, historical, and socio-cultural contexts. To explain such disparity, one may refer to the empirical work by Clifford (2009, 2014), who has examined how academics from different disciplines react to international education. Clifford (2009, 136) found that a universalist orientation characterised scientists working in Chemistry and Computer Science, who would insist that their disciplines were based on generic principles and could therefore be taught in the same way around the world. A similar view was voiced by engineers in Trice's (2005) study of US-based academics' experience with international education, which indicates that lecturers from Natural and Technical Sciences would support Rata's assertion that scientific knowledge is generally applicable, dismissing the possibility that internationalisation requires a rethinking of disciplinary practices. In contrast, informants from the Social and Human Sciences tend to accept the argument that knowledge is tied to specific national, socio-cultural, and institutional contexts. In order to perform successfully within international research and education, academics have to adapt their practices, leading, in the extreme case, to a complete reorientation of a disciplinary field. An associate professor from Law observes:

> [I]t makes a great difference to work in Danish or to work in – well, it is working in English mainly, but also in German. One of the reasons why it makes such a difference is that languages not only bring with them a research tradition, but also a legal tradition. So when you start communicating in English ... you automatically engage with an Anglo-American perception of law and the relationship between law and society. While if you communicate in German, you automatically engage with a Continental European perception of law. (DA)

Arguably, scholars internalise a particular disciplinary orientation as part of their socialisation into a scientific community. Within Natural Science actors are likely to meet an understanding of knowledge as generic and universally applicable, which influences how they present their subject to peers and students. In comparison, a researcher from Law is educated within a field that refers to domestic law, actors, and institutions, and is likely to organise knowledge into distinctive, national traditions. A final group of scholars from 'internationalist' subjects such as Geography, Anthropology, Development Studies, and International Business have learnt to engage with socio-cultural locations around the world and describe this as natural to academic work.

Disciplinary orientations affect academics' assessment of internationalisation processes, prompting some actors to present such initiatives as a major 'catalyst for change' while others see little difference. Yet qualitative research from Norway and Denmark reveals that scholars from a range of subject areas experience pressure to engage with international research and education, which, over time, could change academic norms and dispositions, privileging those already involved in global interaction. An indicator of change is the attention paid to international visibility among young academics. In 2004, Ljosland published an empirical study of the language preferences of Norwegian doctoral students, foregrounding how English had become the default option for knowledge dissemination. According to Ljosland (2004, 143–4) many PhD students considered English the natural medium for research purposes, insisting that this language was more prestigious because of its association with international activities, high-ranking scientific journals, and an outward-looking approach to science. English seems equally important to Danish lecturers, who relate language change to institutional processes that have established international teaching and research as normative practices. An assistant professor (Business) provides an example of how junior academics are encouraged to align their work with standards recognised by international professional associations and publishers:

> [O]ur head of department has … held some publication clinics for the young researchers – PhD students and assistant professors. Where he simply tells [us] about his own experiences with publishing. From the beginning you really get told that this is very important. This thing about performing internationally. For writing articles for international journals, that is part of becoming international. While in the old days you could stay here, writing books, and still be respected for that. (DA)

This represents a formalised approach to academic socialisation where the most senior member of the department presents international publishing to junior scholars, prompting them to accept this as their benchmark for academic success. Even if most describe more informal processes, many informants agree that they experience a growing pressure to internationalise research and education, insisting that scientific status has become tied to one's ability to be obtain international recognition. A contrasting perspective is provided by those who perceive internationalisation as a process working to their advantage because it enables them to pursue a personal interest in international affairs. A social scientist observes:

> I am sure there are some of my colleagues who will see this as pressure from above. That what they are doing, both in research and education, ought to be more international. Both in terms of theme and publishing etc. And that I am certain about, right? For me, well, that is how it is, and that is my point of departure. Hence, well, when pressure comes from above, it is really working to my benefit. (DA)

Across disciplines, the Danish interviews reveal that scholars are encouraged to act and think 'internationally'. This suggests that a new norm has emerged in academia, requesting that scientists align their research with standards set by global communities of practice.

Internationalising research practices

Scientific work involves various forms of action and interaction, including research, teaching, professional networks, collaborative writing, conference attendance, departmental meetings, peer reviewing, and project administration. Yet many academics consider research to be the principal element defining academic identity, providing the setting where they can demonstrate disciplinary expertise by producing new scientific knowledge and thereby gain recognition from peers. Most prestigious is scientific work that achieves international visibility, which explains the ambition of doctoral students to interact with a global community of scholars. Even if some mention institutional pressure, most academics accept international knowledge exchange as a natural part of scientific pursuit, which makes research practices an obvious place to look for evidence of how and where the disciplines have internationalised.

Trowler (2014a, 34) characterises disciplines as a cluster of activities, which in 'each area of practice [involves] different identities, discourses and contextual concerns.' Writing specifically about the internationalisation of academic work Rostan and Ceravolo (2015, 38–9) suggest as characteristics defining international research 'scope or orientation', 'collaborating with international colleagues', 'primarily employing English', and 'funding for research from international organisations'. Rostan and Ceravolo place knowledge dissemination and mobility in separate categories, which seems problematic, given the close relationship between actors' conduct of research, their communication of key results, and participation in international research communities. Instead, the present author has found inspiration in practice theory, using the concepts of *Doings*, *Sayings,* and *Relatings* to organise the experiences conveyed by informants (see Schatzki 2002, Kemmis/Mahon 2017). For the purpose of the present discussion, *Doings* may be defined as scientists' conduct of research, including their identification with specific intellectual traditions, choice of research methods, and use of artefacts such as computer software, lab equipment, and key texts. *Sayings* involve various forms of academic discourse, e.g. scientific publications, guest lectures, conference papers, and outreach activities such as TED talks and media appearances. *Relatings* concern activities building on some kind of relationship and can take the form of co-authoring, project collaboration, professional associations, and short-term visits to foreign research institutions. As discussed in Chapter 2, *Relatings* was added to Schatzki's original framework to acknowledge the importance of networking in academic work.

With regard to *Doings* an international dimension can be identified in relation to disciplinary orientation, intellectual traditions, and material objects such as literature, computer programs, and economic models. In terms of orientation, the majority of informants insist that an international outlook be regarded as one of the elements defining their approach to science. Field researchers from Anthropology, Biology, and Geography present an engagement with locations around the world as natural to their discipline, while specialists in Area Studies explain how their work is distinguished by a great reliance on knowledge produced in other contexts, languages, and intellectual traditions. 'Greek-Roman culture has always been an international field' (DA), a historian observes, suggesting that a global outlook is an integral part of disciplinary culture. A second form of internationalisation involves scholars' positioning of their work in relation to the predominant intellectual traditions within their field. Bourdieu and Wacquant (1999) argue that academic communities increasingly accept American scientific models as their benchmark, and their claim is supported by Burawoy (2016), who notes how in Sociology this has allowed US-based academics to 'remain staunch believers in a positivist universalistic social science' (950). In the Danish interviews, evidence of American hegemony can be found in subject areas such as International Business, Management, and Political Science where informants highlight the importance of US-based authors, institutions, and publications to developments within their field. In contrast, other researchers present knowledge production as multi-sited, distinguishing between Continental and Anglo-Saxon philosophy, Continental European and Anglo-American law, and American and European academic traditions. A final example of *Doings* involves the material objects employed when conducting science. Artefacts include computer software, mathematical algorithms, and statistical models, which are presented as standardised tools that can be used around the world. Yet an equally significant research object is scientific literature, which interviewees often describe as 'English'. One may speculate to what extent such preference for English-medium material influences what theoretical and methodological knowledge is recognised within a discipline, favouring models developed by scholars who are competent writers of English.

The second theme of *Sayings* concerns practices related to academics' use of oral and written discourses to disseminate the knowledge produced through research. Hyland (2012) has identified various genres that academics employ to demonstrate mastery of scientific discourse, although the present discussion will focus on conference presentations and scientific articles, which are the forms of knowledge communication referred to most frequently in the interviews. As regards oral discourse, the Danish data show a consensus across disciplines that researchers will present conference papers in English in order to engage in international debates within their discipline. An informant elaborates on this, noting how within her field of Nordic Studies practices are becoming internationalised:

> [P]erhaps within the last one or two years I have seen that there are more colleagues who will attend conferences abroad, and I can see that more conferences organised in the department are English-medium. And which involves more than locals or inviting [people] from Copenhagen University. So I think there is a tendency towards becoming more internationally oriented. (DA)

Opinions vary more when it comes to academic writing. At one extreme are the natural scientists who insist that they have always used English as their principal medium for scientific publication because, as one professor (Agricultural Science) puts it: '[Our] area is simply too narrow and too small to make it worthwhile to [use] Danish' (DA). In comparison, social scientists describe academic environments split between 'old school' researchers, who rarely publish internationally, and young scholars writing exclusively in English. Most critical is this associate professor from Business Communication, who here problematises the adoption of English as the default medium for academic writing:

> At some point, I wrote an article where I was warned against writing it in Danish because it did not count … Back then it was also okay to write it in German, but it was clearly more prestigious to write in English. But since I was writing about Danish syntax, with Danish examples and Danish references, I found it a bit ridiculous having to write in German or English, for my target audience was neither English-speaking nor [people like that]. Actually, they were some pretty Danish-speaking people. (DA)

The final category of *Relatings* describes research practices that involve some form of collaboration. This group ranges from the loose connections achieved through membership of professional associations to more demanding types of cooperation such as co-authorship, collective projects, and joint funding applications. Common to all is their reliance on contact between individual academics, which, according to Trondal (2010), is one of the factors driving internationalisation within the disciplines. Looking at individual activities, the most accessible forms of *Relating* are performed through participation in professional associations and international conferences. These research practices are important to junior scholars in particular, who can use such forums to meet with senior researchers in their field and thereby extend their networks. International mobility represents a second form of contact, which is shared by junior and senior academics across disciplines. Rostan and Ceravolo (2015) show that short-term sojourns are popular among European academics, who use research visits to build relationships with colleagues based at top-ranking institutions in Europe or North America. Judging from the Danish data, the most attractive destinations are the US, Britain, and Australia, whereas Norway and Sweden come across as not 'international' enough. More demanding are collaborative activities such as co-authorship, partnerships, and joint funding applications. Such practices are pursued by senior academics, who enjoy greater international visibility and therefore find it easier to enlist internationally renowned scholars in shared enterprises. Most committing are large-scale collective projects where researchers cooperate with teams positioned at institutions around the world. A natural scientist mentions how she is working on a project involving several Asian and European countries, and this is common among the informants from Natural Science, who describe cooperation with multiple partners from research institutions, industries, government agencies, intergovernmental organisations, and NGOs. In comparison, references to external partnerships occur less frequently among interviewees from Social Science and the Humanities, which may reflect a disciplinary tradition to perform research alone or in smaller groups.

The previous examination offered examples of research practices that can be characterised as international. What also became apparent was that the choice to act and interact internationally is taken by the academics in an attempt to fulfil a personal ambition to obtain global visibility. This suggests that international activities have become habituated within academia, compelling actors to accept these as 'natural' to scholarly work.

International education and the disciplines

As mentioned in Chapter 3, Trondal's study of internationalisation (2010) identifies two 'worlds of change' at Norwegian universities. First, academic systems may be transformed as the result of a bottom-up process, driven by scholars' participation in disciplinary networks and collaboration. Trondal (2010, 358) describes such change as 'de-coupled from actions and initiatives from the university leadership', and this is characteristic of research where academics willingly engage in international activities in order to gain recognition, opportunities, and an extended network. The second process, 'internationalisation by hierarchy and design' (2010, 354), is initiated by managers seeking to strengthen an institution's global position by implementing new organisational policies, rules, and benchmarks. An interesting example of top-down internationalisation was found at two Danish universities where institutional decision-makers implemented a language change, adopting English as the default medium of instruction for Masters education (see Tange 2012a, 2012b). To the policy writers, the decision to switch from Danish into English may have seemed a minor change, but to academic staff, such expansion of international education affected a bundle of practices, in some cases necessitating a complete rethinking of course design and curricula. When prompted about the concrete actions taken to internationalise education, lecturers mention a number of areas, including curricular design, course reading, academic socialisation, communication style, lecturing format, group work, supervision practices, and exam preparation, which are teaching practices explored in the third part of this book.

Even if there are actors who feel pressured by management initiatives, most informants in the Danish data are positive about international education. Most enthusiastic are academics from subject areas characterised by a strong international orientation, a high degree of staff mobility, and regular interaction with global communities of practice. 'I guess we are all, perhaps, these types who find that we do not really fit very well into quite an ordinary, national context' (DA), an associate professor notes with reference to colleagues in Area Studies, stressing how she actively sought employment in an environment that allowed her to engage in international course development. Similar views are expressed by interviewees from European Studies, Anthropology, Development Studies, Finance, and International Relations, who relate their interest in internationalisation to the global outlook within their disciplines. In scientific communities where an international dimension has been less prominent, academics may use international education as an opportunity to promote a particular area of specialisation. One assistant professor relates how her field of Old Norse proved attractive to international students, which enabled her to demand that more attention be paid to this in a department that had traditionally neglected such research. Other academics have used international teaching to offer alternative perspectives on disciplinary knowledge, allowing the philosopher to introduce a cross-cultural dimension, while the Business lecturer can pursue a special interest in China and India. However, in cases where actors feel hesitant about internationalisation, affiliation with a globally oriented discipline can increase the sense of insecurity experienced by actors. One informant explains how English-medium teaching has become normative within her field of Management:

> [P]erhaps this has also something to do with, well, we are a business school, where this is part of what we teach people. Among other things, this is about entering foreign markets and being able to lead international organisations. And then it would really be a complete admission of failure if we were standing there – oh no, not in English. Wouldn't it? (DA)

The comment serves as a reminder that within all scientific communities one encounters reluctant internationalisers, and that such individuals can experience a sense of vulnerability and marginality if belonging to disciplines that link scientific achievement to actors' international activities. For non-native speakers of English, this can make it difficult to refuse international teaching because they fear that such denial will reflect negatively on their status within the department, suggesting to managers that they lack the linguistic competence to produce, present, and publish scientific knowledge in English.

A second factor affecting academics' attitude to international education is their understanding of disciplinary knowledge. Building on Becher's distinction between *hard/soft* and *pure/applied*, Clifford (2009, 2014) has shown how international education is perceived differently across the disciplines, highlighting the contrast between academic fields where knowledge is regarded as universal, and fields that consider knowledge to be a product of socio-cultural location and experiences. Clifford's mapping of disciplinary positions serves as inspiration for the present analysis, enabling the identification of patterns in the accounts offered in the Danish interviews. As regards the Hard/Soft distinction, informants working in Hard disciplines such as Chemistry, Statistics, and Theoretical Biology confirm Clifford's claim that knowledge within these communities is understood as 'objective, measurable, impersonal and value-free' (2014, 198), requiring minimal adjustment to work in international education. A natural scientist observes: 'Well, it has been Chemistry and Biochemistry, and you make some references to the body and some natural phenomena and things like that, right? But it is really quite international' (DA). In contrast, academics from Soft disciplines present knowledge as context-dependent, tied to particular geographies, socio-cultural conditions, and languages. Educational programmes in History, Nordic Studies, Law, and Public Administration, for instance, often refer to national traditions and institutions. This means that courses within such disciplines cannot simply be translated into English, but demand rethinking and reframing. A social scientist reflects on the difference he sees between his disciplinary practice and the approach requested from students in Natural Science:

> To me the scientific terms represent a form of conceptualisation … [W]hen I start explaining the context in which the concept has to be used, which really is a description of society and the world around us. This is where it starts creating problems. And what I mean is that if they had read Biochemistry or something like that in English, then they would have been privileged because they would only need to acquire the scientific terms. But here, because it is Social Science, then you also need to know … the English word for a building or a road. (DA)

Clifford (2009, 136) places academic disciplines on a continuum from Hard Pure to Soft Pure, suggesting that a marked contrast is found between Hard and Soft positions. A similar divergence characterises the Danish interviews, which thus supports Clifford's argument that academics from Soft disciplines see a greater need to contextualise the knowledge presented to international classes. As regards Clifford's second dimension, the Pure/Applied distinction highlights the difference between disciplines that are mainly theory-driven, and those seeking to develop scientific knowledge that addresses the needs of specific social groups, organisations, and sectors.

Particularly the latter form of knowledge can present challenges in an international course since it requests from the lecturer an ability to establish connections between scientific principles and practices tied to specific geographic settings and experiences. A Danish agricultural scientist reflects:

> Right now I am running a course, which thematically involves plant production, which is really a very applied, practice-oriented course … [P]reviously this has also been the kind of course where students primarily learnt something about Danish plant production, and you know, who are the kind of people acting within the Danish plant production. There are some consultants, there are some farmers, there are some scientists, etc. Where you can tell a lot of anecdotes and history and give examples because, well, I really know that world. But when it is in English, and when it is international, [then] we really have to run it in a way that makes the teaching interesting to a student from Kenya or Portugal. (DA)

The informant's point – that international education demands that localised knowledge be replaced by something generally relevant – is echoed by academics from other applied sciences, including Law, Business Administration, Management, and Accountancy. All explain how in Danish-medium courses they would use personal anecdotes, news stories, and business cases to forge a link between the theoretical models presented in class and the forms of professional practice that students may meet upon graduation. Such teaching practice has proved difficult to implement in international courses because it draws on knowledge connected to particular socio-cultural locations and traditions. In comparison, academics working in Pure disciplines consider internationalisation a manageable task. Examples are informants from areas such as International Relations, Finance, Engineering, and Natural Science, who express a common understanding of disciplinary knowledge as something constituted by generic models, conceptual frameworks, and research methodologies found in English-medium literature and therefore easy to adopt for international teaching. An associate professor (Cognitive Semiotics) reflects: '[We] teach how humans generally understand the world, use their intelligence, you know, human beings' generic, intellectual, cognitive traits, right?' (DA)

When Clifford's two dimensions of hard/soft and pure/applied are brought together, one sees substantial differences with regard to the amount of adjustment that academics find necessary when internationalising disciplinary knowledge. On the one hand, informants from Hard/Pure sciences are able to treat knowledge as generic principles, which may be taught in a similar way to all students. On the other hand, academics from Soft/Applied subjects insist that knowledge is context-dependent and difficult to translate from a national to an international setting. Exempt from this general pattern are academics who in their research have engaged with the global dimension to context-specific disciplines such as Law, History, and Media Studies. Frequently these actors present themselves as 'drivers' of internationalisation within their discipline and department, actively pursuing opportunities to develop international research and education.

Internationalising the disciplines?

A catalyst may be defined as 'a feature or set of features that hasten or bring into being new practices' (Saunders 2014, 169). Inspired by the empirical work of Clifford, Saunders suggests that internationalisation functions as a 'catalyst for change', motivating academics and university managers to reconsider disciplinary practices. The previous discussion has supported the argument that the academic system is currently undergoing a transformation, which is materialised through the internationalised research and teaching practices that have increasingly become the norm within a range of disciplinary communities. The empirical documentation mainly come from academic systems that are traditionally non-English speaking, although Clifford's work suggests that also staff employed at Australian universities experience change.

Together with two empirical studies from Norway and China (Ljosland 2004, Feng et al. 2013), the observations made by the Danish-based academics in the author's research provide evidence that internationalisation, as realised through English-medium publishing, references to US/UK-produced literature, and short-term visits to prestigious, English-speaking institutions, may be considered a normative practice across disciplines. Interestingly enough, even within context-specific subjects such as Nordic Studies, English is now employed as a conference medium, which suggests a general acceptance that international knowledge exchange is essential to academic work. The analysis of the Danish interviews showed how international research practices spread in a number of ways: First, they are promoted through institutional benchmarks and reward systems which will often rank English-medium publications higher than work disseminated through alternative languages such as German or Danish. Second, junior scholars encounter an expectation to engage in international activities as part of their formal or informal socialisation into academia. Finally, researchers have expressed an interest in adding an international perspective to context-specific subjects such as History, Law, and Sociology, which, over time, may cause a change to disciplinary outlook.

With regard to teaching practices, the way internationalisation can be realised depends on the (perceived) nature of disciplinary knowledge. In some areas international education involves only minor adjustments, or, in the case of lecturers located in English-speaking environments, none at all. In contrast, for academics in disciplines that refer to specific geographical locations or professional practices, an engagement in international education represents a major undertaking, causing lecturers to reconsider their teaching style, course contents, and socio-cultural framing of knowledge. Particularly in relation to very context-specific areas one may speculate about the long-term effect of such adjustments, which could cause a reorientation of education from, for instance, Danish History to International Studies or domestic to European Law. When combined with the material presented in the subsequent chapters on language usage, course design, curricular contexts, academic conventions, multicultural teamwork, and exam preparation, this supports Saunders' claim that internationalisation should be considered a 'catalyst of change', which in the long run will cause major 'disruption' to the way individual actors think about, enact, and reproduce academic disciplines.

5 Global and local teachers

Mobility as a structural condition

Movement in the form of mobile people, objects, and ideas may be considered a defining feature of academic life in the 21st century. Every year millions of students and staff travel to new institutional settings in pursuit of educational opportunities, job openings, and research collaboration, and through their action contribute to an internationalisation of disciplinary knowledge, networks, teaching, and learning practices. Three factors underline the importance of mobility as a structural condition in academia. First, the historical precedent of the wandering medieval scholar suggests that mobility constitutes an academic tradition. Healey (2008, 334) compares present-day migration to the talents attracted to European centres of learning in the 15th and 16th centuries, while Hook (1975) has documented how in the 18th century mobile intellectuals connected American and Scottish universities. A second factor is the scope and scale of contemporary academic migration. According to UNESCO (2018) 4.8 million students could be identified as 'internationally mobile' in 2016, to whom should be added a considerable number of academic staff moving overseas to take up new positions or on short-term sojourns as visiting scholars or guest lecturers. The population of academic migrants has risen dramatically since 2000, which testifies to the value attached by individual actors to international experience and qualifications. In terms of scope, institutional and national policies have opened new geographies to academic migrants, enabling South Korea, Japan, Vietnam, and South Africa to become established as new destination countries (Van der Wende 2015, Gunter/Raghuram 2018). A third factor is the power of mobility as a social imaginary. Judging from the literature, the ability to move and attract mobile scholars is increasingly used as benchmarks for individual and institutional success. This has prompted Robertson (2010, 641) to speak of a 'mobilities paradigm', centred on the premise that '[t]he world is on the move, and if it is not, it ought to be'. The implication is that movement has become normative, with intellectual prowess directly linked to actors' capacity to navigate within a global field of higher education and research.

The German sociologist Thomas Faist (2009) has described the socio-cultural change effected by increased migration as a 'transnationalization of social life worlds', defined as 'an increased trans-border integration of social practices ... and cross-border elements of common horizons of meaning and senses of belonging or common identifications' (183). Transnationalisation offers a useful way to conceptualise academic mobility, underlining how ideas of movement shape actors' perception of their profession and the university as a site where global careers can be performed more or less satisfactorily. The reading of academia as a transnational profession can be supported both at the practical and ideological levels. In terms of practice, the previous chapter established how academics commonly identify with disciplinary communities, within which they acquire the shared experiences, understandings, and methods that distinguish their particular field. Most communities of practice facilitate cross-border activities such as scientific collaboration, international networking, conference attendance, and short-term visits to partner institutions or research groups. 'Transnationalism', in the form of identities 'negotiated within social worlds that span more than one place' (Vertovec 2001, 573) may thus be regarded as the norm in academe, installing in actors the impression that international travel and connections are key elements in a scientific career. The perception of movement as 'natural' places academics within the elite group that Calhoun (2008) has labelled 'cosmopolitans'. According to Calhoun (2008), cosmopolitans are privileged people who share an experience of 'global mobility and connection' (106), using this to promote a worldview that takes for granted actors' ability to travel seamlessly around the world. Unlike Calhoun, who criticises cosmopolitanism for its neglect of inequality and power, educational scholars have embraced an ideology of transnationalisation. Sanderson (2008) insists on an 'Internationalization of the academic self', arguing that the concept of cosmopolitanism should be used to rethink teaching and learning practices in globalised educational settings. Similarly, Kim (2017, 987) suggests that mobility be treated as an 'ontological condition', realised through a tribe of *homo viator* – 'itinerant men and women in perpetual (academic) pilgrim condition both in real life and metaphorically' (Kim 2014, 63).

Processes of transnationalisation have transformed the way actors understand the institutional settings in which academic careers unfold. The traditional image of the university as a physical place embedded within specific local and national geographies can no longer accommodate the multi-scalar and multi-sited reality experienced by academics. Through the opportunities provided by technology and travel, scholars engage with multiple localities, co-constructing research practices with peers positioned in other parts of the world, and planning career moves that demonstrate their capacity to navigate in a global system. To capture such change Larsen (2016) proposes that higher education be approached through a theory of 'space, networks and mobilities'. Larsen characterises universities as *connectivity spaces*, comparable to 'airports and roads' in the sense that they constitute 'spaces of transition through which people and objects move around the world, but also within which people encounter one another, face-to-face' (Larsen 2016, 26). Arguably, the purpose of academic institutions has changed as the result of actors' 'mobile practices' (Larsen 2016, 91). While historically regarded as centres of learning that inspired in staff a sense of institutional belonging, universities are now treated as anchorage points enabling international recruits to move in, local staff and students to move out.

Scholars have warned against a 'mobility fetish' (Robertson 2010, 646). Guerin and Green (2016) thus characterise academic transnationalism as 'imaginary' rather than the reality experienced by most migrants, while Bauder et al. (2017, 3) note how movement is treated as unconditionally positive, 'independent of the quality of the scientific experiences obtained abroad'. To these may be added three concerns. First, the academic field is organised hierarchically, which means that actors are not equally capable of moving around the world. This supports the view expressed by Waters (2018), who encourages scholars to address the geopolitics of academic migration. Second, authors tend to focus on scholars settling permanently abroad. This has created a distorted picture, marginalising the considerable number of academics who pursue a career in their countries of birth, yet choose to *internationalise* their teaching and research through short-term sojourns. Third, there is a need for a transformative perspective, which acknowledges how actors' practices change as the result of their engagement with different disciplinary, institutional, and national contexts. Two empirical studies have documented how international recruits undergo a process of *localisation*, adapting their teaching to institutional norms, whereas native staff will *internationalise* through participation in cross-border communities of practice (Tange/Wilken forthcoming, Clifford/ Henderson 2011).

The present chapter examines academic mobility from three perspectives: First, 'Academics on the move' focuses on migration trends, using quantitative data to identify traits shared by mobile scholars. Second, 'Mobility as *habitus*?' engages with movement as a social imaginary, asking how this affects academics' career trajectories and self-understanding. Third, 'Migrants grounded' shows how most academics become embedded in local institutional contexts, which challenges the myth of a global educational space.

Academics on the move

Information about international student mobility is readily available from reports and statistics published by organisations such as UNESCO, OECD, and the EU. In contrast, quantitative data on staff migration has been gathered less systematically, prompting Teichler (2017, 16) to complain about the 'paucity of the information base'. Most comprehensive are two surveys conducted by Teichler and his team, namely the CAP study (2007–8) which included academic staff from 18 countries, and the EUROAC study (2007–10) which focused on 12 European countries (Teichler 2017). The CAP and

EUROAC data constitute the empirical foundation for several analyses of academic migration published in the 2010s (e.g. Galaz-Fontes et al. 2016, Teichler 2016, Rostan 2015, Galaz-Fontes/Metcalfe 2015 Goastellec/Pekari 2013). Teichler (2016, 2017) has since updated the results by comparing the original data to EUROSTAT statistics on the mobility of doctoral students within Europe. Limitations related to the information base present to challenges to the present discussion. First, any findings published describe the situation 10–12 years ago, which means that they do not necessarily provide an accurate picture of academic migration in 2019/2020. Second, empirical research has mostly centred on the Global North and West and does not take into account the fact that the contemporary academic system is multi-centred, with regional hubs emerging in Western Europe, South East Asia, and South Africa. The present inquiry builds on a variety of empirical foundations, comparing results from the two 2007–10 surveys to 1) observations made in the literature on academic migration; 2) material obtained on mobility in Danish academia 2011–17; and 3) patterns revealed through a qualitative analysis of lecturer biographies and interviews.

To identify tendencies relevant to a discussion of academic mobility, a comprehensive literature review was undertaken, which included both theoretical and empirical work. This foregrounded five general themes:

1) Academic migration occurs within a *global system*, which is organised hierarchically. This means that a select number of destinations in Western Europe and North America can claim the position of 'elite' in terms of power and prestige, which enables them to attract a high number of mobile scholars (Bauder et al. 2018, Marginson 2008). At the centre of the global hierarchy are the United States, Britain, and large European countries such as Germany and France, although this traditional hegemony is challenged by emerging powers such as Brazil, South Africa, China, and Singapore, which have invested large sums in developing higher education and research (Van der Wende 2015). Ranked lowest are developing countries in Asia and Africa whose talented academics move north and west in pursuit of career opportunities.
2) Academic cultures can be more or less *open* to international migration. Galaz-Fontes et al. (2016) propose two criteria for assessing system openness. First, one may consider the proportion of staff with foreign doctoral degrees. Here United States and South Africa represent two extremes, with 3% and 82% international PhD holders, respectively, while scores for other countries are: Japan 4%, China 6%, Germany 7%, the UK 14%, Australia 26%, and Hong Kong 71% (Galaz-Fontes et al. 2016, 331). A second criterion is the proportion of staff who have spent at least one year abroad since their appointment. As with foreign PhDs numbers vary between countries, ranging from 62% in Hong Kong to 12% in China.

3) The impact of *language* is relatively unexplored, although Bauder et al. (2017) have suggested that short-term mobility is more valued by academics who are non-native speakers of English, arguing that those 'who began their academic careers in English-speaking countries are sometimes unaware that international experience can be an asset' (9). Similarly, Gimenez and Morgan (2014) present English as a form of cultural capital that migrants seek in order to become recognised as internationally successful.
4) In terms of *mobility forms*, the CAP and EUROAC surveys foreground the importance of short-term stays to academic career development, which is generally overlooked in the literature because of authors' tendency to focus on permanent migration (e.g. Kim 2017, Chen/Koyama 2013). Yet researchers increasingly acknowledge a circular pattern where academics travel as sojourners to engage in network-building and research collaboration, but with the intention of returning to their home countries and institutions (Gimenez and Morgan 2014). Indeed short-term visits have become normative in some contexts, as Leemann (2010) demonstrates in her study of Swiss doctoral graduates.
5) A final theme is *demographics*, which has been examined by Galaz-Fontes et al. (2016) with the aim of establishing possible correlations between mobility trends and traits such as age, gender, social background, career stage, and experience. While these variables are significant when analysing individual career trajectories, the research findings show great national variation, which makes it difficult to identify any general tendencies.

The next section zooms in on migration trends within Danish academia in order to present a nuanced picture of mobility, as this unfolds within a particular national system. The choice of Denmark may be challenged as a 'power geography' firmly placed in the Global West and North (Fahey/Kenway 2010, 269). Undoubtedly, such positionality influences the nature of migration flows, which means that any findings should be read as specific to this context and not applied uncritically to conditions in other parts of the world. Yet Denmark offers an interesting case as a country placed in a semi-peripheral position within the global system. Danish universities have been successful in recruiting mobile scholars, which is reflected in the proportion of non-natives appointed for the positions as professor (11% in 2017), associate professor (12% in 2017), and assistant professor (32% in 2017) (Danish Ministry 2018b, 33). Little information is available on the nationality of foreign recruits, but analyses on student mobility suggest that Danish universities attract migrants from neighbouring countries (Germany, Norway, Sweden), Central and Eastern Europe (e.g. Romania, Lithuania, Poland), and China (Wilken/Dahlberg 2016). Material obtained from Aalborg University on doctoral students reveal a similar pattern (AAU 2017, 5), with a high number of PhDs recruited from Western/Eastern Europe and Asia. Equally important

Table 5.1 Top destinations, PhD sojourners (DK)

Destination country	*All sojourns 2014–17*
United States	27%
Great Britain	12%
Germany	8%
Sweden	5%
Australia	4%
Norway	4%
China	4%
Netherlands	4%
France	4%
Canada	3%

Source: Danish Ministry of Science and Higher Education 2019.

is the peripherality of Denmark compared to the United States and Britain. Denmark offers intrinsic rewards such as relatively high salaries and good working conditions for PhD students, and Danish universities therefore often serve as the intermediary stage for scholars pursuing a global career, 'delivering highly qualified personnel to other countries' (Van der Wende 2015, 80). This means that talented junior staff are likely to proceed to positions in more prestigious locations, which is documented in statistics from Aalborg University, which reveal how five years after obtaining their degree more than 50% of Aalborg-educated PhDs have left the university (AAU 2017). As regards short-term mobility, the information available suggests a high outflow of academics. Particularly PhD candidates are expected to undertake 'a change of environment', which in many cases involves a short-term stay abroad, while senior staff travel as visiting scholars, guest lecturers, and field workers. The top 10 destinations for PhD sojourners, as listed in Table 5.1, offer an indication of power geographies recognised by Danish-based scholars.

The statistics on PhD mobility shows a clear preference for English-speaking countries, which receive more than 47% of visits (Danish Ministry 2019), followed by Continental Europe, Scandinavia, and, as the only non-Western location making the Top 10, China. A parallel trend can be seen in the lecturer biographies, which indicate that Danish academics tend to travel to English-speaking countries (USA, Britain, Australia), prestigious research institutions in Western Europe (e.g. Science Po, European University Florence), and, occasionally, other Nordic countries.

Even if short-term mobility is the most common form of migration in Danish academia, it seems worthwhile to end with a consideration of five factors that can motivate a permanent move to a new national or institutional setting. First, actors' embeddedness in either a national or an international field determines to what extent they regard migration as a possible career choice. An academic educated and employed at the same Danish university can be expected to stay in this environment, unlike one who has worked in multiple locations, and to whom mobility constitutes a natural part of professional development. Second, university staff may be motivated to seek transfer into more prestigious settings. Generally, migration flows from south to north, east to west, which explains why Danish universities attract talent from Central and Eastern Europe, but see gifted scholars move westwards to Britain and the United States. The third tendency supports this as academics navigate within a well-established global hierarchy, seeking to boost their reputation by obtaining a position at high-ranking universities such as Harvard, Stanford, Oxford, and Cambridge. Many prestigious institutions are located in the United States and Britain, which contributes to the position of these destinations as power geographies. A fourth tendency is actors' move to a new institution to obtain a promotion, e.g. from post-doc to assistant professor or associate to full professor. This type of mobility is as likely to occur between institutions situated within the same national system as internationally. A final possibility is migration motivated by disciplinary concerns. Hence, a PhD trained in English literature may be willing to accept a position as a Business School lecturer in Professional English, but can be expected to move on as soon as a university post becomes available within her area of expertise.

Mobility as *habitus*?

Habitus, Bourdieu wrote in *Outline of a Theory of Practice* (1977), 'designates *a way of being, a habitual state*' (214). Bauder (2015, 87) proposes that mobility be treated as 'an element of the academic habitus', predisposing actors to seek recognition through collaboration with overseas colleagues, sojourns at prestigious foreign institutions, international conference attendance, and publications. Bauder's characterisation of mobility as 'habituated action' suggests that movement has obtained a taken-for-grantedness in academia, distinguishing successful 'global' scholars from those pursuing careers within a single institutional or national context. Yet academics' trajectories vary greatly, which means that one will find within the same environment both researchers navigating within a global system and those capable of demonstrating intellectual prowess from a relatively narrow home base. The following excerpts from interviews with British-based lecturers illustrate these opposite positions:

> [A]t that point I was about 55 and I thought I had one more, maybe, move in my career. Maybe this is the time … when I do something else. My partner had just retired, he was absolutely able to travel. I said, well, what if I get a job in England? Let's go to England and I'll be close to the theatre, I'll be able to do that research instead of being the outlier in the, always the outsider trying to kind of keep up.
>
> (International, Theatre Studies)

> I stayed in this locality, yes. Yes, I have been at university since – well, for 42 years – and I've never ever moved out of the Midlands except for two years. And I am also from, originally from the North Midlands. So I've never been abroad to teach, never been abroad to do research.
>
> (British, Biology)

The domestic orientation conveyed by the second respondent is shared by other UK-born staff employed at this British university, which supports the observation made by Bauder et al. (2017, 9) that native English speakers working in Anglophone contexts may be less prone to accept international experience as important to professional career development. In contrast, international recruits present short- and long-term migration as a natural part of academic work, which is a view common also to academics based at Danish universities. Mobility can take many forms so, in order to establish what academics more precisely mean by 'international movement', an analysis was performed of the Danish and British interview data, attending to comments that suggest long-term or short-term migration. As regards long-term migration respondents' examples include *lengthy or permanent settlement abroad* (either present, e.g. international staff in tenured positions, or past, e.g. as a child growing up in Brussels), *international work experience*, *international education* (typically at Masters or PhD level), and biological or ethnographic *fieldwork* (which at least in the traditional sense involves an extended period in the research site). In terms of short-term mobility, most references were made to appointments such as *visiting scholars*, *PhD sojourns*, participation in *teacher exchange* programmes (e.g. Erasmus), and *capacity building* in Eastern Europe or Third World countries. To these should be added research collaboration and conference attendance, which feature so regularly in the interview and biographical data that they can be treated as 'normalised' elements in an academic career. The implication is that any actor failing to demonstrate an engagement in such activities falls short of the disciplinary and institutional benchmarks used to evaluate scientific achivement.

Increasingly, writers on academic mobilility present international sojourns as normative for ambituous scholars because, as Morley et al. (2018, 540) observe: 'Professional stays abroad are often perceived as essential for academic identity formation, recognition and credibility and capacity building'. To explain the value attached to migration authors have relied on a terminology inspired by Pierre Bourdieu's concept of cultural capital. Early explorations of transnational movement as a strategy employed by migrants to boost their professional reputation and networks are Waters' (2007) and Munk's (2009) analyses of student mobility, which indicate that international education constitutes a conscious career move for local elites seeking to position themselves as 'cosmopolitans' competing in a global rather than national field. Cosmopolitans build their identity on the idea of a world connected through technology and travel, acknowledging the importance of educational migration as a way to acquire English-language proficiency, extended networks, and international experience (Waters 2007). Changing the focus to academic staff, Kim (2010, 2017) argues for mobility as a strategy for acquiring 'transnational identity capital', defined as 'a mode of cosmopolitan positioning to forge and sustain multi-stranded social relations, which can facilitate free movement among diverse groups and contexts' (2010, 583–4). Because such theorisation primarily builds on biographical analyses of migrants settling permanently overseas, Kim does not consider the importance of short-term movement, which is problematic given the popularity of temporary sojourns as a way to further professional development. A different approach is offered by Larsen (2016, 27), who proposes that the term 'network capital' be used for the variety of assets that individual actors can obtain through participation in research networks, international travel, and virtual collaboration facilitated by technologies such as the internet and social media. In contrast to Kim's somewhat idealised picture of a cosmopolitan elite, Larsen provides a conceptualisation that can embrace the range of international activities that academics engage in on an everyday basis. Nevertheless, the image of 'academics on the move' has maintained its appeal in some institutional and national contexts, prompting Nikunen and Lempiäinen (2020, 554) to observe that '[t]he "entrepreneurial university" demands that its researchers be mobile and have international careers'. Nikunen and Lempiäinen build on interview data collected from Finnish, Italian, and British academics, which reveals a contrast between informants working in Finland and Italy, who generally recognise migration as a form of professional development, and British-based staff, among whom 'attitudes towards geographical mobility were positive, but the need for internationalisation as a career move and person value was less visible' (2020, 13). Similarly, Bauder et al. (2017) have highlighted the difference between staff located in non-English-speaking Europe and those working in Britain or Canada. Generally, Bauder et al. (2017, 11) observe, 'mobility seems more desirable in non-English speaking countries', which is also a tendency noticed by Gimenez and Morgan (2014), who argue that non-native speakers consider academic migration a way to improve their English proficiency and thereby acquire linguistic capital. Gimenez and Morgan's claim is confirmed by the list of destinations visited by Danish-based PhD sojourners (Table 5.1), which included four Anglophone countries: United States, Great Britain, Australia, and Canada. That English-speaking environments have become the default destination in some disciplinary or institutional contexts is evident also in the interview data. When choosing an alternative location in neighbouring countries such as Norway or Sweden, some interviewees thus find it necessary to justify their decision, as seen in this comment by a Danish assistant professor (Business):

> I have been to Sweden during my PhD, and I have been extremely happy about this. It was really what determined what direction my PhD took, so [academically] it was a success. And I could see myself working in Sweden again, if I had to become a researcher somewhere else. And this has a lot

> to do with their methodology. Where I find that both England and the United States are very quantitative in orientation. But of course this has not given me a lot of experience when speaking about English. And this is what [people] focus on when talking about internationalisation. (DA)

The respondent comes across as vulnerable, suggesting that her international profile has been weakened as the result of her choice to visit Sweden rather than an Anglophone country. Such uncertainty may be caused by a sense of linguistic inadequacy as well as the awareness that she will have to qualify for the senior post as associate professor within an environment prioritising English-medium publication and teaching. In comparison, this professor from Political Science is confident about his gains from moving within a global field:

> I have only been employed at [Danish University], but simultaneous with that I have been abroad relatively often [as a visiting scholar]. And here I have been in Canada, I have been attached to a department in Brussels, I have been two years in Florence at the EUI, and twice I have been on shorter visits to Barcelona, and now, most recently, I have spent half a year in Turkey. And there, of course, I will make contact with … people and get a really good network, while getting an insight into how things are done differently in different places. (DA)

Common to both is the representation of international travel as natural to the academic profession. This supports the initial claim that mobility functions as a form of habituated action in academia.

Migrants grounded

The cosmopolitan academic uses the opportunities provided by travel and technology to navigate in a global field, treating her present university as a nodal point in an ever-expanding network of transnational connections and sojourn destinations. In contrast, *grounded* migrants are actors who have found their dreams of seamless travel shipwrecked against the constraints that national, institutional, and disciplinary cultures make on those seeking to transfer into a new environment. Experiences conveyed by international recruits in Australia indicate that transition is rarely as swift as the idealised pictures evoked by some authors writing on transnationalisation (Saltmarsh/Swiski 2010). Instead one must recognise how academic work is embedded in a variety of social contexts, which, according to Richardson (2009), challenges the myth of 'geographic flexibility'. The literature provides three examples of the limitations that contexual factors can impose on academics' room for manoeuvre.

1: Anne Metcalfe's (2017) account of her experience as a US national in Canada highlights how the flexibility of the migrant scholar working in a neighbouring country is constrained by political questions of nationhood and citizenship. After an initial transition period, Metcalfe is requested to renew her work permit, and pressure from her employer prompts her to reconsider her position:

> Becoming a [permanent resident] of Canada was not a choice if I intended to remain continously employed in my present position. My work permit would eventually expire, and my university warned me that they would not be pleased if they had to go through the bureaucracy necessary to renew it.
>
> (2017, 140)

Once they apply for citizenship, academic migrants establish a permanent connection with a specific nation state, obtaining the rights and responsibilities that this involves. Often this comes at the expense of special treatment such as expatriate bonuses or tax rebates which international staff have received because of national and institutional policies supporting the recruitment of foreign labour. In response, some may choose to terminate their employment relationship as soon as the transition period ends. Hence, a Danish-based informant explains how her co-teacher, an internationally renowned professor, was not expected to return to the programme because he no longer qualified for a tax rebate.

2: Heike Jöns (2007, 2011) foregrounds constraints related to particular academic and disciplinary cultures, using the example of Germany where junior scholars are expected to serve an extended period as an apprentice to a professor, with no guarantee of this leading to a permanent position:

> The *Habilitation*, a postdoctoral qualification often still required for applications to permanent academic posts, has tied young scientists and scholars to the research group of a professor for many years beyond the PhD. This has led to great job insecurity as it remains uncertain whether one will be able to secure a professorship at the age of about 35 to 45 and if so, where in the country this will be.
>
> (Jöns 2011, 204)

Academics aiming for a career in German higher education are bound to a specific environment where any disagreement with their professor can hinder advancement within the system. To talented scholars, such a culture can become a push factor, motivating junior researchers to seek appointments overseas rather than wait for recognition at home. As a result, a relatively high number of German-born scholars are employed by universities in neighbouring countries such as Switzerland, the Netherlands, and Denmark.

3: Stephanie Kim's (2016) examination of Western faculty at a Korean university demonstrates how an exclusive institutional culture may become an obstacle to academic career development. The international staff were originally hired to boost the university's global profile, receiving perks such as free accommodation in return for delivering American-style education at a newly founded 'international' college. In practice, the foreign recruits were isolated from the main university, leading separate lives that effectively cut them off from the power circuits and networks that they needed to enter in order to advance within this institutional environment. As a result, the internationals never became integrated, experiencing a 'growing disconnect between [their] needs and ambitions' and 'expectations of them at Yonsei University' (Kim 2016, 86).

The embedded nature of academic work means that migrants recruited from different national, educational, and institutional cultures undergo a process of experiential learning as part of their settling into a new position. This has motivated the current author to suggest that international staff become 'localised', which means that they internalise the tacit knowledge and norms that govern professional practice within their present academic context (Tange/Wilken forthcoming). As suggested by Richardson (2009), context-dependent rules of action can be detected in relation to both research and education, and mobile scholars may therefore end up fighting a battle on several fronts. An American professor reflects on her transition to a British university:

> [Y]ou think because you all speak English that there's not going to be any cultural adjustment and there is. And I suppose I thought even more so, because I've been coming over here for years, and because my research was based on British institution theatre etc. I thought, well, I'm not going to notice very much. And that's not true. You do notice, and I think the things I noticed was – I'm not sure if they are particular to [University] ... but there are many unspoken, unformal ways that a university operates. And trying to learn how to get what you need from the various [places], it's not transparent.
>
> (Theatre Studies)

Judging from the frequency of interview references, processes of *localisation* often happen in relation to teaching, which is perhaps to be expected, given that research can be carried out within transnational communities of practice, unlike education which is shaped by national regulations, institutional policies, departmental traditions, and collegial interests.

Based on informants' comments on international staff members' transition, one can identify four stages of *localisation*. First, the migrant scholar will have to realise that the rules of action and interaction may differ from practical knowledge acquired in other educational settings. Particularly in the early stage of transition international staff may be tempted to ignore such differences, resting on the assumption that academia is global, which means that their ways of teaching should be immediately recognisable to domestic staff and students. As a consequence thereof, they will attempt to structure and perform their lectures in the manner that has worked for them in the past. If such teaching practice deviates from local norms and traditions, the international lecturer is likely to encounter noise from local students and staff. This is the second stage of localisation, which is the point when the academic migrant realises that she cannot take for granted that the same rules apply. A German associate professor (Business) relates how his approach was challenged by a group of Danish students:

> One thing that I remember from my very beginnings ... was that I was actually used from Germany [to] give a more detailed solution of homework on the blackboard in the following lectures. And that, actually, for the students, they were coming to me and complaining. They were saying, oh ... we're are spending too much time on this and we can [do] this ourselves, and you can just upload the solution and then check if we have any questions and then you should move into detail. But otherwise just assume that we are able to do it.

Student complaints in class or course evaluations can be dismissed by teachers who believe that such reactions are caused by biases related to nationality, gender, age, and accent. However, if it becomes the rule rather than an exception, negative feedback draws the attention of programme convenors and colleagues who may choose to intervene in order to align the international lecturer's approach with normative practices recognised within the department or institution. This *disciplining* represents the third stage of localisation and may involve formal procedures such as enlistment in teacher training programmes or collegial mentoring. Stage four sets in when international staff have acquired enough local knowledge to function seamlessly in their various capacities as course teachers, supervisors, examiner, and administrators. If working in a non-English-speaking context, actors can demonstrate their dedication by learning the local language, which is a strategy distinguishing many of the Danish-based internationals who have progressed to the senior positions as associate or full professors. In contrast, junior staff seem less willing to invest resources in language training, which can be ascribed to their temporary appointment as well as a possible ambition to migrate into a different instutional and national context.

Mobility and teaching practices

Mobility undoubtedly shapes the way contemporary academics plan and perform their work. A growing number of scholars move abroad either as permanent migrants or short-term sojourners and through their action contribute to the organisational transformation generally known as 'internationalisation'. Less obvious is the impact of migration on teaching practices, but, arguably, the structural condition of mobility affects education in several ways. First, migrant experiences expand lecturers' knowledge of diverse academic and institutional cultures, thereby enhancing their awareness that educational practices vary around the world, which will improve their ability to support students in transition, as discussed in Chapters 7 and 8. Second, mobile scholars have lived in multiple socio-cultural, political, and linguistic contexts, which has enabled them to acquire a comparative perspective on the world. In the classroom such an approach can be used to construct a learning platform where reality is presented as multi-sited rather than a space dominated by a limited number of power geographies. Finally, long-term migrants who have worked or studied overseas for an extended period have developed an intercultural orientation that makes them capable of analysing educational practices from an outsider as well as an insider perspective. This is important when seeking to identify tacit rules and routines that need to be explicated to students moving into an unfamiliar academic environment.

Despite the gains, academic mobility is by no means unproblematic. The previous discussion demonstrated how scholars operating in a global field treat their university as a temporary mooring, investing resources in boosting their 'international' profile instead of engaging with the development of higher education. These cosmopolitans can be found teaching in international courses where they may assume that their pedagogic approach is 'global' and therefore recognisable to all students. The section on 'localisation' showed how this creates noise in the encounter with local students. Hence, departmental managers and course convenors will have to attend to the transition needs of international recruits, supporting their exploration and possible internalisation of institutional practices and norms.

6 The languages of internationalisation

Internationalisation or Englishisation?

Essential to teaching practice is language, which is used by university lecturers to disseminate disciplinary knowledge and establish positions of authority in the classroom. Bourdieu and Passeron (1994) use the term *academic discourse* about the particular linguistic practice found in universities, arguing that professors rely on an elaborate, elevated style to create a distance from students, who speak and write in a more ordinary manner. Bourdieu builds on the image of a linguistic market (1991, 67), where the value of language variants is established by laws of demand and supply within specific fields. The implication is that academics can only be considered successful once they have mastered the forms of speech and writing that are recognised within their discipline, demonstrating such linguistic capability through lectures, engagement in collegial debates, and publications in top-ranking journals. This makes language an extremely powerful vehicle in academia, enabling the distinction between actors who are capable communicators of specialised, scientific knowledge and those who are not. The Danish socio-linguist Bent Preisler (2014) notes on the relationship between language, teaching, professional identity, and power: 'Their reputation as teachers (their *authenticity*) is the result of performance (their endeavour to *authenticate* themselves) in their first language or a language (other than English) in which they have near-native proficiency' (223). Preisler's observation resembles that of Bourdieu and Passeron (1994), yet it is motivated by a fundamental change in the linguistic market. Unlike Bourdieu, whose thinking was developed in relation to a field that was primarily French-speaking, Preisler engages with an internationalised academic setting, accepting that in non-English-speaking parts of the world actors' struggle for linguistic power involves both the national language and an English lingua franca.

The linguistic internationalisation of academia can be traced in quantitative studies of English-medium instruction. Focusing on Europe, Wächter and Maiworm (2014) have documented the expansion of English-taught BA and MA education, pointing to an increase in absolute numbers, from 725 English-medium programmes in 2001 to 8,089 in 2014 (16). Beyond Europe, the appeal of English as a teaching medium shows in case studies from Cambodia (Keuk/Tith 2013), Vietnam (Duong/Chua 2016), Qatar (Kane 2014), and Japan (Bradford 2016, Chapple 2015). Common to all is the assumption that English, as the 'international' language, facilitates academic migration and knowledge exchange, enabling individuals and institutions to compete in a global market. The understanding of English as 'global' has been explored in sociolinguistic research by Jan Blommart (2010), Alastair Pennycook (2017), and Suresh Canagarajah (2013). Particularly enthusiastic is Jennifer Jenkins (2011), who has argued for English as a Lingua Franca, or ELF, insisting that non-native speakers of English rely on linguistic, cognitive, and cultural strategies that deviate from the linguistic norms taught in traditional language classes. Canagarajah (2013, 63) has challenged Jenkins' ambition to establish ELF as a new, *internationalised* variant of English, arguing that it assumes a neutrality that does not match reality in globalised settings where prestige and power are commonly attached to actors' command of English. A second critique is voiced by Shohamy (2013) and Ammon (2012), who insist that the massive growth in English-medium education has happened at the expense of multilingualism, causing the neglect of alternative teaching languages. Supporting this is Robert Phillipson (2006), who characterises English as the 'cuckoo in the European higher education nest of languages', which because of its status as the language of global scholarship lures away academics 'whose origins are in vibrant research and teaching communities that have used, say, Danish or Dutch for centuries' (14). Phillipson's criticism builds on an idea of the university as a multilingual setting, against which the spread of an English Only approach can only represent a narrowing of institutions' and actors' linguistic repertoire.

In the Nordic countries of Denmark, Sweden, Norway, and Finland a vivid debate on the language(s) of internationalisation has taken place over the past 20 years. The background is the rapid growth in English-medium programmes, which in the 2010s placed Denmark and Sweden among the European countries with the highest proportion of English-taught courses (Sandström/Neghina 2017, Wächter/Maiworm 2014). Some Scandinavian researchers have interpreted the trend towards English as a break with the tradition of multilingualism at Nordic universities where the national languages of Scandinavia historically coexisted with French, German, Latin, and, from the 20th century, English (Mortensen/Haberland 2012, Bull 2004). Other scholars have focused on the impact of English on institutional practice, highlighting how policy-makers have engaged with a reality of multilingualism by explicating what functions are attributed to *global* English, the *national* languages, and any alternative *regional* or *minority* tongues (e.g. Bolton/Kuteeva 2012, Hult/Källkvist 2016, Saarinen 2012). To describe a condition of linguistic coexistence linguists have coined the term *parallel language usage*, which Gregersen et al. (2017, 5) define as follows:

> By *parallel language usage* is understood … that two or more languages are employed for the same purpose within a particular context or societal

> domain, in this case universities in the Nordic region. Most will probably think of English and another language, but the concept is equally applicable to the use of Swedish and Finnish in Finland or the use of Danish and Greenlandic in Greenland. When English is added, as part of the internationalisation of the universities, this means that three languages are involved and not just two. (DA)

To Hultgren and Thøgersen (2014) parallellingualism represents an ideological discourse disconnected from the linguistic practices that can be observed at Nordic universities. Instead, Hultgren and Thøgersen (2014) insist that one recognises how academic discourse has been subjected to a process of Englishisation. This Hultgren documents through an analysis of Danish data from 2005 to 2011, which reveals a rise in the proportion of English-medium publications, doctoral dissertations, BA and MA programmes (2014, 2013). In a recent inquiry Tange and Millar (forthcoming) tested such findings on information collected on academic publishing in Denmark 2015–17, and this confirmed Hultgren's assertion that English functions as the default medium for scientific communication. Similar observations have been made in relation to the situation at Swedish and Spanish universities (Hult/Källkvist 2016, Lasagabaster 2015), which indicates that the rules of price formation within Bourdieu's linguistic market increasingly recognise English as the global currency in academia. This is supported by qualitative studies, which reveal that many academics choose to teach and write in English instead of their native speech, thus consolidating through their linguistic practices the symbolic power of English (Sälo 2017, Tange 2012b, Ljosland 2007).

Language constitutes one of the principal structural conditions underpinning academic practice. A switch from teaching in the native language to delivering education in English should therefore be regarded as a major transformation, which means that lecturers have to develop new communicative and pedagogic strategies. This chapter examines the impact of internationalisation on academic language usage from three perspectives, foregrounding the themes of 1) *language politics*, 2) lecturers' *linguistic practices*, and 3) global English as *classroom pedagogy*.

The politics of language

The previous section highlighted how in academia internationalisation has become synonymous with Englishisation. Perhaps this linguistic change was inevitable given that many of the early movers in international education were universities based in English-speaking countries, which took advantage of the fact that they were using a teaching medium that had become accepted as global in scale and orientation (Pennycook 2017). To many academics working at British, American, and Australian institutions the recruitment of students from non-English-speaking backgrounds was probably never seen as anything that might affect their own linguistic practice, although some undoubtedly engaged in staffroom exchanges about learners' limited English. In contrast, internationalisation in non-English-speaking countries has sparked an ideological debate about the spread of English-medium research and education, inspiring politicians, intellectuals, journalists, and academics to consider the present and future balance between English and the national language. The topic of Englishisation has been addressed from various perspectives, ranging from Japanese policy-makers' ambition to strengthen the presence of English in education to Scandinavian worries about a possible disappearance of the Nordic languages in science communication (Rose/McKinley 2018, Hultgreen 2014). In relation to this, two themes have been particularly prominent, namely an ideological concern with the spread of English and the question of institutional policy-making, which relates to universities' everyday management of English.

The worldwide Englishisation of academia can be interpreted as an ideological process because, as Pennycook (2017) observes, cultural meanings are tied to English as an international language. An interesting example is Kane's (2014) field study of Weill Cornell Medical College, Qatar, which shows how the immersion of local students into an English-speaking American college environment causes learners to question to what extent they have become 'Westernized' (104), disconnected through linguistic and professional practice from the Arabic-speaking community surrounding them. Writing from Japan, Bradford (2016, 346) notes that a similar connection can be made between English-language usage and pedagogic practices characterised as 'Western-centric', causing some Japanese academics to worry about a possible loss of local traditions. In Northern Europe, the language discussion has been characterised by a discourse of parallellingualism, with debaters insisting that universities are obliged to serve the national as well as an international community (Hult/Källkvist 2016, 59). With reference to Scandinavia, Hultgren (2014, 69) notes how policy writers will contrast *international* English to languages such as Danish or Swedish, which are described as 'society-bearing', thus acknowledging the expectation that key functions in education, health, law, and civil society are carried out in the native speech. Yet researchers from all academic disciplines increasingly accept English as their principal medium for research dissemination, which has caused politicians and linguists to voice concerns about domain loss, the threat of English, and a possible disconnection of academia from civil society.

To what extent are university lecturers influenced by ideological debates about English in academia? In the first interview study, 36 staff working at Danish universities were prompted about the impact of internationalisation on their linguistic practice. Their responses suggest that many informants were aware that a language-political discussion was taking place, using the interview as an opportunity to position themselves in relation to ongoing institutional and national debates. Most willing to accept English as an inevitable part of contemporary academic work were Business lecturers, who describe an institutional climate where actors are expected to teach and publish in

English. 'Our' ability to work in another language was never questioned, an informant observes on a managerial decision to expand English-medium education, relating this to the internationalist orientation of a recently arrived head of department:

> [He] really is a cosmopolite, who has lived in Hong Kong for 20 years. And Hong Kong – we are talking a city of five million people. So a truly international centre. And he has no understanding that it may be a problem for some to teach in English. (DA)

Academics from other disciplines were more sceptical, arguing that English-taught courses widen the distance between academic discourse and language usage in civil society. A Law lecturer offered a historical analogy, comparing the present challenge from English to the situation in the late 18th century when the first Danish-medium programme was introduced: '[T]his Danish education in Law, you know the one in Danish rather than Latin, which was the international one, the Danish Law exams have contributed to the creation of a Danish academy and a Danish civil society' (DA). Equally concerned with the connection between academia and the surrounding society were informants from Agricultural Science, who highlight the asymmetrical communication situation that emerges when MA education is conducted in English, while practitioners in agriculture and the dairy industry use Danish. The lecturers provide several examples of students adopting a scientific vocabulary inspired by English, which, as one associate professor explains, creates problems when graduates have to interact with farmers who know only the Danish phrases. Interestingly, the Danish agriculturalists describe a situation comparable to that of Kane's Arabic-speaking medical students, who had difficulties relating to patients in Qatar because they had encountered professional practice through American case studies and scientific English.

Equally important is the theme of policy-making, which concerns institutions' attempts to manage linguistic practice within an environment where two or more languages coexist. Language policies are found at universities around the world and have been used in Britain, for instance, to address issues such as the provision of bilingual education in Wales. A review of recent literature suggests that language management has become particularly important in non-English-speaking parts of Europe, where institutions confront the question of how to manage English in contexts that have traditionally relied on alternative tongues. University responses can be political, with policies expressing an ideological commitment to principles such as parallel- or multilingualism. Examples are the Multilingual Programme at the Basque University, which promises trilingual education in Basque, Spanish, and English (Doiz et al. 2014, 348), and the Copenhagen policy of parallel language usage (Siiner 2016, 448–9). However, most institutional strategies have emerged for pragmatic reasons, responding to the presence of non-native students, a wish to recruit international students and staff, or invitations to develop Erasmus or dual degree programmes. A key issue concerns implementation, which can involve either a top-down or a bottom-up process. In relation to this Airey et al. (2017) note the disparity between universities' strategic decisions about language and the actual learning facilitated by staff teaching in a second language. This corresponds to the findings of the current author, whose research on 'linguistic organisation' shows how institutional approaches to international education affect university lecturers' perception of and willingness to engage in English-medium teaching (Tange 2012a).

English Only represents the most direct attempt by managers to control university lecturers' linguistic practice. The term English Only refers to the situation where English is adopted as the sole teaching medium within an entire discipline or department, leaving academics no choice but to accept English-medium courses. Staff from two faculties have experienced this type of organisational change, describing how English-medium education spread as the result of a management decision, without any prior consultation of students or staff. A lecturer from Agricultural Science reflects on the process:

> I have felt a bit unhappy about the very dogmatic attitude … that at least our management has had about the need for everything to be in English at Masters level. And that it has almost been the case that we, as course convenors, were hit in the head with it … that from 2008 all our Masters programmes had to be in English. And we do not really discuss that. (DA)

A different approach is the *single course* organisation where English-taught courses happen on the initiative of individual lecturers and course convenors. Within this institutional context, language policies are a practical rather than strategic matter, arising from the need to guarantee non-native students' academic and administrative services in English. An anthropologist observes:

> [B]efore we have not had a lot of English-medium courses at BA level, and this is something I try to push for or sneak in by providing more and more single courses in English … so that the students [realise] this is a possibility, but also so we can gradually move towards an English-taught BA programme. (DA)

The difference between informants' experiences with the English Only and Single Course approaches offers one explanation why some lecturers consider English a threat, while others welcome it as an opportunity. Yet all lecturers' ability to manage in English depends on their linguistic competence, which affects the form, content, and tone of academic discourse.

Englishising linguistic practice

To Bourdieu and Passeron (1994) language is central to higher education, facilitating knowledge exchanges between the professor, who occupies a position of academic and institutional authority and students, who are presented as novices, seeking to internalise the professional practices and discourses associated with a particular field of study. Bourdieu and Passeron (1994, 6) see the purpose of pedagogical communication as two-fold, requesting that lecturers 'maximise the absolute quantity of information conveyed', but do so in a manner that 'minimize[s] loss of information'. In other words, successful university teachers are capable of disseminating scientific insights through a medium that simultaneously demonstrates the speaker's disciplinary expertise and ensures comprehension from learners who are in the process of acquiring the specialised vocabulary of academia. Bourdieu and Passeron never question that the language underpinning academic discourse could be anything other than French, describing a linguistic environment where any variation relates to actors' social or geographical background. Yet the previous discussion suggests that monolingualism can no longer be treated as the norm at European universities, many of which have internationalised by increasing their number of English-taught courses. In consequence, a growing number of academics are expected to work in English, which is to them a foreign language, prompting Preisler (2014) to ask if lecturers can maintain their professional 'authenticity' in English? According to Preisler, effective teaching requires a combination of linguistic, communicative, and pedagogic skills, which he documents through observations made of natural scientists involved in the *doing* of English-medium education. The current author has studied the impact of Englishisation through interview research, inviting Danish-employed academics to reflect on the linguistic and communicative challenges that they have experienced in the international classroom. The preliminary findings were presented in the article 'Caught in the Tower of Babel' (Tange 2010), which highlights linguistic register, classroom atmosphere, and student evaluations as particularly significant to the informants. All can be related to teachers' ability to convey information in a persuasive manner, which indicates that the change into English affects academics' perception of their own capability as scientific communicators. The subsequent discussion explores this through an examination of three themes: Actors' *linguistic competence*, *communication management*, and *professional self-image*.

The theme of *linguistic competence* relates to university teachers' (perceived) command of English, involving, for instance, their pronunciation, written proficiency, semantics, pragmatics, vocabulary, and access to a variety of registers. Lecturers' linguistic capability is central to any examination of English-medium education because teaching constitutes a highly complex form of communication, requesting a degree of fluency that may be hard to achieve for people working in a second language. In spite of this, language problems are often invisible in academic environments where a mastery of English is regarded as the prerequisite for an academic career, thus making it hard for individuals to admit to difficulties when asked to teach or write in English (Tange 2012b). When interviewed face-to-face, lecturers are generally open about any linguistic weaknesses, identifying challenges related to grammar, a limited vocabulary, preparation time, and the sense that the message delivered is inadequate. Featuring prominently is the question of English repertoire or register. When asked to describe the difference between pedagogic communication in English and their native speech, informants mention a lack of nuances, variety, sophistication, and precision, which leaves the impression of classroom communications restricted by a medium that is too narrow to fulfil lecturers' needs. An associate professor (Business) reflects:

> Because my vocabulary is greater in Danish, I think I find it easier to express myself. So there will be things that I cannot say in English – which I cannot formulate and I can therefore not say. In this way I believe my lectures become more of a shortcut than they would have been in Danish. Well, it might be such a thing as [using] more anecdotes – where it can be hard to find the precise vocabulary, where you cannot cover as much ground as in Danish. Because linguistically speaking you do not feel entirely on safe ground. (DA)

Few refer directly to problems such as grammatical mistakes, pronunciation errors, a lack of appropriate discourse markers, and semantic awareness, which is interesting because these linguistic features are employed by language centres to assess academics' English proficiency (see Kling/Stæhr 2011, Dimova 2017). This suggests a discrepancy between the way international educators perceive their own English and the professional approach represented by the English-language specialists. One explanation is that actors consider their English 'global', in the manner proposed by Jenkins (2011), which means that they do not feel constrained by the normative standards used for purposes of language evaluation and training. 'We' are not language teachers, several interviewees insist, stressing that their principal responsibility is content, not form:

> Well, I would never step in and assess English, for example. I am not the person to do so. But I can use it as [a teaching medium] – after having been thrown into it, I have gradually acquired that confidence. That I know I can do this. And then, I will need to swallow that it is not pretty and eloquent and grammatically correct … And this I have also become better at. Because I have reached the point where, if English is what they are after, they will get what I have to offer.
>
> (Associate professor, Business; DA)

The perception that one is limited by linguistic capability relates to the second theme of *communication management*. When asked for examples of how the switch into English affects teachers' communication, interviewees explain how they have cut down on their story-telling, examples, and humour, adopting what is best described as a focused and formalised style of lecturing. When so many express concerns about the stories that go missing in English-medium education, they foreground an important teaching practice: The use of examples to support the students' comprehension of abstract scientific knowledge. Judging from the interviews, story-telling serves two purposes. First, personal anecdotes can be brought in to illustrate a theory or model, thereby connecting academic concepts to examples that are more immediately relevant to learners' everyday practice. Second, story-telling is used as a strategy for initiating classroom interaction. Lecturers may choose to narrate a personal experience or joke in an attempt to invite students to engage in dialogue, which suggests that the disappearance of such a component could result in a more teacher-centred communication style. An assistant professor (Business) observes on her use of stories as a way to break the ice:

> But basically, I also believe this is about finding techniques that will work in [an English-speaking] context. Where we have been accustomed to Danish students, where you arrive and then test the waters, and if you feel that the mood is a bit restrained, then you will try to say something provocative about the election or other local matters, some kind of shared joke, and ease things up like that. (DA)

What emerges from the informants' comments is the general feeling that lecturers' messages have become more limited in English, containing them within the specialised vocabulary of science, which prevents them from building rapport with students and thereby ensuring that knowledge is disseminated in a way that is accessible to all. Following Bourdieu and Passeron (1994), one could argue that these actors are no longer in command of academic discourse, which means they cannot claim the disciplinary authority expected from the successful classroom performer. This causes some informants to worry about the impact of inadequate English on their *professional image and identity*. Often such concerns are expressed in relation to student evaluations, where some academic staff see a need to defend themselves or colleagues against accusations of linguistic inadequacy:

> We have teachers who have dropped 1½ to 2 points in evaluations – falling from being good, steady communicators to becoming rubbish teachers. Because they cannot speak English, and it is sad, and it is terrible … It is a difficult thing to be thrown into, to become engaged with. Yes, it is fine for me because I do not have a problem. So yes, in principle I can say – well, I guess, I do not need to worry. But I have seen bright colleagues, who do have [this problem], and who, unfortunately, hit the bottom because of it.
>
> (Associate professor, Business; DA)

An alternative strategy is to project the problem onto the learners, stressing how students of Engineering or Agricultural Science are not capable of understanding sophisticated, scientific English, which justifies to the academics their use of a limited linguistic repertoire. Interestingly, only a few suggest that lecturers could improve their English by partaking in language classes. An associate professor (Natural Science) explains this with reference to the stigma that some colleagues attach to the faculty-run English courses, which might expose any linguistic weaknesses, signalling to peers and local managers that actors are incapable of working in an internationalised institutional and disciplinary environment.

Global English in the classroom

Undoubtedly, the switch into English has affected some academics' ability to convey information in a satisfactory manner, causing them to question their capability as international educators. Yet the lecturer as producer of academic discourse is only one aspect of pedagogic communication. Equally significant is the need to 'minimize the loss of information' (Bourdieu/Passeron 1994, 6), which involves students' reception skills, including their access to the specialised, scientific register employed in academia. Bourdieu and Passeron see language as something separating teachers and students, underlining that learners are vulnerable until they have cracked the professorial code employed by lecturers in the classroom. Arguably, English-medium education increases such distance, creating learning environments where a teacher, whose first language is German, may confront a class composed of students recruited from Germany, Poland, Sweden, Spain, and China. Such linguistic situations can fuel ethnocentrism because students and staff carry into English idiosyncratic practices adopted from their native language and will therefore find it easier to comprehend speakers from a similar background (Risager 2006). A social scientist observes:

> I guess this relates to all who are not from an English-speaking country, right. There is no difference between Danes and Peruvians in that respect. But the Dane will then have the advantage that I do not speak perfect English either, so I will choose some English words that resemble the Danish word for the same thing, and which makes it easier for the Dane to understand another Dane speaking in English. (DA)

The realisation that 'global' English concerns more than the quality of teachers' language foregrounds the need for pedagogic strategies that can support knowledge exchange in academic settings where the actors work in their second language. Examples of such approaches are *adaptation*, *translanguaging*, and *scaffolding*.

Adaptation refers to a change of register, communication speed, and linguistic sophistication undertaken by international educators in order to prevent students' linguistic weaknesses from affecting their comprehension of the scientific knowledge disseminated. Adaptation is an important technique in international education where a common problem is that student and staff language levels are asymmetrical, which means that one party has a greater command of English and is therefore required to make adjustments to ensure mutual understanding. Particularly easy to spot are linguistic discrepancies emerging within academic environments located in countries such as Britain, United States, and Australia, which are traditionally English-speaking, and where classes of non-English-speaking students from Asia, Africa, and Europe will commonly be taught by native speakers of English. A British natural scientist conveys his experience of teaching a Masters class composed of 75% Chinese:

> We've got to monitor them. And if we see someone struggling, then we take steps to rectify it. So they're not left to sink or swim. We do carefully monitor what's going on. That's why they have a formative assessment to do very early on, both oral and written, and from that we then assess, well, what is the standard of both spoken English, which is the first one, and secondly, what is their written English like.

The informant's reflection suggests that international educators, regardless of their linguistic background, have to attend to students' linguistic capability and comprehension. In other words, native speakers of English also have to adapt, which is a theme often overlooked in the literature on English-medium education. Hence, the teacher's English can be too fluent or idiosyncratic for an international class, necessitating that students have the ability to decode social or regional varieties of English. A British natural scientist observes on a teaching situation where he happened to use the Scots word 'wee' in class:

> I never ever forget the first time I stood up with undergraduates, and I literally said that. I said 'this is a wee bit different from', and you could hear everybody just stopped. It's normally quiet, but they just stopped and, 'what the hell is he talking about?'

The lecturer's experience underlines that the pedagogic strategy of adaptation can involve the standardisation of academics' English accents and vocabulary. Interestingly enough, the observation that international educators have to learn how to teach in English thus seems equally applicable to native speakers, who require tools that help them accommodate students who are accessing scientific knowledge through a foreign language.

Translanguaging has been employed in multilingual contexts such as South Africa to support learners whose English was inadequate to manage education conducted exclusively in this language (Van der Walt/Kidd 2013). Doiz et al. (2013, 218) define translanguaging as 'the adoption of bilingual supportive scaffolding practices', recommending that this be used to enhance learning in international education. Judging from the interview data bilingualism is a common feature in English-medium education, used by university teachers to ensure that students' academic accomplishment is not hindered by inadequate language skills. In relation to this, informants have pinpointed a number of situations in which a code-switching strategy is employed. Shared by many is the experience of local students changing into their native speech when initiating a conversation with teachers during a break. Lecturers find such a practice challenging, stressing how this compels them to make a difficult choice between answering in English and accepting a medium that may not be shared by all. If responding in the medium selected by the student, lecturers allow for the possibility that learners' need for further clarification may arise from insufficient linguistic skills, which may have prevented them from voicing their concerns in class. Yet interaction carried out in the local language excludes most international students, who consequently miss out on any additional explanations given. Some teachers have resolved this dilemma by offering English summaries of any informal exchanges, thus establishing an even knowledge base for all. Alternatively, one may introduce a practice of code-switching in class, encouraging students to contribute in any medium known to the teacher. A professor (Agricultural Science) describes such a multilingual approach:

> I have said it, again and again, that if there are Danish students who find it difficult to ask their questions in English, then I would much rather that they raise the point in Danish, and then I will translate for the rest of the class and so on. But it is really not acceptable if they remain silent because they feel uncertain about their English. (DA)

One final example concerns language usage in exams. In relation to this several respondents mention what is best characterised as multilingualism, motivating this by their need to assess learners' scientific knowledge rather than linguistic capability. A natural scientist observes:

> [W]e always accepted that they answered exam questions in whatever language they preferred. So we received answers in Danish, Swedish, and English. Or we told them to switch – if they got stuck with anything, then they might just switch into another language. (DA)

The teaching practice of *linguistic scaffolding* is comparable to translanguaging in the sense that it involves a conscious choice by university lecturers to adopt pedagogic techniques that can support learners whose linguistic competence is deemed insufficient to benefit fully from English-Medium education. Where translanguaging mainly concerns spoken and written discourse, scaffolding practices are more varied in form, using multiple modalities to enable learners simultaneously to hear, read, and see an illustration of core concepts and models. A Humanities lecturer describes the combination of speech, writing, and visuals that he has developed in order to prevent his own or students' linguistic competence from disrupting knowledge transmission:

> [T]he only thing I can do ... is to make the effort to ensure that if there will be noise, this is not on the language side. So sentences have to be short etc.

> I also make sure that … I prepare some slides which are detailed, meaning that they can use them when preparing for their exam. Then they can use those slides as a resource. This does not mean that I am reading from them in class. I do not do this at all, but I make sure that they contain the essence; that is, something to support [the students] afterwards so they are not dependent on notes they have taken, which may not be quite precise. (DA)

The use of scaffolding techniques can explain why some informants find that English-taught classes require additional preparation time. One should thus be careful of reading such comments as symptomatic of inadequate skills on behalf of the teachers, acknowledging that the extra hours could be spent working on written and visual resources that can supplement the verbal message. A lecturer from Engineering relates how he attempts to support students' acquisition of scientific vocabulary as well as knowledge:

> [I have] taken a list of terminology from Supply Chain Management, which is publicly available, more or less everywhere, but I have placed this in their folder so they can actually find it and keep it in front of them. So when he uses this term, what exactly is it that this implies. Then there will be a short explanation of it, to which I have added some of the phrases I know that I commonly use … [T]his helps them to have some kind of idea of what is actually going on. (DA)

Judging from the interviews, scaffolding techniques are common in Natural Science and Engineering, which indicates that students from these disciplines are challenged by scientific English.

Teaching global Englishes

The switch from education in the native language to English-medium instruction represents a major reconfiguration of the teaching and learning environment, requesting that staff develop strategies for working in and with a second or foreign language. Not surprisingly, the literature engaging with the impact of language change has mainly been produced in contexts that are traditionally non-English speaking. However, as the British examples showed, native speakers of English also require strategies for managing language usage in classes composed of learners with different linguistic backgrounds and skills. Teaching global Englishes involves the role of the lecturer as sender of scientific knowledge. Ideally, the teacher's message should be conveyed in an effective manner, demanding a clear pronunciation, a precise vocabulary, and the ability to explain and expand through story-telling. With reference to these, non-native speakers of English describe a sense of inadequacy, stressing their need for additional preparation time and language training. Yet academics also highlight pedagogic strategies developed to accommodate students' divergent language needs, which suggests that scientific communication be treated as a two-way process, involving both teacher and learners.

This second approach to the teaching of global Englishes is student-centred, emphasising the lecturer's need to minimise the information lost in translation. Teaching practices inspired by such a perspective focus on comprehension, which can be supported through a variety of pedagogies, reflecting the linguistic skills and requirements characteristic of a specific programme and subject area. Adaptation can thus demand both a simplification of the teacher's academic discourse and the request that British students accept non-native varieties of English as equal to their own. Scaffolding techniques are connected to academics' disciplinary needs and traditions, inspiring bilingualism in Agricultural Science, glossaries of scientific terminology in Engineering, and visualisation in Media and Cultural Studies.

Part III

Teaching practices in international education

Teaching practices involve the concrete *Doings* and *Sayings* performed by lecturers and students engaging in international education. In Part III, the discussion will focus on practical knowledge related to programme design, academic routines, curricular contexts, multicultural teamwork, and assessment, highlighting any challenges and changes that academic staff associate with internationalisation. As shown in Part II, educational practices are shaped by structural conditions such as macro-level globalisation, disciplinary orientation, academic migration, and the spread of English. What was also made clear is that international education is realised differently around the world, which problematises any attempt by educational scholars to propose a one-size-fits-all model.

Starting from experiences narrated by academics teaching in Danish and British institutions, the author should like to stress that the practical understandings explored in subsequent chapters relate primarily to conditions found in Northern and Western Europe. As discussed in Chapter 3, international education can assume many forms, ranging from EU-facilitated student exchange to offshore campuses and education hubs, and they have different implications for the lecturers' position and possibilities in the classroom. The Danish and British universities that served as research sites for the present inquiry adhere to Knight's *classic* model, which means that educational activities are mainly delivered at campuses situated in a single national environment, and that internationalisation is manifest through partnerships, academic migration, programme design, and international benchmarking (Knight 2015, 110). Of crucial importance is the socio-linguistic environment since international education in Denmark generally calls for a translation of course activities into English, whereas no similar linguistic adjustment is required in Britain. Hence, one may distinguish between international education, as realised through an Englishisation of existing courses, which characterises institutions located in non-English-speaking contexts, and internationalisation, as found in Anglophone countries such as the UK, US, and Australia, where international students can be admitted into programmes developed with native learners in mind.

Three forms of international education can be identified in the interviews conducted with Danish and British academic staff. First, there are examples of *exchange agreements* where students from other European countries or partnership institutions are invited to join modules developed for existing educational programmes. In the 1980s and 1990s, the arrival of exchange students at Danish universities would have necessitated that the teaching language be changed from Danish into English, but as the result of a post-2000 expansion of English-medium education many courses have become accessible to non-Danish speakers. Second, some programmes are designed as *international*, targeting students from diverse national, socio-cultural, and linguistic backgrounds. International programmes are often found at post-graduate level and interdisciplinary in nature, which enables them to admit learners from a variety of undergraduate courses. A third form is the *Erasmus Mundus* programme. This type of education involves a partnership between institutions situated in different European countries and can offer EU-sponsored scholarships, which means that it is often perceived as elite education, attracting a select group of learners.

7 Designing international education

Planning for global learning

Designing involves the planning of education, including curricular concerns such as learning objectives, programme structure, course contents, class activities, assessment forms, and evaluation criteria. In recent years, questions of design have become prominent in the literature on international education, motivating scholars to emphasise the need to construct study environments that enable all actors, native and non-native, staff as well as students, to participate as equals in intercultural dialogue and knowledge co-creation (e.g. Leask 2015, Killick 2015). Internationalisation requests that all actors be taught 'engagement with one another', Spiro insists (2014, 65), suggesting that universities fail as international communities of practice if they cannot resolve the challenge of segregated international and domestic student communities. Similarly, Kahn and Agnew argue for 'global learning through difference' (2017, 52), invoking an image of international education as collaborative and transformative learning:

> Global learning classrooms provide a form of practiced mimicry, where students incorporate perspectives, overcome challenges, transcend differences, and seek answers collaboratively. Collective work puts knowledge into practice, transforms students into educators, and allows learners to see themselves as nodes within global learning communities.
>
> (Kahn/Agnew 2017, 58)

Scholars' growing interest in promoting intercultural education can be read as a reaction to literature inspired by cross-cultural psychology. Reviewing early research on international education, Marginson and Sawir (2011) note how this builds on work by authors such as Oberg (1960) and Berry (1997), foregrounding cross-cultural experiences related to foreign students' transition or 'culture shock'. A central concept is acculturation, which is individualised in a way that places the responsibility for successful internationalisation on non-native learners, who may be more or less capable of assimilating host university norms and practices (e.g. Andrade 2006, Lewthwaite 1996). The cross-cultural approach has been criticised for its positioning of international students as deficit learners who lack specific insights and skills (Marginson/Sawir 2011, 69). This results in an understanding of international education as a process of unilateral adaptation by foreign students, which, the critics stress, defies the purpose of creating global learning environments (Tran 2016, Volet/Jones 2012). As an alternative, scholars propose that pedagogies be developed to further inclusion, equality, and integration, relying on terms such as *interconnectedness* (Spiro 2014), *transnational learning communities* (Singh 2005), *synergy* (Zhou et al 2008), *transcultural wisdom* (Chang 2006), and *global learning* (Kahn/Agnew 2017), which all suggest an ideology motivated by principles of internationalism and intercultural relationship-building. Characteristic of such an approach is the insistence that 1) international education be considered a transformative experience, and 2) pedagogies be adopted that enable non-native as well as native learners to participate as equals in the co-creation of knowledge.

The growing awareness of internationalisation as a holistic process transforming practices for all actors has inspired scholars to suggest changes to the way institutions design internationalised education and learning environments. One example is the European *internationalisation at home* policy, which has emerged in response to the realisation that not all students participate in mobility programmes. The aim is for all students to have 'an international higher education experience' (Harrison 2015, 414), which means that the focus for institutional policy-makers shifts from student exchange to the development of learning environments that allow all learners to develop intercultural and international competences. A key element is the *internationalised curriculum*, which Nilsson (2003, 31) defines as: 'a curriculum that gives international and intercultural knowledge and abilities, aiming at preparing students for performing (professionally, socially, emotionally) in international and multicultural context'. Nilsson's ideas resemble those of Australian educationalist Betty Leask, who proposes an interventionist approach, working with academic staff to align course contents and learning objectives with an overall institutional ambition to 'educate for global citizenship'. Leask's strategy for *internationalising the curriculum* (2015) involves an evaluation and modification of practices related to *learning* (e.g. outcome, organisation of activities), *teaching* (e.g. flexibility, adjusting for diversity, facilitating dialogue), and *assessment* (e.g. integration of an intercultural dimension in exam tasks). Leask's recommendations may be read as a response to conditions in Australian higher education, which has seen a dramatic growth in the number of non-English-speaking Asian students, who have reportedly been subjected to domination by Western students and staff (see Doherty/Singh 2005, Singh/Shrestha 2008). Leask's (2015) and Nilsson's (2003) models recommend that internationalisation be addressed at the institutional level, engaging all academics, administrators, international, and domestic students in the building of globalised learning environments. Yet one may speculate on the extent to which one can develop a generic model, given the great diversity found within the global field of higher education. Addressing this issue, Otten (2009) argues how within the same institutional setting *academic communities* perceive their need to develop inclusive, intercultural pedagogies very differently. Otten (2009, 410) suggests as key factors the demographic profile of a department or research group, as well as their area of specialisation, which can be more or less global in scope and orientation. A second element is *learning cultures*. According to Hodkinson et al. (2007), learning cultures emerge as the result of teachers' and students' negotiation of expectations tied to the roles that they perform within specific settings, or fields. The implication is that the same practices will not necessarily apply in all parts of the university. A final consideration is the impact of organisational culture. Wu (2002) describes significant variation in the forms of supervision provided at two British universities, while Tange and Jensen (2012, 186) note how an institutional learning philosophy such as Problem-Based Learning can influence academics' perception of international students.

The current author does not seek to produce a generic design for international education, but will start from issues identified by lecturers engaged in this teaching practice. Three themes serve as the focal points: 1) *design*, including purpose, form, and academic level; 2) *socialisation*, which involves students' admission into the academic community; and 3) *progression*, which addresses subject specialisation and assumptions tied to this.

Designing international education

An important question, which has attracted scarce attention in the literature is *how do university programmes become internationalised*? This calls for an examination of the specific circumstances under which international education is produced, including the national and institutional environments, which can be more or less conducive to internationalisation. British higher education, for instance, may be considered a relatively open system, which means that it is accessible to migrant academics, who benefit from the use of English, which many will accept as global, and an undergraduate-postgraduate structure that facilitates the recruitment of MA students from diverse educational and national systems. Historically, non-natives have been admitted as exchange and postgraduate students into courses developed for a domestic audience, which explains some British scholars' preoccupation with international student 'adjustment' (e.g. Peelo/Luxon 2007, Brown/Holloway 2008). However, educational researchers increasingly challenge this model, foregrounding the need for British universities to adopt a holistic approach to internationalisation, designing study environments that can inspire all learners to engage in intercultural dialogue and relationship building (e.g. Jones/Brown 2007, Killick 2015). In comparison, the Danish system of higher education has traditionally been closed to many students, relying on a language accessible mainly to migrants from other Nordic countries. This changed as a consequence of the growing interest in student exchange in the 1990s, which motivated Danish universities to expand their range of English-medium courses. To academic staff, translating a module into English might require a rethinking of course syllabi, contents, and assignments, and, arguably, this represents an example of designed international courses, albeit limited in scope. By 2000, when international education, in the form of English-medium BA and MA programmes targeting both global and domestic students, became a strategic priority at Danish universities, many academics had therefore already been engaged in processes of internationalisation. In some environments, such effort inspired the development of a new form of higher education: The *international Masters* programme. In terms of contents and structure, such courses can be compared to the one-year taught MAs found in the British system since they allow learners to be recruited from a variety of disciplinary and institutional backgrounds. Yet the Danish programmes were designed for internationalisation, which means that they had been developed with a linguistically and nationally diverse student body in mind.

The generic history of international education in Britain and Denmark draws attention to the structural conditions that inevitably shape the way academics engage with internationalisation. Yet a simple comparison, based on system differences alone, may cause one to overlook similarities in the experiences conveyed by British and Danish lecturers as well as the possible influence of alternative factors such as actors' disciplinary backgrounds, institutional environments, research interests, and personal biographies. To obtain a deeper understanding of the concerns underpinning the design of international education, the author proposes a framework of four questions:

1. What is the purpose of offering international education?
2. What forms of education are involved?
3. Is the programme designed for undergraduate or postgraduate learners?
4. Is the programme targeting subject specialists or generalists?

With regard to *purpose*, a distinction should be drawn between academics who use economic arguments to motivate internationalisation, and those inspired by an ideological principle of internationalism. This difference is manifest in the way staff talk about international education, as illustrated by two observations made by British-based lecturers:

> [I]f you ask my head of department, what more can the university do, is to get us more international students because they bring in more money. The department is always in need of money, so therefore they have to bring more of them in for us. Give us an opportunity to sell our wares abroad more easily.
>
> (Biology)

> [T]his course wouldn't be the same if the make-up of students was not international. Because that internationalism in class works for the

> internationalism that's part of the curriculum we are trying to develop. And that it's really them challenging each other or bring in perspectives, sharing perspectives, is what really makes the course dynamic.
>
> (Theatre Studies)

The Danish interviews reveal a similar contrast between informants insisting that internationalisation is driven by economic incentives and those expressing a professional or personal interest in using international education to create spaces for global knowledge sharing. Undoubtedly, such perceptions influence academics' attitude to incoming students, causing them to position learners either as 'customers', in need of specific skills, or 'co-creators' of an international learning community.

The three main *forms of education* described in the interview data are *student exchange*, *international Masters*, and *Erasmus Mundus* programmes, which make different demands with regard to course design and contents. Least significant are the changes caused by exchange agreements, which can often be realised by admitting foreign students into existing modules. Where the medium of instruction is English, lecturers may pretend that this is 'business as usual', making little effort to adapt course content and activities to a diverse student body. In comparison, *international Masters* involve a substantial rethinking of the way lecturers design and perform education. Many programmes are planned with internationalisation in mind, which means that allowances have been made in terms of how knowledge is framed, communicated, and evaluated. In relation to this, a key concern is the demographic make-up of the student cohort. Across disciplines, lecturers appreciate diversity, stressing how a 'good' international class will attract learners from a variety of educational and socio-cultural backgrounds. Informants stress that class dynamics change if the proportion of internationals drops below 10% or exceeds 50%, which is similar to the observation made by Harrison and Peacock's (2010) in relation to British student perceptions. A final type is the *Erasmus Mundus* programmes, which rely on partnerships between European universities. These courses are prestigious because they can provide scholarships to the most gifted students, which explains why academics are generally enthusiastic about this type of international education, insisting that it enables them to work with a select group of talented learners. Although they may incorporate modules developed for other courses, *Erasmus Mundus* programmes are mostly designed from scratch and have to accommodate mobility between partner institutions.

The two questions of *undergraduate/postgraduate* and *subject specialisation* relate to the academic level and disciplinary knowledge that lecturers expect from the students admitted into a module or course. The literature on international education has foregrounded stories of foreign students as deficit learners in need of special academic and linguistic support. Empirical studies reveal a similar preoccupation with international-ness among academic and administrative staff, which causes these actors to explain any problems arising in relation to non-native learners with generic references to national culture (see Friedman 2018, Tange 2016). As a result, lecturers may overlook alternative explanations for international student failure, including the importance of clear admission criteria and course descriptions that specify to incoming students what academic level and disciplinary knowledge are expected in a course. Indeed, the lack of transparent course requirements can leave academic staff with a very random mix of students, as seen in this example from Denmark:

> [T]here is a fair group among the international students, who have only had Philosophy for a year or maybe no Philosophy at all … But who may yet be interested in a specific course which we have and offer, and because our study regulations allow free topic modules … it is formally an option students can use. And of course this leads to the problem that in [class] we have, at least as a starting point, experienced, Danish Philosophy students, who have had a foundation course for two years and are now in their third or fourth year of Philosophy; on the other side are international students, who have no qualifications or only very few, basic qualifications, and that is a pedagogic challenge.
>
> (Associate professor, Philosophy; DA)

The first asymmetry relates to academic level. Most lecturers will assume that Masters students have internalised particular disciplinary routines and practices, and are challenged when confronted by exchange students who lack such practical knowledge. To resolve the problem international educators have to spend time explicating the rules relating to specific activities or assignments, which can fuel discontent among the graduate students, who already possess such knowledge. A second asymmetry is the contrast between subject specialists and generalists. While Danish Philosophy majors expect an in-depth engagement with core principles and theories, most visiting students require an introductory course. Here the informant resolves his dilemma by asking the Danish 'experts' to teach their international peers, thus producing some form of knowledge-sharing within his classroom. Yet one might argue that internationalisation happens at the expense of the local students' ability to acquire a deep understanding of their chosen subject, which highlights the importance of addressing disciplinary socialisation and progression when designing international education.

Academic socialisation

Socialisation involves the formal and informal learning processes that students engage in to acquire the practical understandings deemed essential to successful performance within an academic community. All students new to a department or institution may be considered *learners in transition*, which means that the learning needs of a postgraduate, recruited from another country, discipline, and institution, are comparable to those of undergraduates entering a university for the first time. Instead of reducing international students' transition to a question of language and culture, Straker (2016) recommends that one looks at participation, identifying the specific forms of action and discourse that *all* learners have to master to become recognised as experts within their programme and discipline. Straker proposes that international education be approached through Wenger's theory of *Communities of Practice* (1998), which foregrounds the social learning occurring through collective sense-making, engagement in shared practices, participation in a community, and the identity formation that happens as a result thereof. The Communities of Practice model is useful in relation to higher education because it identifies a variety of possible learner positions within a learning culture. Students new to their programme and discipline perform the role of novices, who observe and thereby develop an awareness of the *Doings & Sayings* characteristic of their academic community, but later, as they acquire the practical knowledge underpinning action within their field, they move towards the central position of a disciplinary expert. All students are expected to undertake a similar movement from periphery to core, which means that they can be treated as equals rather than actors with 'special needs' defined by socio-cultural background, nationality, and language.

A second approach foregrounds the practical knowledge that students require in order to perform successfully within their discipline. Hodkinson et al. (2007) underline the importance of *learning culture*, which they define as 'the social practices and meaning through which people learn' (23), stressing how context (institutional, disciplinary, national, and departmental) influences the way students and staff negotiate teaching and learning practices. This has inspired Blasco (2015) to an empirical investigation of the sense-making processes used by international students to decode and adjust to the tacit rules and routines tied to their role as students at a Danish business school. Blasco works from the assumption that '[a]ll students can learn in new ways if they know what is expected from them' (2015, 86), arguing that learners' transition into an unfamiliar environment can be supported by a conscious effort by teachers to 'conceptualise and excavate the tacit dimensions of local learning culture' (2015, 85). As examples Blasco mentions students' preparation, class participation, project supervision, and exam assignments, to which can be added disciplinary canons of theory/theorists, methodological awareness, academic writing and speech, and an appropriate scientific terminology (see Tange 2016, 2019, Gerholm 1990). Most students internalise tacit disciplinary practices as undergraduates, which makes the transition from BA to MA relatively smooth as long as it happens within the same institution and discipline. In contrast, Masters students transferring to a new institution, subject area, and department are challenged because they are supposed to perform the role of a postgraduate expert learner, but lack tacit knowledge about local rules and routines.

In her conceptualisation of the international curriculum, Leask (2015, 8–9) distinguishes between a *formal* (e.g. syllabus, schedule, planned tasks), *nonformal* (e.g. support services, study groups), and *hidden* (e.g. tacit knowledge) dimension to education. In a similar vein, one may differentiate between *formal* and *informal* processes of academic socialisation. Formal socialisation is planned either at *programme-level*, involving course convenors, key lecturers, support staff, student counsellors, and mentors, or with reference to specific *modules* or *learning activities*, in which case it can happen on the initiative of academic staff in response to a particular student need. In comparison, processes of informal socialisation may be hard to detect because they typically require an exchange of tacit knowledge, performed in social settings such as a project group or student association. However, in practice, learning situations may combine processes of formal and informal socialisation, as illustrated by a series of observations made by the programme convenor of one international Masters in Business, located at a Danish university. First, the informant describes action taken at programme-level, where he, as convenor, is responsible for explicating to new students the formal requirements and expectations tied to their role as postgraduates. In many programmes such practical knowledge is provided before or in the first week of term, although the programme convenor may return at a later stage to address student queries arising in relation to specific tasks such as internships or dissertations. Second, the informant explains how the programme sponsors 'homework cafés', which are module-specific and meant to support students' acquisition of skills required within a particular class:

> [Here] we have study cafés. Which means that we have some doctoral students, who will join in and then prepare a case for each week. And what I know is that most of those attending are the international students. First, because many of them, they have only just arrived [to] Campus ... So as I have just said, it is very, very important that they will be put in some groups there, and they will gain some reference points and ... well, get started with things. (DA)

Here academic and social learning overlap. The convenor describes how the study cafés not only function as a means of providing teaching support, but also as a social venue where incoming students can come, interact, and thereby build a network of peers. Finally, the programme convenor plays a role in relation to students' informal learning systems, insisting that he cooperates with student representatives and programme 'clubs' in order to obtain a student perspective on any issues arising in relation to specific modules, teachers, or individual learners:

> [I]f there is a student who comes to me, I say: I listen to you, but tell this to your representatives in the [Business] Club, for they are the ones I take seriously. Because they may perhaps get more [response]. Before people

> complain to me, there is a certain barrier. But that [barrier] is not present in front of their peers. (DA)

Across disciplines and institutions, interviewees highlight a range of programme and module-specific activities developed in an attempt to support students' transition into an unfamiliar learning culture. Certain types of academic socialisation have been incorporated into the formal course structure, including modules presenting key concepts and theories, principal research methods, and project management tools. Particularly at Masters level it is important that such foundational modules be placed as early as possible, as they draw students' attention to key areas that may demand a rethinking of practices they have acquired at an earlier stage of education. To supplement the activities organised at programme level, lecturers have adopted pedagogic strategies that enable them to support academic and social learning within a specific module. Examples are workshops on academic writing, reading groups dedicated to core literature and theories, study cafés where students practise technical skills, and group assignments which can simultaneously encourage collaborative learning and facilitate social interaction. When motivating their decision to engage with student socialisation, informants generally refer to a learner strategy of either *assimilation*, *integration*, or *strategic coping*. Lecturers relying on the *assimilationist* approach will focus on non-native learners who are presented as a special needs group, meriting attention from the teacher in order to acquire practices that are labelled as national, e.g. 'Danish' or 'British'. Actors use expressions such as 'British academic tradition' or 'Danish group culture', which indirectly place internationals in the position of outsiders who will have to 'go native' in order to succeed within their new academic environment. A second group highlights *integration*, explaining how teaching practices should contribute to building an awareness of the international class as a global community where all learners partake as equals. Among the activities mentioned by informants are ice-breaker exercises, discussion groups, and lecture topics that encourage students to add their own personal or national perspective to a collective story. In addition, some actors attempt to support informal socialisation by arranging extra-curricular activities such as field trips or social gatherings. A third option is *strategic coping*. Unlike assimilation and integration, which demand that students develop identities as 'almost native' or 'global' learners, this approach is task-specific, engaging only with the practical knowledge that students need to manage a specific assignment or module. A Law professor notes about his class:

> They will need a bit of knowledge about – well, if you want to know something about international [studies], you will also need to know something about the international legal system, and how that works etc. And whether we bring anything in from the Law tradition? Oh yes, we

> do knowledge-wise, of course, in the sense that they have to learn what 'sources of law' are and so on ... [But] they are not aiming to become lawyers. This means that the assignments they write need not ... be papers like those written by a Law student. Because they need to know other things, right? (DA)

The informant's stance is pragmatic, identifying areas where students lack certain skills and then focusing his attention on the development of these. By reading the lecturer's study guides and feedback students gain enough practical knowledge to perform satisfactorily in the exam, but they are not asked to acquire an identity as 'experts' in Danish or Law culture. Arguably, this makes strategic coping an egalitarian approach where students are allowed to form individual identities that reflect their unique combination of different disciplinary perspectives, past and present educational experiences, sociocultural knowledge, and personal interests.

Progression in international education

Regardless of discipline, a key concern when designing higher education is to ensure learners' growth from novice to subject expert. Educational theorists Jan Meyer and Ray Land (2005, 2006a, 2006b) propose that academic progression be approached through the key notions of *threshold concepts* and *troublesome knowledge*, envisioning learning as a sequence of doorways that students can only cross by acquiring a deep understanding of discipline-specific theories, discourses, and practices. Taylor (2006, 87) compares threshold concepts to a 'transformative gateway'

> that leads to the understanding of new and conceptually more difficult ideas. Such concepts are the key to subsequent higher order learning within a discipline and a lack of ability to progress past such a threshold may lead to ongoing problems in subsequent understanding and application.

Transformation is realised differently within the disciplines, requesting, for instance, from Biology students an expanding awareness of their subject area, which eventually enables experienced learners to bring together modules that were initially understood only as 'isolated islands of knowledge' (Taylor 2006, 89). In comparison, Philosophy students are expected to adopt from the start a new way of thinking and talking about reality, which is bound to challenge any non-specialist learner joining an advanced Philosophy class (Booth 2006). Meyer and Land's second notion of *troublesome knowledge* foregrounds the difficulties that some learners have in mastering particular disciplinary concepts and practices. According to Savin-Baden (2006) these students are placed temporarily in a state of *disjunction*, which they can only exit by rethinking core frameworks or practical understandings obtained at previous stages of education. Building on Perkins (1999), Meyer and Land (2006a) characterise as 'troublesome' knowledge that is *ritual* (9), *inert* (10), *conceptually difficult* (11), *foreign* or *alien* (11), *tacit* (12), and involving a specific disciplinary *language* (14). Several of these overlap with the hidden routines and expectations foregrounded in the previous section, which suggests that a connection can be established between academic progression and students' socialisation into unfamiliar institutional and disciplinary environments. A final example of troublesome knowledge is interdisciplinarity. According to Land (2014, 181) most academics identify with a mono-disciplinary community of practice and are challenged when asked to engage with the *Doings & Sayings* recognised by other academic tribes. In interdisciplinary education this creates 'trouble' for learners when they encounter lecturers who insist that their disciplinary practice be used as a benchmark, demanding, for instance, that the bachelor in English write and speak in the manner of a political scientist.

Exempting Wilken and Tange's 2014 article on Danish higher education, the theme of progression has not been discussed in relation to internationalisation. Such neglect is unfortunate since progression represents a significant source of dissonance in internationalised learning environments, but should probably be ascribed to structural differences in the way that higher education is organised around the world. In English-speaking countries such as Britain, United States, Canada, and Australia, university education is structured around an undergraduate-postgraduate cycle, assuming no direct connection between the discipline students choose for their BA and their subsequent enrolment in a MA course. In such a system, one can graduate as a BA in Medieval History and yet enlist in a professional MA course in Accountancy (as indeed one of the current author's British acquaintances did). In comparison, European systems such as the Scandinavian and German have treated university education as a four- or five-year period of disciplinary specialisation, enabling MA students to acquire a deep understanding of their chosen subject. This organisation of higher education was modified as a result of the post-Bologna implementation of the BA-MA structure across Europe, easing postgraduate students' transfer into new institutions and subject areas. Yet a formal policy such as Bologna does not necessarily change how academics perceive MA education, which means that lecturers trained in the Scandinavian or German tradition may continue to demand from postgraduates a substantial, foundational knowledge within their discipline. Their understanding is supported by official definitions such as the one provided by the Danish Ministry for Higher Education and Science: 'The Masters education will enable a further development of the knowledge and qualifications a student has gained through the BA education. The purpose of the education is that students develop their competences through in-depth disciplinary learning.' (Danish Ministry 2018a; DA).

Arguably, examples of noise arising from students' failure to master the threshold concepts that lecturers deem essential to academic progression can be found in all modules targeting learners in their second or later years of studying. However, such tension becomes particularly evident in advanced-level classes that bring together various types of troublesome knowledge, e.g. by admitting students from various disciplines, socio-cultural backgrounds, and learning cultures. To establish how progression challenges academic staff, one may examine asymmetries identified by actors involved in the teaching of international, interdisciplinary MA education in Denmark. In relation to this, the interviews foreground three themes that can be related to progression: 1) the *BA-MA connection*; 2) students' *socio-cultural knowledge*; and 3) *interdisciplinarity*. To these will be added a fourth asymmetry: *institutional learning cultures*.

First, the *BA-MA connection* emerges as a strong theme within academic contexts such as Danish higher education, where Masters education has traditionally been understood as the opportunity for students to acquire sophisticated disciplinary understandings, and practices. Within this system, academic staff expect to be able to build in their Masters class on discipline-specific, foundational knowledge acquired by students as part of their undergraduate training, which works as long as students are recruited from institutional programmes that are well-known to the lecturers and can easily be checked for any changes to course structure and contents. This is no longer the case once MA education is internationalised and postgraduates are recruited from a broader range of programmes and institutions. Even if they are admitted on the basis of a BA degree in, say Business, learners have internalised diverse understandings of what it means to be a 'Business student', and their subject knowledge does not necessarily match the expectations of academics teaching in their new environment. In consequence, the MA teacher cannot take any knowledge for granted, as noted by this associate professor (Business):

> [A]s soon as there is some diversity, and that is always the case even if it is only a few, and even in the other programmes … where there are less international students, maybe, but there is still some diversity and some, also Danish students coming from other universities and so on. I would always start like this, the first two weeks kind of repetition for some, but to make sure that everybody is somehow on the same page and not lost from the beginning. (DA)

A second theme is asymmetries arising in relation to students' *socio-cultural knowledge and background*. When prompted about Chinese students' ability to access Western Accountancy models, a lecturer admits that these frameworks are not applicable to the situation of Chinese firms, which places Asian learners in a disadvantageous position compared to their European peers. A similar observation has been made by Zhou et al. (2005), who demonstrate through qualitative research how learners may be silenced in Canadian higher education because of lecturers' tendency to depend on themes needing insider knowledge of Canadian culture and society.

The third theme foregrounds a key challenge in MA education, which is frequently designed as *interdisciplinary*, taking broad themes such as International Business, Global Communications, and European Studies instead of disciplinary specialisations such as Political Science, Law, and Medicine. Land (2014, 180) characterises interdisciplinarity as a 'venturing into strange places', claiming that this makes knowledge *unclear, uncertain,* and *unpredictable*. Several respondents working in interdisciplinary programmes confirm Land's observation, including this associate professor (Biology), who here reflects on the pedagogic challenges related to the teaching of Natural Science methods to a class composed of Social Science and Humanities graduates:

> I had difficulties working out if they – if I hit the right level, right? Also because from the beginning we had just set the academic level far too high. Even if we did know that they were not from Biology, so we could probably not assume a great deal. But even then – that surprised me quite a bit. For I had taught 3rd semester for some years, after all, and ... we lowered the level even further. (DA)

Related to dissonance arising from interdisciplinarity is noise created by students' transfer between diverse *institutional* or *learning cultures*. This theme is particularly strong in data collected at universities building on a specific pedagogic approach such as Problem-Based Learning. At these institutions learners are expected to develop their capacity to resolve self-selected 'problems' in peer groups during their undergraduate training, which means that learners arriving at a later stage (e.g. as exchange students or postgraduates) may come across as 'deviant', meriting special attention from support staff and lecturers (see Tange/Jensen 2012, Tange 2016). Negative perceptions have reportedly caused home students to de-select learners from other institutions and disciplines when forming project groups, and at the Danish University of Aalborg some international MA programmes have therefore added to their curriculum an introductory module on Problem-Based Learning, attempting to remove any asymmetries related to students' previous educational experiences.

International educators as 'transition managers'

Educational design has become increasingly important to researchers on international education, shifting the focus away from international student adjustment to institutional and departmental planners' responsibility for creating internationalised study environments. As highlighted in the previous discussion, designing can happen at different levels of organisation, ranging from the holistic, institutional approaches proposed by Nilsson (2003) and Leask (2015) to the concrete actions taken by individual lecturers and programme convenors in relation to a specific class or module. Central is the idea of students in transition. Particularly in MA courses, university lecturers meet learners recruited from different socio-cultural contexts, institutions, disciplines, and learning cultures, which means that they can no longer take for granted that a common practice exists. This places academics in the role of 'transition managers' (Tange 2019), responsible for working out what learners already know and explicating the practices they should attempt to acquire in order to perform successfully within their new academic environment.

An understanding of international educators as transition managers foregrounds two themes. First, academic staff have to engage with students' academic socialisation, attending to formal as well as informal learning needs. In this respect, one can compare the situation of MA students recruited from a different institution, country, or discipline to first years arriving at the university at the beginning of term. Both have yet to internalise the practical routines and understandings governing action and are dependent on information provided through induction workshops, study guides, and feedback from course teachers and peers. A second concern is progression. In programmes that recruit broadly, one cannot assume that all students have mastered the same threshold concepts, and, in consequence, MA lecturers must begin their modules by establishing common theoretical and practical understandings. The interviews suggest that these induction sessions can provoke negative responses from students native to an institution or discipline, who see such activities as unnecessary repetition. To avoid such tension, course lecturers and convenors may opt for voluntary workshops instead, which can address any task or concern that arises within a specific module or class.

8 Roles, rules, and routines

Doings & Sayings in the classroom

Action and interaction in university education are shaped by practical knowledge developed in relation to specific disciplinary, institutional, national, and, in some cases, supernational settings. By bringing together actors socialised into diverse practices, international programmes almost inevitably create dissonance, necessitating that lecturers and students with divergent experiences and expectations co-inhabit a shared learning space. Educational scholars have attempted to resolve this problem in a variety of ways, enabling Ryan (2011) to identify three stages in the research on teaching and learning for international students. The first stage was dominated by a cross-cultural perspective, which demanded that one 'fixes' the international students, insisting that they assimilate into the academic culture found at their host institution (638). The second phase turned the attention to academic staff, stressing how teachers had to 'accommodate' international students, which might involve their acquisition of new pedagogies that could support learners' transition into an unfamiliar environment (639). The third, 'current' stage (639) foregrounds curricular issues, including the design of international programmes, learning objectives, contextual frameworks, and the transformative learning occurring in the meeting between academics, local, and migrant students.

To capture the *Doings & Sayings* involved in international teaching one may draw on the academic literacies model proposed by Lea and Street (1998, 2006). This framework distinguishes between three forms of literacy that students have to master: 1) *study skills* (e.g. reading or producing academic texts); 2) *academic socialisation* (e.g. practices tied to particular disciplinary communities); and 3) *academic literacy*, which 'is concerned with meaning making, identity, power, and authority, and foregrounds the institutional nature of what counts as knowledge in any particular academic context' (Lea/Street 2006, 368–9). Applying the academic literacies model to international education, Sheridan (2011) notes the relationship between the forms of knowledge highlighted by Lea and Street and Bourdieu's concept of *habitus*. The implication is that *all* students' ability to fit into a new academic environment depends on their internalisation of the practical understandings rewarded within a specific institutional and disciplinary field. This takes the discussion beyond the simplistic distinction between local *experts* and foreign *deficit learners* that many critical scholars see as the principal outcome of research applying a cross-cultural perspective (Straker 2016, Ryan/Viete 2009). Instead, Madge et al. (2015) argue for a change of focus from international *students* to international *study*, emphasising that the mobilities now shaping international education mean both students and staff have to reconceptualise knowledge, learning/teaching practices, and academic routines. Ideally, higher education should become a dialogic space that reaches beyond the '[porous] lecture room walls', enabling academic migrants to connect simultaneously to multiple locations, academic traditions, and institutional cultures (Madge et al. 2015, 689). In order to achieve this, university teaching will have to be *done* differently, requiring academic staff to engage actively with the variety of educational experiences present within a diverse student cohort.

To understand what kind of expectations lecturers encounter in international education, one needs to look more closely at the learning cultures that have shaped actors' perceptions of roles, rules, and routines in higher education. The literature offers three perspectives on this. First, there is a strong *cross-cultural tradition*, which tends to ascribe student behaviour to national culture. This has been particularly visible in relation to Asian learners where it has inspired a somewhat stereotypical representation of Chinese students as *passive*, *silent*, and *dependent* on guidance from teachers (e.g. Valiente 2008, Wong 2004). Many contemporary scholars question such an image, insisting that Asian students' behaviour should be interpreted in the light of their previous learning experiences, a marginal position as newcomers in an unfamiliar institutional environment, and communicative difficulties related to the need of non-native speakers to master academic discourse in English (e.g. Tran/Pasura 2019, Heng 2017). Such critique echoes the approach taken by a second group of researchers who insist that actors' expectations be related to their socialisation into specific institutional, disciplinary, and socio-cultural *communities of practice*. Gutierrez and Rogoff (2003, 22) have argued that learner practices commonly explained by national difference should instead be treated as distinctive *repertoires of action* that actors acquire by 'observing and otherwise participating in cultural practices' found within primary, secondary, and higher education. When moving into an unfamiliar academic setting, students draw on practical knowledge internalised at earlier stages of education, which creates dissonance in situations where such action repertoires differ substantially from the rules and routines recognised within their immediate environment. To overcome this barrier, learners require assistance in the form of guidance from academic staff, who can explain what types of academic literacy are considered important within a particular educational, disciplinary, and institutional community of practice (Straker 2016). A third body of literature relates actor experiences and expectations to *beliefs about teaching and learning*. With reference to this, a distinction can be made between teacher-centred and student-centred approaches, which has implications for the perception of classroom teaching, student/staff relationships, and the educational activities that learners are expected to engage in (Maclellan 2015, Samuelowicz/Bain 2001). If socialised into an academic culture where the teacher is considered a disciplinary authority, transmitting 'knowledge from experts', students will experience difficulties when moving into a student-centred learning environment where, in Maclellan's words (2015, 174), teachers 'share authority with learners, encourage positive exchanges among learners ... and help learners to develop effective ways of generating and validating knowledge'.

Lea and Street's academic literacy model suggests that the *Doings & Sayings* of higher education are manifest in individual actors' study skills, practices acquired as a result of previous disciplinary and/or institutional socialisation, and academic literacy, in the form of normative beliefs and power structures that govern action within a specific educational system. Academic socialisation has been addressed in Chapter 7, while skills relating to group work and course assignments will be explored in subsequent chapters on multicultural teams and assessment. This leaves the question of academic literacy, which is here approached through an examination of the roles, rules, and routines that university lecturers highlight when reflecting on their experience with international teaching. To identify areas where practices may diverge, the author performed a review of empirical research on international study environments, noting down any findings relating to student/staff roles, learning/teaching styles, classroom interaction, and dissonance, in the form of conduct labelled 'problematic' because it seemed to violate local norms and routines. The results were compared to themes foregrounded in the interview data, enabling the identification of three topics: 1) *Roles and expectations*, which focuses on teacher positions and styles; 2) *Participation and silence*, which examines assumptions tied to student–staff interaction; and 3) *Critical thinkers?*, which looks at norms attached to the understanding of students as independent, critical learners.

Roles and expectations

The classroom provides the shared space where academic staff, local, and international students meet and engage in mutual knowledge exchange. Increasingly, scholars argue for international education as a global learning environment constructed in a way that is inclusive, enabling all actors to partake as equals regardless of linguistic, socio-cultural, national, and disciplinary background (e.g. Mitzi 2017, Kahn/Agnew 2017). This idea of education builds on an understanding of the university classroom as a neutral space, which allows academic migrants to move relatively easily between institutions located in different parts of the world. Yet the classroom can easily become a 'faux ami' for international students, persuading them that they have entered a setting similar to the lecture halls encountered at earlier stages of education (Kastberg/Tange 2014, 43–4). This may cause them to rest on the assumption that they are 'good' students, who have already achieved academic success, and who can safely continue to act and interact in the manner mastered previously. That such complacency can be risky has been demonstrated in several empirical studies, which reveal how Asian students entering postgraduate programmes in Australia and Britain often experience failure as the result of their transfer into an unfamiliar educational environment (e.g. Tian/Lowe 2013, Yates/Trang 2012, Ryan/Viete 2009). The implication is that no setting is value-free, but each comes with its own set of distinctive roles and expectations.

To identify what associations *lecturing* carries for staff working with international education in Denmark, 25 academics were interviewed about the forms of action that they associate with the practice of classroom teaching. What was shared across programmes and disciplines was the perception that a lecture is made up of various educational activities, including knowledge dissemination by the teacher, exercises to test learners' understanding, group or class discussions, case work, and student presentations. An associate professor (Media Studies) explains:

> [W]hat we had [in] a lecture: 45 [minutes], about, talking, maximum 45, and even I think that is sometimes too much. It is too much. Or that we show examples or that we show videos or that. And then there was discussion, and questions, and a break. And the group presentation-discussion.

The observation that 45 minutes teaching is 'too much' indicates that to this informant it is important that lecturers do not monopolise classroom communications. Arguably, this implies that the informant favours a learner-centred educational culture, which privileges student–staff interaction and joint knowledge construction. In comparison, a teacher-centred approach positions the lecturer as disciplinary authority, who, in the words of Maclellan (2015, 174) '[dominates] class discussions and [creates] few opportunities for students to develop their own questions'. In the interviews, several informants characterise such a format as old-fashioned, which suggests that within a Danish academic context 'innovative' lecturers are expected to rely on a dialogic, student-oriented pedagogy. Academics who find it difficult to achieve this, make excuses, as seen in this comment by an anthropologist:

> [T]here is a part of it, which is a bit like classic teaching where you communicate some material or other, and they take notes … They will of course ask some questions but it is not so. It is not my impression [that] they abstain from asking the questions they want. (DA)

The way the informant presents her practice indicates that she is using the student-centred approach as her benchmark. First, she characterises her action as 'classic' teaching, which carries associations similar to the 'old-fashioned' used by other interviewees to express distance to a more teacher-centred pedagogy. Second, she refers specifically to the students' questioning, or lack thereof, which shows that she considers student–staff dialogue an essential part of 'good' university teaching.

Educational scholars increasingly explain the differences observed in international classes with reference to *learning styles* (Eaves 2011) and *cultures of learning* (Yates/Trang 2012), highlighting how the pedagogic approaches that learners have encountered as part of primary, secondary, and tertiary education shape their present perceptions of classroom roles and routines. In the cross-cultural literature, there has been a tendency to foreground the contrast between a Western, student-centred approach and an Eastern, teacher-focused style (e.g. Valiente 2008, Wong 2004, Chan 1999). Yet case studies relating to contexts such as China and Iraq show that such a distinction is too simplistic, producing a dichotomous representation of academic cultures instead of acknowledging how teacher- and learner-centred approaches coexist in most national systems (Ma/Wen 2018, Jordan et al. 2014). Having said that, one may see a tendency within specific educational environments to privilege one pedagogy over the other. Judging from comments made in the Danish interviews, one could argue that the student-centred approach has become normative within this context, which has implications for teachers' perception of their role and responsibilities. One area where this is evident is teacher–student relationships. Informants generally agree that Danish *teaching culture* can be characterised as egalitarian, which to the lecturers means that students engage with them as equals rather than disciplinary experts. Such an approach may challenge students socialised into a more hierarchical academic system since it demands that learners assume responsibility for speaking up and thereby contribute to the co-creation of knowledge in class. An associate professor from Media Studies observes:

> [T]here is also a difference in how teacher–student relations might work in Germany and the Netherlands and here in Denmark. You know, we also talk about authority relations. That we have a more casual approach. Which does not mean that you do not respect your peers and teachers. Of course, you do. But it is appreciated if you contribute to discussions, engage in scientific debates, and also challenge the teacher. (DA)

When reflecting on teaching and learning cultures, informants highlight the contrast between a Danish approach, characterised by dialogue, student activity, and a withdrawn role for the lecturer, and *Other* pedagogies associated with a monological lecturing style, student passivity, and an authoritarian teacher. In the international classroom, *Other* styles are mainly ascribed to the non-natives and explained with reference to national cultures (e.g. China, Eastern and Southern Europe) or academic traditions (e.g. Anglo-American, Asian). Yet lecturers' comments about 'foreign' pedagogies suggest that they employ the term rather loosely, using it to signify anything deviating from the student-centred pedagogy favoured by the informants. The implication is that dissonance should be related to divergent beliefs about teaching and learning rather than national difference. This places academic staff in a key position as they can help students crack the codes of an unfamiliar system by explicating what kind of relationship they prefer. An associate professor (Agricultural Science) observes:

> [T]hey clearly experience me, as the professor, and their relationship with me as different … And really, this is also a big part of the first week [that] they discover me as a person who is interested in them. I am a person who wants to [do] something with them. I have thought about what I should like to achieve … and we work together on this. I shall not arrive, deliver a lecture and then leave. I am not authoritarian. I have opinions, but I am not authoritarian. (DA)

Tange and Jensen (2012) have identified lecturer and student roles as a common source of tension in international education, provoking strong emotional responses to actors who defy preconceived notions of 'proper' student or teacher conduct. Such dissonance can derive from expectations tied to the lecturer's status as disciplinary authority. From the perspective of students socialised into a teacher-centred system the lecturer role involves taking responsibility for directing learners, helping them understand canonical disciplinary texts, and ensuring that any knowledge required to pass an exam will be explained in class or during supervision sessions. In contrast, an actor relying on a student-centred approach works on the assumption that learners can only acquire deep disciplinary insights if put in charge of all stages in the learning process. A social scientist reflects on the asymmetry this creates between his teaching practice and the culture that some international students bring into the classroom:

> [A]nother thing is their study culture. Where they have not been used to the kind of exams that we use here, and a study form like the one we have here. Where I give them very wide conditions for learning. Really, I just introduce themes briefly, and whether they should like to acquire more knowledge about those themes, is really for them to decide. I do not expect that they will have time to read the entire book, I expect them to read those parts of the chapters that they think are most exciting. (DA)

Inevitably, this very open approach confuses students who in earlier stages of education have become accustomed to professors acting out the role of disciplinary authority by providing clear instructions on how learners should solve particular tasks. Such actors may react negatively when exposed to a student-centred pedagogy, questioning the teacher's scientific qualifications or reading her unwillingness to offer directions as incompetence.

Participation vs. silence

Learner participation can be defined in a variety of ways, including students' ability to follow lectures, take notes, partake in class discussions, present information orally, and contribute to joint knowledge construction by suggesting new theories, socio-cultural experiences, and disciplinary perspectives. Cross-cultural researchers generally treat participation as normative in higher education, positioning international students who seek to avoid interaction as *deficit learners* in need of special attention (see Murray/McConachy 2018). Prominent among these 'passive' learners are Asian students, whose mythical silence in Western-style, international education has routinely been attributed to cultural and linguistic differences. Recently, interview studies have questioned the stereotypical picture of reticent Asian learners, inviting Chinese and Vietnamese students to share their experience of participation in American, Australian, and Canadian higher education (Heng 2017, Yates/Trang 2012, Zhou et al. 2005). These studies involve researchers from an Asian background, which means that students have been able to express themselves in their native languages rather than English. The findings provide a different perspective on Asian non-participation, highlighting how learners abstain from classroom interaction when 1) this requires Western or country-specific knowledge (Zhou et al. 2005, Heng 2017); 2) moves too fast for non-native speakers of English (Yates/Trang 2012, Heng 2017), or 3) is too 'chatty' for learners trained to accept only contributions that are 'useful, relevant and to the point' (Yates/Trang 2012, 29). In addition, Heng's Chinese respondents request that university teachers 'consider our background' and 'be patient with and caring to us' (2017, 839–40), which underlines the importance of turning the focus from the reticence of individual students to the practices that teachers can adopt in order to facilitate dialogue.

Increasingly, scholars acknowledge that the degree of classroom interaction partly reflects the lecturer's beliefs about education (e.g. teacher-centred vs. student-centred pedagogies), partly derives from concrete actions taken to engage students actively in knowledge production. One example is Jude Carroll (2015), who has developed a set of pedagogic 'tools' that teachers can use in order to increase student participation. Among the actions recommended for lecturing Carroll suggests an explicit structure, language adjustments, and scaffolding techniques such as Power Point slides and video recordings. Participation at seminars is encouraged through an active use of students' socio-cultural resources and attention paid to 'silent' learners. Yet Carroll's advice reflects her position as educational consultant rather than practitioner, which makes her propositions somewhat generic and detached from the actual performance of international education. In comparison, Murray and McConachy (2018) take British university lecturers' experiences with participation as their point of departure, using focus group interviews to highlight how classroom strategies are shaped by individual actors' understanding of cultural and linguistic difference. According to Murray and McConachy (2018, 259) academics are concerned with students' 'lack of participation', described by one lecturer as a 'blank wall' that is created simultaneously by learner silence and missing 'non-verbal responsiveness to [the teacher's] attempts to create an animated classroom'. The findings foreground strategies that teachers have developed to resolve the problem of non-participation, including 'providing discussion questions and tasks in advance', 'experimenting with group size', and '[flipping] the classroom' by making lectures available online (Murray and McConachy 2018, 261). A final take on participation suggests that classroom interaction, or lack thereof, can be explained with reference to experiences and expectations tied to the physical space in which education is realised. Confronted by international students' reticence, Mangan et al. (2016) conducted an experiment, adding to a management course workshops set at a nearby theatre, thereby breaking 'expectations about how to behave in the classroom' (292). The effect of such action was clear, compelling *all* students to accept roles that demanded communication in English (Mangan et al. 2016, 298). Subsequently, the authors conclude, learners previously identified as 'quiet' became more outspoken in class, implying that the classroom is a setting that can inspire or prevent particular forms of interaction. A similar move to break out of the classroom is described by this Danish associate professor (Agricultural Science):

> [O]n the second day of the course … then we go on a one-day field trip, where they are all standing there, … freezing in a ploughed field in Denmark. And find out that it is cold, and the soil can freeze and so on in the month of January. And it is dark and it is slippery. And then we go to my place … I have bought a lot of food and then we cook together. And this is day number two after their arrival, and they are all so shy, and, ooh, how it is so difficult because they do not know anyone. And after we have been on that field trip, and we have been sitting at my place, and they have cooked together … then they are a team. (DA)

The literature suggests that educational scholars generally agree that 'good' teaching practices are participatory, inviting all students to partake as equals in classroom interaction. Yet the research has primarily been conducted in English-speaking countries such as Britain, Australia, and North America where classroom encounters are highly asymmetrical, bringing together international students, who may use English as their second or third language, and locals, who enjoy the fluency of a native speaker. One may compare such observations to research carried out in educational systems that are traditionally non-English-speaking, asking if academics working in Danish higher education perceive participation in the international classroom differently.

Across disciplines, Danish-based informants share the assumption that student–staff interaction is critical to 'good' university teaching and learning.

To use the term proposed by Murray and McConachy's British respondent, lecturers fear 'the blank wall', evoking the image of students who remain silent despite all the teacher's attempts to stimulate dialogue. An assistant professor (Business) describes her frustration when failing to achieve interaction: '[W]hen this happens, there is no interaction, then it is really a feeling that … I am a clown in front of the [class]. I mean, you have the feeling you give yourself … you are prepared, and there's absolutely nothing.' Other respondents convey similar experiences, describing their international classes as more 'silent' or 'less fun' than a homogeneous group of Danes. A noteworthy difference between British and Danish higher education is the impact of language. When referring to 'Danish' courses, the lecturers are comparing to a situation where both teacher and students work in their first language, unlike 'international' classes, which at Danish universities normally involve a change into English, which is a second or foreign language for most. As demonstrated in Chapter 6, this affects the nature of classroom communications, silencing local as well as international students. A social scientist reflects:

> Even the Danes, whom I had first taught in a Danish-medium course and then, subsequently, in an English-medium module. And those who had been keen to ask questions in the Danish course, they were quiet as the grave in the English one. So, really, they might as well have watched a film with a lecturer, right, for there wasn't a lot of interaction. (DA)

Interestingly enough, the use of English creates symmetry in a Danish international education, preventing both local and non-native students from speaking up in class. As a result, few informants ascribe learner reticence solely to international students' English proficiency, but note how Danish students are as likely to remain silent in English-medium courses. Yet, a historian observes, it is important that academic staff acknowledge that divergent approaches to teaching and learning can be found in the international classroom, and that 'it is not the most natural for all people that there is dialogue, that you interrupt the teacher' (DA). The informant adds that international educators should accept their responsibility for managing interaction, training all learners through a combination of dialogue-oriented activities and explicit advice on dos and don'ts in participatory education. A social scientist reflects on his effort to 'break the ice' in a class on European Studies:

> Perhaps, [it is] special when you start up? May be a kind of modesty, or whatever you want to call it, about managing in a second language? Perhaps the insecurity is greater? Perhaps it takes more to break the ice in the beginning? But having said that … It's really not a problem. Thankfully, it is so easy to be teaching in EU-related stuff, right? Then you can always ask or provoke them: Well, that is not problem in Bulgaria, is it? And then you get an immediate reaction from the Bulgarians. (DA)

The Danish interviews indicate that many teachers actively seek to facilitate dialogue, designing educational activities such as teambuilding exercises, group assignments calling for different socio-cultural, linguistic, and disciplinary perspectives, and debate topics on global themes and conditions. Even if student–staff interaction is clearly normative within this educational setting, the lecturers seem to have accepted their responsibility for guiding students unfamiliar with participatory education, adopting practices that can support these learners' acquisition of a more interactive, student-centred approach.

Critical thinkers?

Connected to classroom participation is the third theme of critical thinking. When commenting on classroom interaction, Danish university teachers frequently link learners' willingness to *speak up in class* to their capacity to *ask critical questions*. Critical questions may be defined as challenges that learners present to lecturers in class, requesting that they defend a particular theoretical position or consider alternative theories or interpretations. The interviews indicate that academic staff enjoy such conversations, describing as 'good' students those who do not accept their disciplinary authority at face value. In a review article, Yershova et al. (2000, 41) proposed *critical thinking* as one of three 'major competencies [considered] essential to functioning effectively in culturally diverse learning environments', the others being *intercultural competence* and *comparative thinking*. Yershova et al. characterise critical thinking as a problematic concept because it is acknowledged to be an essential skill in higher education, yet lacks a clear definition or guidelines as to how such a competence can be taught and assessed. In the article Yershova et al. (2000) list a number of traits characteristic of a critical thinker, including the *disposition* '[to come] up with the best, most unbiased answer' (50), an ability to *evaluate academic knowledge* (52), *analytical* and *argumentative* skills (53), and *reflective skills*, which involves 'questioning one's own beliefs and values' (55). The authors insist that the elements used to define critical thinking are linked to culture, reflecting the norms and assumptions found in particular academic traditions and environments. In consequence, critical thinking may be considered troublesome knowledge – a threshold concept that will challenge incoming learners until they have cracked the code of a new educational and disciplinary culture (see Meyer/Land 2006a, 2006b).

In the literature, several scholars present critical thinking as a 'problem' confronting non-native students admitted into international programmes at British and Australian universities (e.g. Shaheen 2016, Vandermensbrugghe 2004). Egege and Kutileh (2004) name critical thinking a 'foreign notion' to be taught to 'foreign students', positioning Asian students as deficit learners who present difficulties to the Australian lecturer because they lack a 'critical thinking capacity', which is associated with a 'Western academic model' and defined as an 'understanding of the requirements of analysis and critique' (2004, 78). Egege and Kutieh's identification of critical thinking as the key attribute distinguishing graduates educated within Western educational cultures from those trained in non-Western contexts is typical of the way the concept has been used in the cross-cultural tradition. Hence, Asian students are constructed as 'deviant learners', who merit special attention from 'good' international teachers in order to successfully manage the transition into Western academic culture. A recent article by Song and McCarthy (2018) has documented how such deficit discourses are reproduced in Australian policy papers, which rely on an essentialist conceptualisation that presents critical thinking as 'both a totem pole of Western superior thinking and a yardstick to measure international students' deficiency' (354). As a result, international students are placed in the position of an undesirable *Other* in Australian higher education, which encourages teaching and administrative staff to turn academic failure into a question of cultural difference rather than the outcome of mismatching educational norms and experiences.

A similar tendency to use critical thinking as the benchmark distinguishing 'good' from 'deviant' learners is found in the Danish interviews. When reflecting on their encounters with international students, informants offer anecdotes about individuals who act in a way that is 'different', which suggests that, consciously or unconsciously, the lecturers consider certain forms of learner behaviour as normative, assessing any alternative practices with reference to these. Informants' stories are often motivated by supervision experiences, which shows the importance attached to this practice in Danish higher education where university teachers are expected to engage in a close relationship with students working on group or individual assignments. Project-writing involves a high degree of student autonomy, and interview comments on the supervision process can be used to obtain a deeper understanding of norms attached to the perception of learners as independent, critical thinkers. Judging from the data four themes seem particularly important.

First, lecturers work on the assumption that they should seek an *egalitarian relationship* with their students. Academics acting in the capacity of supervisor will not assume the position of a disciplinary authority or instructor, for, as one associate professor (Law) observes, learners 'should be challenged to think for themselves' (DA). The insistence that all partake as equals creates dissonance in situations where learners expect their supervisor to perform in a more authoritarian, teacher-like manner. A Business lecturer observes: '[Y]ou have this very extreme attitude that the supervisor possesses the right answers – he just does not want to tell me, and I have to turn up until I get the answer' (DA).

A second norm concerns *decision-making*. The lecturers regard project-writing as an autonomous learning process, which means that they hold students responsible for organising their work and making their own theoretical and methodological choices. In order to avoid taking over a project, supervisors will seek a passive role, where they respond to any questions raised by their supervisees, but abstain from providing instructions as to how supervisees may solve their task. A social scientist describes his practice:

> I do not have any methodological discussion with them. Because I will say, well, now, we have to get to this point, and then we need to accumulate enough knowledge to become wiser when we get there. And when I then start telling these foreigners that there are many roads leading there, then they already start to question my judgement. Because there must be one way of doing this. (DA)

A third assumption is that students must work *independently* with any material used for exams or projects. Informants describe 'independence' in various ways, including the ability to synthesise information, compare different theoretical perspectives, offer a new interpretation, and highlight limitations attached to a specific scientific paradigm or method. Shared is the understanding that a 'good' paper contains more than knowledge reproduced from literature or lectures, which motivates this anthropologist to make the following distinction between 'good' and 'deviant' learners:

> Well, there are those who will write half a page on something, having no clue what is actually said. It has just been copied. And then you really discover the cultural gap between the independent student, right, and s/he who only parrots the teacher. (DA)

A final norm is the lecturers' expectation that *they be challenged* during the supervision process. A challenge may involve students arguing for the decisions made, their defence of a theoretical position, or the correction of misunderstandings caused by the teacher, which informants present as essential to an egalitarian relationship between supervisor and supervisee. However, as noted by this Engineering lecturer with reference to a group of exchange students, such a learning approach does not come natural to all:

> Culturally they come from a very different place where one may not be accustomed to counter the teacher or argue, because what the teacher says must, per definition, be correct ... And here it becomes difficult when I am sitting as supervisor for their projects and say: What is your idea about this? If I have just said that I think, perhaps, the focus should be here, then I can see that when I look at [the exchange students], they do not feel comfortable about saying: But we think that maybe the focus should be there. (DA)

The informant adds that his presence at group meetings may have prevented some students from contributing, and that he has asked local students to report if debates change when he is not in the room. If so, he continues, 'I shall have to change my conduct' (DA). Interestingly enough, the category of 'local' includes all students registered for a degree programme, internationals as well as Danes. Hence, the lecturer seems to relate any divergence to incoming students' need to settle into an unfamiliar learning environment rather than a generic difference distinguishing Danish from *Other* learners.

As a concept in international education critical thinking has proved troublesome for several reasons: First, there is no clear definition, which means that academics have no common reference point that can be used to explain and assess such a competence. Instead actors rely on comparisons, contrasting a somewhat vague and idealised notion of 'being critical' with learner actions dismissed as 'uncritical', 'parrot-like', or 'passive'. Second, critical thinking has been used to *other* international students. Particularly Asian learners have been described in the literature as uncritical rote-learners, who need to change their approach to teaching and learning when entering a Western academic culture. This places the responsibility for managing transition solely on the learners, whilst fuelling any discourses of deficit circulating among local students and staff. Third, critical thinking is a hard thing to teach. Such an approach builds on principles such as egalitarianism, independence, and student control, and a more active involvement by academic staff could prove counterproductive, persuading students to rely on the teacher's instructions instead of accepting their role as autonomous learners.

Teaching roles and routines

The past discussion has shown how the teaching roles and routines that can be observed in the classroom reflect normative understandings of how a university teacher should act and interact in higher education. Judging from the interview data, internationalisation processes have drawn lecturers' attention to academic rules and conventions which are exposed in the intercultural encounter with learners whose previous educational experiences have caused them to internalise other approaches to learning. Yet academic staff enjoy a position of power that is unrivalled in the international classroom. This means that, at the end of the day, it is up to the teacher to decide whether she will rely on an assimilationist strategy, insisting that international students need to adapt, or rethink her teaching practice, developing pedagogies that enable the equal participation of all learners in knowledge creating and sharing.

Working with the normative understandings underpinning teaching and learning practices is difficult as they frequently involve tacit knowledge, of which actors are not necessarily aware. The author used research interviews to pinpoint some of the roles and routines governing action in Danish higher education, and even if the findings apply to a specific academic context, a similar approach can be used to obtain information about other educational cultures. First, it is important to establish what experiences and expectations shape people's practical understanding. This is in order to identify academic norms and routines, which will subsequently have to be discussed in relation to international education, enabling a distinction between rules that are non-negotiable and those allowing for flexibility. A second step is to describe the principal norms, preferably in relation to a particular course or discipline as these may build on divergent beliefs about notions such as independence or critical thinking. Finally, international educators should consider what action they will take to support students in transition and thereby ensure that all learners know what is expected from them.

9 Curricular contexts and concerns

Mapping contextual practices

Context refers to the geographical and socio-cultural framing that lecturers use to explain and ground the abstract scientific knowledge presented in class. In programmes that educate domestic learners for a national labour market, context can often be taken for granted, with teaching staff working primarily from examples that refer to local and national conditions. However, once education is internationalised, university teachers have to reconsider and perhaps change their curricular contexts, shifting the frame of reference from the national to a supernational or global scale. In the light of that, it is not surprising that contextual practices have become an important concern for educational scholars, foregrounding a possible need to internationalise course curricula.

In 2002, human geographer Martin Haigh challenged universities to create an even platform for all students, 'irrespective of their national, ethnic, cultural, social class/caste or gender identities' (51). This, Haigh continued, demanded a curriculum that was global and polyphonic, engaging with geographies beyond the 'Northern White Empire' (Haigh 2002, 55, quoting Stott/Sullivan 2000). Haigh offers a postcolonial reading of curricular practices in British higher education, insisting on the need to 'remove the notion that ideas from non-Western traditions are "exotic" and to establish them as normal' (2009, 271). Postcolonialism has also inspired case studies from several Australian-based scholars (e.g. Collyer 2018, Joseph 2008, Rizvi 2007), who highlight the contrast between a hegemonic space typically named as Eurocentric, Euro-American, Western, and Northern, and alternative, *Other*-oriented geographies described as indigenous, non-European, non-Western, and Southern. While important to a debate on colonial relations, such binaries may be problematic in relation to international education since they narrow the discussion to a question of North versus South, West versus East. According to Berg (2004), one finds within the 'global North' core, semi-peripheral, and peripheral geographies, which suggests that a more nuanced approach is required if one is to capture the multi-centred reality enacted by international educators.

Another researcher concerned with the importance of location to the selection and representation of academic knowledge is Betty Leask, whose approach to internationalisation has been introduced in previous chapters. Leask et al. observe that '[i]nternationalisation of the curriculum is highly context dependant and may look different in different disciplines, in different regions, in different nations and in different institutions' (2013, 188). Unlike advocates of a postcolonial perspective, Leask acknowledges that it can make perfectly good sense for French universities to privilege Pierre Bourdieu and Michel Foucault over theories emerging from Brazil and China. Leask (2015, Leask/Bridge 2013, 84) works from a model that incorporates four 'layers of context' (institutional, local, national/regional, and global), suggesting that this be used to engage academic staff in a dialogue about curricular practices. Leask's framework orders contexts vertically, reproducing the scalar approach found in human geography where space is commonly conceptualised as a hierarchy of nested scales, 'ranging from the national to the regional and local' (Leitner/Sheppard 2009, 232). Geographers have criticised scalar models because they fix space, encouraging an interpretation of spatial processes as a mono-directional movement from the micro to macro level (see Marston et al. 2005, Mahon/Keil 2009). Within international education, a scalar approach seems equally problematic since an awareness of such hierarchical ordering may encourage international educators to abandon systematically all local or national references in favour of geographies perceived to be 'international'. Given the domination of English-medium publishers, media, and institutions within the global academic system, this would privilege locations such as the US and UK, possibly motivating academics based in non-English-speaking contexts to replace indigenous literature with standardised, American textbooks.

Common to both Haigh and Leask is the normative belief that curricular contexts can be conceptualised in terms of fixed categories such as Western/non-Western and local/national/global scales. Hence, space is taken for granted, while academic staff are positioned as novice learners in need of educational experts to teach them how to manage 'properly' the internationalisation of course curricula. The current author should like to propose an alternative approach, reading curricular contexts as social constructs created and possibly transformed by university teachers when enacting the practice of international education. This understanding is inspired by Larsen and Beech (2014), who suggest that one engages with spatial theorising in education, foregrounding the *relational* and *productive* functions of space. Larsen and Beech (2014, 199) explain the *relational* function of space as 'sets of relations between individuals and groups', which is manifest, for instance, in social networks and virtual communities. The *productive* function of space refers to the critical spatial theory of Henri Lefebvre (1991), which contains three core dimensions: 1) *spatial practices*, 2) *representations of space*, and 3) *spaces of representation*. Larsen and Beech (2014, 200) define these as 1) space 'interpreted or perceived and referred to as common-sense'; 2) space 'as used in the media, maps [etc.] which operate in ways to represent and make sense of space'; and 3) space 'lived, felt, and experienced'. Lefebvre offers three access points to the contextual landscapes produced in international education. First, *spatial practices* refer to academics' interpretation of space, including ways in which internationalisation processes inspire lecturers to question and rethink curricular practices. Second, one may investigate the *representation of space* in international education, focusing on the geographies produced when lecturers select course readings, case studies, and topics for class discussion. Three, *spaces of representation* involve an engagement with the contexts 'lived, felt and experienced' by students as well as staff, which is manifest through pedagogic practices adopted to embrace the diverse geographies co-inhabiting the international classroom.

Spatial practices

Scale matters when internationalising. That was the message of Martin Haigh and Betty Leask, and they are supported by a 2016 survey conducted among international students at American universities, which reveals that 28% of respondents would like their professors to use more non-US examples in class (Redden 2017). As mentioned in Chapter 8, Zhou et al. (2005) have explored the myth of the 'silent' Chinese learner in interviews conducted with Mainland Chinese students enrolled at Canadian universities. Challenging the popular view that Asian learners' passivity can be explained by culture, Zhou et al. demonstrate that the problem is scale, arguing that Chinese students withdraw from classroom discussion when this demands contextual knowledge about Canadian and Western culture that these actors do not possess (2005, 295). Investigating the performance of Chinese doctoral students within Australian higher education, Singh and Meng reach a similar conclusion, ascribing Asian learners' silence to a systematic 'devaluation of non-western theoretical knowledge by western peers' (2013, 908). Hence, empirical research indicates that lecturers' spatial practices constitute a possible barrier to successful international education, resulting in the exclusion of certain groups of learners. Participants in the author's interview studies offer a different view, with several informants highlighting how internationalisation processes have caused them to reflect on their spatial practices and, in some cases, rethink curricular contexts and scales. An associate professor (Agricultural Science) comments on the translation work required when a course originally framed within a national context was opened to international students:

> [We] have certain competence areas, which are tied to a Danish context. Well, they need to know something about Danish agriculture … It is really difficult to think these into an English-medium situation, where you have foreign students, because suddenly you need to shift one level up and start teaching principles, and then, perhaps, use Danish examples … Because you have English-speaking [students] there, who may come from Nepal, and what, precisely, would they need [the Danish cases] for? (DA)

The lecturer's distinction between a Danish and an 'English-medium situation' is significant as it foregrounds the connection between space, curricular choices, and language in academic fields that are traditionally non-English speaking. At Danish universities, it is common to find that disciplines such as Danish history, literature, and law, which predominantly relate to domestic settings, are taught in Danish, unlike programmes titled *European* Law, *International* Studies, and *Global* Communication which are offered in English and refer to contexts wider than the nation state.

Based on the interview data one may identify two spatial practices characteristic of international teaching: *Recontextualisation* and *upscaling*. *Recontextualisation* is defined as a change in the spatial framing of knowledge, causing academics to abandon local and national settings in favour of contexts perceived to be wider in scope and therefore expected to be recognised by a greater number of learners. For lecturers located in non-English speaking environments such as Denmark, Sweden, and the Netherlands recontextualisation may involve a lateral move, which means that examples referring to countries perceived as 'small' or 'marginal' are replaced by cases from larger geographies such as the US and UK. In a situation where a Media Studies lecturer replaces a story heard on the Danish news with a feature article from the *New York Times*, the scale will remain national, zooming in on a particular American debate, but the teacher works on the assumption that most students follow American news, which makes the chosen example more accessible. Alternatively, recontextualisation is a vertical move where academics broaden the context by moving from local/national settings to a supernational or global scale. Another name for such a strategy is *upscaling*, which is signalled by adding to course titles adjectives such as *European*, *international*, and *global*. When signing up for a module on *Global* history, students expect a curricular context embracing diverse geographies, whereas programmes in *Scottish* history, *English* literature, and *Celtic* civilisation make no such promise.

In *The Production of Space* (1991) Henri Lefebvre warns readers against the treatment of space as an unproblematic category, reminding them that space is a social construct, constituted by the theoretical practices found in academic disciplines such as Mathematics, Philosophy, and History. Yet there is a taken-for-granted quality attached to the idea of space in academia, which becomes apparent when prompting lecturers about their curricular contexts. To test the importance of space 25 academics involved with international higher education in Denmark were asked to describe the geographical and socio-cultural contexts that they consider important to their course. Surprisingly few were able to answer the question without cues in the form of suggested scales such as local, national, regional, international, and global. This confirms Lefebvre's assertion that space represents a neglected dimension in many academic disciplines, which poses a challenge when attempting to understand the meanings attached to an internationalised curriculum. Central to the discussion are three concerns: 1) to what extent are processes of recontextualisation motivated by a hierarchical perception of scale; 2) what does *international* connote to the lecturers; and 3) has internationalisation made local/national scales irrelevant?

According to Larsen and Beech (2014, 197) researchers working with globalisation tend to foreground 'the global', conceptualising the alternative national and local dimensions as '[places] influenced by outside forces'. Similarly, international educators rely on a distinction between specific locations or countries, which may serve as the backdrop to specific examples or cases, and generic, macro-level institutions and processes that merit a thorough, theory-driven exploration. An anthropologist observes:

> [W]e have different [cases] from Asia ... But all the time there is this added global dimension both in the form of those Millennium Goals outlined by the UN, or climate change or all the global economy and international politics stuff etc. So you could say that this is really the local and global contexts integrated. (DA)

The informant presents the local and global frames as interdependent, acknowledging that the scale extension that follows from internationalisation does not necessitate an exclusion of the local and national dimensions. Yet a common view among the interviewees is that geographical scales constitute a hierarchical order, motivating the conclusion that the proper framing for international education is one that is either transnational, international, or global. 'Europe: That is not international enough', a Law professor observes, adding: 'We are not European Studies' (DA). To this informant *doing* 'international' means engaging with global conventions such as the Human Rights Declaration, and although they may be discussed with reference to the particular conditions of a single country or region, cases are read against a global system constituted by international institutions and treaties. A Business lecturer offers an alternative interpretation, defining as 'international' the countries with which 'we' trade. This results in a triadic organisation of the world, foregrounding key geographies in (Western) Europe, North America and South East Asia. 'I have nothing called *The South African Journal of Finance*' (DA), the informant observes on his syllabus, which suggests a spatial hierarchy where some geographies are privileged and others ignored.

Emerging from the interviews is the general understanding of internationalisation as spatial upscaling where academic staff will either abandon local and domestic frames altogether or connect them to international or global settings. Hence, actors rely on a hierarchical ordering of space, which is likely to motivate their deselection of examples from domestic businesses, media, and institutions. Some informants consider this internationalisation of contextual practices a strength since it enables the standardisation of course cases and contents, which increases the transparency of university curricula for employers worldwide, thereby easing graduates' ability to move in a global labour market. Other interviewees are less convinced that global reference points are always preferable, suggesting that one might include occasional local examples to build rapport with classes composed mainly of domestic students. An assistant professor (Business) notes:

> For example, [I was looking for a good case] that we could work with, and I was hoping that this might lead to interaction and stuff like that. But, you know, I am trying to find cases. Either a company in Denmark, but then I am always thinking, [to] those not from Denmark that's ... maybe [it's] not that interesting.

Here the lecturer expresses uncertainty about her right to include in an international course a domestic example. This suggests that some academics perceive internationalisation as a process that necessitates *upscaling*, demanding that all units of analysis be shifted up one level from Danish to European, national to international, and European to global. What is the likely effect of such perceptions on academics' choice of course contents and syllabi? To answer this it is necessary to examine the representation of space, including the material production of geographies that occurs when academics compile reading lists for international education.

Representations of space

Academic staff actively engage with the social production of space when putting together a list of reading for an international module. At this point lecturers need to select literature, and because many texts are framed within particular socio-cultural and geographical contexts, their choice inevitably signals to students what spaces are important, and what geographies can be ignored. Ideally, a historian observes, examples for a global course come from everywhere: 'So, I pick examples from national, transnational, global, so, let's say, European but also Asian, African, Latin American, North American.' On a more pragmatic note, the historian adds that curricular choices reflect what is available within the discipline, which means that some perspectives become more dominant than others:

> [O]f course, I have limits to the language I can read, and there are certain actors who write about global history and they are Americans – and Europeans. So I would say, the course literature is a mix of Germans writing in English, Americans, and British, and English, plus Indian, Chinese, and some African authors.

A second informant from Media Studies voices a similar concern with the global orientation of international education. Reflecting on the contents of his MA programme, he notes that course syllabi are imbalanced in favour of Eurocentric and Anglo-American perspectives, with only limited representation of alternative geographies such as Africa, Asia, and South America. The lecturer has attempted to resolve the asymmetry by developing for his own module a comprehensive biography composed of obligatory, Western texts and recommended readings from other parts of the world:

> I give them a course outline which is about 32 pages long. But why it is 32 pages long is because the key [readings] were from the US or any other European country or Australia. But for every suggested reading session I made sure that I included literature from the non-Western world. So I told them very clearly that of course in my lecture I am going to make reference to Africa, I am going to make reference to Asia, but the core of what we are reading is about the experience in the West.

What is described here is an interesting experiment in *internationalising* course curricula. The informant accepts that all students have a right to see generic, theoretical themes applied to a context that is local to them, which motivates him to compile a reading list of case studies from around the world. Yet his syllabi reproduces a hierarchical organisation of space, labelling some texts as 'key', while others are 'suggested' reading only. Arguably, this encourages learners to distinguish between *core* literature, which, according to the quotation above, refers mainly to a Western/Northern context, and *other* material, which can be ignored by students with little interest in African, Asian, or Latin American affairs. As a result, the effort to produce a global curriculum ends up reinforcing an existing core–periphery structure.

The geographer Lawrence Berg (2004) has proposed that a core–periphery model be used to analyse academic knowledge production, insisting that academic journals, funding agencies, and conference networks privilege certain geographies. According to Berg (2004, 554), the predominant pattern reflects a hierarchical order, which places Anglo-America at the centre of international scholarship, whereas other spaces 'are seen as "limited" (read as local, parochial, case study, etc.)'. Hegemonic knowledge, Berg argues, predominantly come from two places: 'Britain (especially England, Wales and Scotland) and the United States' (2004, 55), whereas institutions located in English-speaking countries such as Canada or Australia represent a semi-peripheral position being 'less "marginal" than other locations' (2004, 553). A similar claim has been made by Bourdieu and Wacquant, who describe an asymmetrical academic field where scholars representing specific geographies assume the power 'to universalize particularisms linked to a singular historical tradition' (1999, 41). The problem, Bourdieu and Wacquant stress, is American domination constituted by scholars' general acceptance of the US as a *commonplace* '*with which* one argues but *about which* one does not argue' (1999, 41). Empirical studies have confirmed such a representation of the US as the dominant space in global academia, documenting how peer reviewers and journal editors request from scholars located in non-English speaking contexts an engagement with theories, methods, and discursive practices developed in American and, to a lesser degree, British research (Bauder et al. 2018, Meriläinen et al.

2008, Aalbers 2004, Gregson et al. 2003). Exempting the single case study by Tange/Millar (2016) no similar effort has been made to investigate core–periphery structures in international course syllabi, which seems paradoxical, given educational scholars' insistence that one internationalises curricula.

Course literature provides an insight into the social production of space for several reasons. First, most lecturers are active researchers, and their choice of literature is likely to be influenced by this. Hence, one may expect academics, who as scholars identify with disciplinary traditions associated with US- or UK-based institutions and theorists, to be affected by this when designing international courses, which could prompt them to include a high number of American texts in their syllabi. Second, literature presented as obligatory often serves as the point of departure for classroom debates, receiving more attention than texts marked as supplementary. In a situation where mainly Western geographies are represented among the key readings, students are indirectly encouraged to accept a core–periphery model, which could motivate their de-selection of non-Western texts for assignments or exams. Finally, the representation of space shapes students' perception of geographical frames within their discipline, encouraging them to evaluate scientific knowledge on the basis of a hierarchical distinction between West/non-West or North/South. Over time, this adds to the power of Western geographies, possibly causing learners originating in alternative spaces to neglect any indigenous knowledge. Several interviewees foreground problems related to spatial hierarchies, underlining, for instance, how this can lead to the spread of a 'North helps South' discourse within disciplines such as Development Studies and Anthropology. Other informants see it as the natural condition within global academia, mirroring a reality where 'the West' constitutes the centre for theoretical and methodological development and therefore attracts talented students. A political scientist reflects: 'If you are bright in a Third World Country, you would normally go to USA or Europe to continue your studies, right. There is a reason for that' (DA).

To take the debate beyond the level of subjective interpretation one needs a method that can objectively map the spaces produced in international education. For this purpose, Tange and Millar (2016) have designed a tool that uses author information to establish what countries and regions are represented in course syllabi. In Tables 9.1 and 9.2 results are summarised for seven international MA programmes (five Danish, two British), covering disciplines situated within faculties of Arts, Natural Science, Social Science, and Business.

To produce the numbers reading lists were collected from a minimum of six modules per programme, equalling one year's worth of student activity. The total sample is 1,013 texts (789 Danish/224 British), which were analysed according to a system inspired by Berg's core–periphery model, placing authors on the basis of 1) nationality and 2) institutional affiliation in one of five groups: US/UK, English-speaking countries (incl. Eire), Europe, BRICS (incl. South Africa), and Miscellaneous (incl. Turkey and Israel). Where no

Table 9.1 Authors' national origins

	Sample	*UK/US*	*Eng. Sp.*	*Europe*	*BRICS*	*Misc.*	*Unknown*
UK 1	116	56.9	9.5	19.8	3.4	3.4	6.9
UK 2	166	61.3	13.7	11.3	1.2	4.8	7.7
Total UK	**284**	**59.5**	**12**	**14.7**	**2.1**	**4.2**	**7.4**
DK 1	243	49.8	3.3	21.8	6.2	6.2	12.8
DK 2	258	33.0	4.3	31.8	6.2	6.2	18.6
DK 3	257	45.5	5.4	22.6	18.3	6.2	2.3
DK 4	254	46.5	5.9	25.6	6.3	4.7	11.0
DK 5	176	59.1	1.7	29	0	1.7	8.5
Total DK	**1188**	**45.8**	**4.3**	**26.0**	**7.9**	**5.2**	**10.8**

Table 9.2 Authors' institutional affiliation

	Sample	*UK/US*	*Eng. Sp.*	*Europe*	*BRICS*	*Misc.*	*Unknown*
UK 1	116	59.5	11.2	15.5	0.9	2.6	10.3
UK 2	166	63.9	17.5	10.8	0.6	1.8	5.4
Total UK	**284**	**62.1**	**14.9**	**12.8**	**0.7**	**2.1**	**7.4**
DK 1	243	65.0	7.0	18.1	1.7	3.3	4.9
DK 2	258	38.8	3.9	29.5	1.9	4.7	21.3
DK 3	257	67.7	4.7	20.2	2.3	2.3	2.7
DK 4	254	53.9	7.5	17.3	2.4	3.9	11.0
DK 5	176	65.3	6.8	25	0	0	2.8
Total DK	**1188**	**57.5**	**5.9**	**21.9**	**1.8**	**3.0**	**9.9**

clear marker of geographical location was found, authors, and institutions were categorised as Unknown.

Looking at the nationality of authors (Table 9.1) the pattern emerging confirms the postcolonial argument that international higher education is dominated by Western knowledge. In both the Danish and the British sample UK/US, the English-speaking countries, and Europe together make up more than 75% of all texts, while alternative geographies amount to less than 15% in all but one programme. Comparing Denmark and the UK, the Danish curricula include more European authors, while the British have a greater proportion of authors originating in English-speaking countries such as Canada and Australia. If one examines the distribution of countries within these categories, the Danish preference for European-authored material can partly be explained by lecturers' selection of literature authored by themselves or Danish colleagues. Similarly, most common on the UK lists are authors of British nationality, amounting to 96 altogether (compared to 73 Americans). Accordingly, the data suggest that ethnocentrism is a factor when compiling reading lists, prompting academic staff to favour texts produced in their home country and institution. A final observation relates to the relatively high proportion of BRICS authors in DK programme 3. This MA course focuses on international business, and the high BRICS numbers may reflect the perception of 'international' within this disciplinary community. Hence, most authors represent growth economies such as India (20 authors) and China (15 authors), which confirms the observation previously made that 'international' in Business means an engagement with countries 'with which "we" trade'. A comparison with the scores for institutional affiliation suggests a second explanation. Here the BRICS number for DK3 drops, from 18.3% to 2.3%, which can be ascribed to the significant number of authors who are born in India or China and now working at institutions in Western Europe and North America. Many authors of BRICS nationality are employed by British and American universities, which could affect their perception of space, causing them to promote a Western rather than an indigenous perspective.

The institutional affiliations shown in Table 9.2 provide a more reliable picture of curricular geographies than a map based on national origins alone. First, information about authors' institutional affiliation is easier to obtain than nationality, which is not always specified on academic CVs and staff profiles. Second, academics move in a global field, and one may speculate whether a prolonged presence in a non-native institutional environment will have a greater impact on actors' spatial orientation than their country of birth. Table 9.2 reveal three general patterns. First, there is a clear privileging of Anglo-American institutions. Bourdieu and Wacquant (1999, 41) suggested that America has become a commonplace that all scholars need to relate to, and this is supported by the data analysed here. Perhaps such a finding is not surprising in relation to the British data where the high proportion of UK/US-based institutions suggests a strong national or local bias. More interesting is the identification of Anglo-America as the dominant geography in Danish course syllabi. This relates to a second curricular trend, namely the relatively low score for European institutions. In the Danish material, the proportion of Europe-based authors reaches a maximum of 29.5% (DK2), while the average score in the British curricula is 12.8%. This makes it difficult to uphold a postcolonial charge of Eurocentricity, for even when adding together the numbers for Europe and the UK, the total rarely exceeds 50%. A final tendency is the low representation of institutions outside North America and Western Europe. This supports Berg's thesis that global academia is constituted by a core–periphery structure, relegating non-Western geographies to a position on the margins. Learners can pursue studies of all countries and cultures, the lecturers asserted in the interviews. Yet the quantitative data reveal that the inclusion of non-Western spaces is not a priority when academics compile 'international' syllabi.

Spaces of representation

Zhou et al.'s 2005 empirical investigation highlighted the importance of curricular contexts to international students' willingness to partake in classroom debates, challenging academic staff to look beyond local and national frames of reference. The analyses presented in the previous sections suggested that informants were aware of their need to extend the geographical framing of education, foregrounding processes of recontextualisation and upscaling. What also appeared was that lecturers relied on a hierarchical ordering of space, allowing a limited number of geographies to dominate. These *power geographies* included: 1) the *national* scales of US and UK, 2) the *regional* scales of North America and Western Europe, 3) an *international* scale constituted by disciplinary constructs such as "Global North/South' in Development Studies or triadic trade networks in International Business, and 4) a vaguely defined *global* scale structured by intergovernmental institutions, alliances, and NGOs. International educators' preference for certain curricular contexts reflects their disciplinary grounding, socialisation, and area of expertise, supporting an interpretation of academics' spatial practices as a conceptualisation of geographies 'lived, felt and experienced' by these actors (Larsen/Beech 2014, 200). Yet successful education should involve the co-creation of knowledge by students and staff, which, arguably, demands that the spaces of representation produced in international modules include geographies that are equally accessible to all learners, enabling them to connect scientific concepts to spaces relevant to their everyday experience. A pedagogic strategy that addresses such concerns is *scale diversification*, which involves the construction of learning platforms that allow learners to approach class debates and assignments from multiple socio-cultural and geographical positions. The notion of *scale diversification* is inspired by Singh and Shrestha's principle of 'double knowing' (2008), which departs from the perception of international students as nodes in a network connecting to diverse educational cultures, disciplinary traditions, socio-cultural conditions, and geographical settings. A teaching practice of double knowing builds on the understanding of learners as experts in possession of valuable indigenous knowledge that can be used to develop a global orientation, e.g. by inviting a class to listen to the experiences of students speaking from divergent, socio-cultural positions (Tange/Kastberg 2013). Scale diversification engages with the more specific theme of context, requesting the construction of a learning space that encourages all students to relate abstract scientific knowledge to cases found in their native countries, cultures, and languages. Lecturers argue that such a strategy widens the pool of knowledge available in their course, allowing a class in European Studies, for instance, to compare various national perspectives on the European Union and thereby obtain an understanding of Europe as a social construct that assumes different forms and meanings depending on the speaker's spatial position. Another way to employ scale diversification is in written assignments where freedom to depart from a familiar context can be used to support exchange students' transition into an unfamiliar academic culture. An associate professor (Media Studies) observes:

> [Here] I have found that it is a good pedagogical trick simply to include experiences from students' own cultural and media systems. And this means that the students will then arrive with a very different motivation to write a paper. For they then have the opportunity to take a comparative approach in their paper. (DA)

Informants generally agree that it is beneficial to provide a contextual framing for written and oral assignments that allow both local and international students to use indigenous geographical, cultural, and linguistic knowledge. Particularly learners who experience difficulties in cracking the linguistic and cultural codes of an unfamiliar educational system can then maintain an image of themselves as resourceful actors, using written papers or presentations to connect any new knowledge to practices established in previous education. Yet some interviewees warn against the ethnocentrism that can emerge from learners' exclusive choice of cases set in the home country or region. A historian notes how one finds in international education 'plenty of students, who really only see things from their own [perspective], which could be Lithuania or Ghana or something else' (DA). Similarly, an anthropologist insists that students engage with a variety of spaces, explaining how, for instance, a Bosnian student may submit one essay on Bosnian themes, but will have to choose alternative socio-cultural and geographical sites for subsequent papers.

From the discussion of scale diversification emerges a picture of international education as an even platform that allows students to enrich class discussion with a variety of indigenous geographical and socio-cultural perspectives. Yet previous sections have suggested that spatial practices are constituted by and possibly constituting a scalar hierarchy, which privileges a limited number of 'power geographies'. In class, students will often encounter a fixed, scalar system which can be manifest in lecturers' framing of a course, selection of examples, as well as the labelling of literature as either obligatory (i.e. important) or supplementary (i.e. less important). Arguably, one may expect that students are influenced by such teaching practices, which could motivate them to evaluate curricular contexts in a similar way. A political scientist provides a glimpse of how his students perceive space, explaining how in a course on International Political Economy he invited students to bring to class *any* news item, local, national, or international, that to them illustrated a specific course theory or theme:

> From this year, I have started to request that the students bring some news. Something. Has anything happened in the wide world that is relevant for us? Not necessarily for this lesson, but for the entire course, and

> then we do a round to discuss this. ... And then the idea was that perhaps they would bring news that was more local, but could be approached internationally from our position. But they don't do this a lot. (DA)

This teaching practice is an example of scale diversification meant to encourage learners to relate abstract concepts to a context familiar to them. The informant expected learners to consult news sites from their home countries, but found that they would use internet sources instead, referring to examples published by English-medium sites such as the BBC and *New York Times*. The students' approach suggests that they have already accepted a spatial hierarchy, privileging stories from Britain and the US, whilst ignoring news from Central Europe, Russia, and the Baltic States. Such a learner practice may be motivated by two factors. First, students have been exposed to the same power geographies as the lecturers, navigating in an academic system where spaces such as Anglo-America and Western Europe are associated with the best authors and institutions. Regardless of their background, students who have made the conscious choice to study at a Danish, British, or American university are likely to be predisposed towards Western knowledge, which could prompt them to consider any non-Western examples symptomatic of a less progressive mind-set. Second, students are influenced by the representation of space in the classroom. As discussed previously, the lecturers' scaling is frequently manifest in the form of a hierarchical order which distinguishes between a select number of geographies treated as *commonplace*, and any alternative sites, which can be used only to exemplify generic course concepts or themes. Arguably, the teaching practice of scale diversification may consolidate such a spatial hierarchy. When asked to contribute indigenous knowledge to class discussions, students find that their national and local cases are used in class to illustrate universal principles, but not as geographies that can inspire new theoretical and methodological developments. As a consequence, international education can leave the impression that 'real' scientific knowledge is produced in the core geographies of North America and Western Europe, whereas the *Other* spaces of Central/Eastern Europe, Asia, Africa, and South America offer case-study material only.

Teaching contextual practices

The examination of spatial constructs in international education has foregrounded three pedagogic practices that lecturers may adopt in order to internationalise course curricula. First, internationalisation involves a process of *recontextualisation*, prompting academics to replace curricular frames that demand from students knowledge of particular local or national conditions with sites accessible to most. A second practice is *upscaling*, which occurs when lecturers shift the framing of their course from a local or national scale to a level perceived to be international or global. A final practice is *scale diversification*, where educators acknowledge students' divergent socio-cultural and geographical positions, inviting learners to add their indigenous resources to the common pool of knowledge created in class.

What has been equally clear is that academics are active participants in the social construction of space, supporting through their curricular framing, reading lists, class discussions, and examples a scalar hierarchy where a select number of power geographies are placed at the centre, whilst alternative sites are relegated to a position on the margins. Through their spatial practices international educators reproduce the core–periphery structure identified by Berg (2004), signalling to students that Anglo-America and Western Europe represent the only truly global reference points in academia. Even when seeking to challenge this order, for instance by evoking postcolonial charges of Eurocentricity, learners inevitably refer to the core geographies, which, directly or indirectly, confirms the special status of such sites.

10 Multicultural teamwork

Working across cultures?

Multicultural teamwork can be defined as a specific form of group activity that seeks to enhance processes of cross-cultural understanding and reflection by bringing together individuals from different socio-cultural, linguistic, and disciplinary backgrounds. As a teaching practice, multicultural teamwork is inspired by a principle of collaborative learning, seeking to achieve 'gains in cognition and problem-solving abilities, increased motivation and higher satisfaction and the development of learner autonomy-responsibility' (Cruickshank et al. 2012, 798). In addition, diverse teams can be used to integrate international and domestic students, which explains the popularity of this practice with academics involved with international education. Yet the literature supports Moore and Hampton's argument that multicultural teamwork is a 'contentious issue' (2015, 390), with empirical studies documenting learner hostility, anxiety, and segregation.

According to Halualani et al. (2004), theorists on intercultural communication have generally relied on a *contact hypothesis*, assuming that the co-presence of actors from diverse ethnic, national, religious, and linguistic groupings within a shared location would be sufficient to ensure cross-cultural dialogue and relationships. The contact hypothesis has been equally popular in literature on international education, where it has been used to promote an 'internationalisation at home' ideology, foregrounding how intercultural learning inevitably occurs when domestic and international students are admitted into the same courses and learning environments (see discussion in Harrison/Peacock 2010). Less optimistic are empirical researchers who have tested the contact hypothesis in a variety of university settings, concluding that co-inhabitation does not guarantee intercultural communication. One example is Halualani (2008), whose interview study of student perceptions at one American campus indicates that learners either understand intercultural encounters as mere coexistence within a shared space, or as a meeting that involves *strangers* identified as outgroup members, who are 'nationally different' (2). With reference to group activities, White and Jerome (2013) have shown how students prefer to self-select into teams characterised by homogeneity in terms of nationality, ethnicity, language, and religion, which echoes the findings of Harrison and Peacock (2010). Hence, the ideological principle of intercultural learning seems to be shipwrecked against the rock of social homophily, which persuades learners to group with peers perceived to be culturally similar and therefore trustworthy (McPherson et al. 2001).

Homophily, as an organising principle in group activities, has been documented in studies from Australia, New Zealand, and Britain, which challenges the idea of multicultural teamwork as an effective pedagogic strategy in international education (Reid/Garson 2017, Kimmel/Volet 2012, Turner 2009, Ledwith/Seymour 2001). Research has shown that students who have experienced multicultural group work often believe that diversity affects group dynamics negatively, which has fostered a hostile attitude towards this form of international education (Sweeney et al. 2008, Elliot/Reynolds 2014). According to Woods et al. (2011), social cohesion is key to successful team achievement, and this can be difficult to achieve in a diverse group. Indeed, Strauss et al. (2011) argue, multiculturalism transforms collaborative learning processes into an encounter with *strangers* from an unfamiliar socio-cultural, linguistic, and academic background, and in situations where the degree of perceived 'foreignness' is high, students may experience affective and cognitive stress, which can disrupt a team's academic performance. To avoid such risks many pursue an ethnocentric strategy, accepting to work only with peers regarded as similar to themselves. Building on Stephan and Stephan's Integrated Threat Theory (2000), Harrison and Peacock (2010, 87) have examined British students' perceptions of multicultural group work, uncovering attitudes ranging from fears related to academic performance to discriminatory practices such as racism and stereotyping. Judging from the literature on multicultural teams, exclusive practices are mainly found among domestic students, although the pioneering study by Volet and Ang (1998) suggests that international students can be equally critical, avoiding local learners in their groups because these are considered less committed and hard-working.

In their account of intercultural conflict management, Okech et al. (2016) identify as sources of conflict: *Communication* (incl. language), *attribution*, and *microaggressions*, which is defined as 'bias demonstrated overtly or covertly' (355). Similar challenges have been foregrounded in relation to students' group activities (Spencer-Oatey/Dauber 2017, Popov et al. 2012), which indicates that such issues must be considered when designing and evaluating teamwork in international education. A key actor is the course lecturer, whose classroom practice may sanction particular forms of student action and interaction. One may thus speculate whether local staff in Britain or Australia contribute to segregation by expressing impatience with non-native speakers' English usage, which could justify to domestic students a withdrawal from multicultural teamwork. Even if the literature offers no clear examples, empirical studies point to English proficiency as a source of tension in diverse groups, which implies that language differences may not have been addressed adequately by academic staff (Moore/Hampton 2015, Ledwith/Seymour 2001). Similarly, lecturers can signal through words and acts that there is a specific national or institutional way of *doing* group work, which could encourage domestic students to position themselves as experts, who may claim the authority of a teacher of practice to incoming, international students. Christensen (2016) has identified what she describes as a 'Danish' approach to group work, which indicates that one finds among lecturers within this academic context the normative understanding that *all* Danes have 'a natural disposition to act as a good co-worker in a group situation' (170). Such an idea of a national learning style is exclusive, suggesting that domestic learners possess certain skills, which, indirectly, places non-natives in the position of *Others*, imagined as academically inferior and therefore in need of special attention (Tange 2016).

The possible existence of a normative, *Danish* understanding of group work makes it interesting to approach the theme of multicultural teamwork through experiences narrated by academics involved with international education in Denmark. To structure the discussion, informants' reflections have been organised into three sections: 1) the *status* of group work, 2) *team formation*, and 3) group *routines, roles, and resources*.

The status of group work

The initial review of research on multicultural teamwork has foregrounded both key arguments supporting this practice (e.g. integration, intercultural learning) and student responses hindering the achievement of such goals (e.g. ethnocentrism, homophily, segregation). What also emerged from the literature was that perceptions are linked to the status attached to group activities in a programme, which means that students are more likely to resist multicultural teamwork if this involves collective assessment and carries the risk that one may achieve a lower mark as the result of poor performance by peers (Strauss et al. 2014). Experiences and expectations are tied to particular ways of practising multicultural teamwork, which makes it necessary to establish what forms of group activities can be found in international courses.

A useful typology has been proposed by Christensen (2013, 189), who distinguishes between student groups used for in-class activities, home assignments, academic writing, and project work. Combining Christensen's types with descriptions offered in the two Danish interview studies, produces the following list:

- *The discussion group*: Used for problem-solving in class. May be formed spontaneously to debate a particular topic or function as a work unit throughout a course.
- *The study group*: Meets between classes to discuss course readings, theory, or home assignments. Study groups are mostly established on the students' initiative, and in a system such as the Danish, where students

may study for five consecutive years within one institution, can become consolidated and closed to newcomers at MA level.

- *The presentation group*: Put together with the purpose of preparing an oral presentation or poster in class. Typically dissolved once the presentation has been delivered.
- *The feedback group*: Functions as respondents to oral presentations in class. Typically dissolved once an allocated task has been accomplished.
- *The writing group*: A formal or informal grouping of students seeking to improve their writing skills. In international programmes, writing groups can happen on the initiative of lecturers aiming to support students with inadequate skills in English or academic writing.
- *The project-writing group*: Established to complete a written assignment on a self-researched topic. The group will define its own research problem, guided by a project supervisor. A grade, individual or collective, is awarded on the basis of the project report.
- *The project and exam group*: Involves a written and an oral component. Once the project report has been submitted, the group will prepare for an oral exam where they answer questions relating to the project. Students may be examined individually or as a group and awarded a grade based on both their written and oral performance.

The forms make different demands on participants with regard to the level of engagement and risk, which explains the diversity of opinions expressed by students and staff when prompted about group work. At one end of the scale one finds the relatively safe approaches described by Turner (2009) and Ippolito (2007), who place students in multicultural teams, but evaluate achievements individually, which means that ambitious learners do not risk lower marks as the result of forced collaboration with peers perceived to be academically or linguistically weak. In contrast, Christensen's (2013, 2016) 'Danish' project work model builds on a principle of shared responsibility, where group members are accountable for all parts of the assignment and graded in accordance with that. As a result, students fear involving themselves with the 'wrong' team, which implies that the practice of homophily should not necessarily be treated as symptomatic of ethnocentrism but rather as a learner strategy emerging in response to the realisation that not all class members are socialised into the same academic culture. A social scientist explains:

> [T]here is a great difference for the [institution name] students that we have in the [Masters] programme, it is their fourth year at [this university]. They know something … [T]his is also why they have difficulties forming those groups, with foreign and Danish students. For the foreign students simply have a different work approach. In part, they are reluctant about project writing, in part they have a different attitude to their supervisor. (DA)

The interviews provide examples of all group types listed previously, with informants reflecting on the pedagogic issues emerging from the particular organisation of teamwork that they have chosen for their module. The subsequent part of the discussion will look more closely at some of these, suggesting that obligatory and voluntary group assignments meet different needs in international education.

Courses that include a *compulsory* group component request that all students partake in collaborative learning processes. Frequently, group work is based on a project model and presented by informants as an activity furthering students' development of skills in areas such as interpersonal communication, project organisation, conflict management, and problem-solving. An associate professor (European Studies) reflects on the group component developed for her course:

> [W]hat we then worked with was how we might provide these students with a more systematic introduction to things like organisational structure, which is what they do. How does an organisation function, and how do you create an organisation to match your specific project? ... [Students] have some groups which both [reflect] the international and an interdisciplinary part. And then they need to make this work. And work in relation to each other and work in relation to the final project. (DA)

This framing of multicultural teamwork is interesting. Even though her references to 'international' and 'interdisciplinary' indicate that the intervention is motivated by the ambition to bridge national and disciplinary differences, the informant highlights organisational skills and capability, establishing a connection between the particular tasks performed in student teams and competences required in the global workplace. A similar concern with employability has inspired other course teachers to involve external partners, requesting that learners design projects that can be realised in business, international organisations, or NGOs. Such assignments aim to enhance students' capacity to apply theoretical knowledge to real-life problems, while teaching them the benefits of interdisciplinarity. A professor (Biology) relates:

> [T]he idea is that over the 7 weeks after the mid-term break they work in that project group to design a development project. And that's when the strength of their different backgrounds comes into play. Because, obviously, the Biology student can focus on the Ecosystems part of the proposal. A student from International Relations can look at the political system, the conflict issues that might arise if the project is implemented.

An alternative approach is the organisation of *voluntary* group activities for students with special interests or needs, and the prototypical example is the study group. Such units are typically formed by students themselves and rarely mentioned in the interviews, although some informants present study groups to international students as a 'desirable model', for instance during an induction workshop. Lecturers may choose to intervene in situations where they see a need for reading groups to debate course theory or workshops to train technical skills such as academic English or report-writing. One example is the 'homework café' developed by this Business lecturer:

> We just have this kind of, we call it study cafe, where they can get support with their homework, and now we just have it, that they have some hours in which they can get supervised homework so there are tutors sitting there and they can just come and go as they like … [W]hen I was there, I could see that they are also forming little groups and sitting together at tables and doing their homework. But it is less formal.

In addition to instructional scaffolding, study cafés have an important social function. MA students new to the programme and institution can go there to meet peers in a similar situation, enabling them to build relationships whilst solving course tasks collaboratively.

Forming diverse teams

> There are many cuts. There is gender, and there is region. Of course, we are all Europeans – both newer and Central European and … Then there is maturity, seniority in the programme. We have in [our programme] many generalists. In [the other programmes] they are relatively homogeneous academically, but our large international courses also attract people from Marketing and Organisation. It is a very heterogeneous group I have taught. I don't actively make use of that except that when [there is] a natural spread in class, I do not need to take diversity into account when forming groups because it will automatically be present. (DA)

This observation was made by a lecturer from Engineering when asked to describe the diversity found in his international class. The comment reveals how multi-faceted multiculturalism can be, which challenges educational scholars and practitioners to clarify what, more precisely, they mean when insisting that students work in diverse teams. Characteristically, experienced international educators tend to abstain from exact definitions of diversity, stressing that one should not generalise about culture, which carries a multitude of meanings, including nationality, first language, ethnicity, religion, gender, age, social class, educational background, disciplinary specialisation, institutional socialisation, personal and professional experience. As suggested above, the cake can be cut in many ways.

To unravel the practices involved when diverse teams are formed, one needs to dig deeper into the meaning of 'diversity', and one way to do so is to use as a point of departure the illustrative example of nationality, which features prominently in the literature on multicultural teamwork. Perhaps this is natural, given that processes of internationalisation have inspired such research, but narrowing the discussion down to a question of *internationalness* is problematic for several reasons: First, a native/international distinction may colour lecturers' perception of learners, motivating them to relate academic ability to national origins, as seen in the example of the Danish project model. Second, a categorisation of diversity based on nationality alone overlooks the importance of language as a factor binding students together, ignoring how, for instance, the situation for an Australian student at a British university may be different to that of a Chinese. Finally, one needs to acknowledge that lecturers' categorisations reflect local circumstances. Comparing interviews performed with Danish and British academics, it is noteworthy that the Danes highlight diversity within the cohort of European students (e.g. Scandinavian, Central European, Southern European), whereas British informants refer to UK and Europeans as 'home' students, defined in opposition to the category of 'overseas' or 'international'. The British interpretation can be ascribed to numbers (one lecturer describes a postgraduate class of four 'home' students to 60 'overseas'), as well as economic factors, since at the time of the interviews EU and UK residents paid 'home' fees, while non-EU citizens were charged the higher 'overseas' fee (Spencer-Oatey/Dauber 2017, 223). Yet the grouping of EU citizens together with domestic students sends a symbolic message about cultural proximity, which could explain why researchers have found UK students to be more open to cooperation with European than Asian peers (see Harrison/Peacock 2010, Ledwith/Seymour 2001).

In addition to nationality, language and discipline are recurring themes when lecturers are prompted about aspects of diversity that they consider important to multicultural teamwork. As regards language, informants tend to differentiate between learners who are capable users of English, and those who are not, which confirms the findings of research conducted in English-speaking contexts (e.g. Turner 2009, Moore/Hampton 2015). Interestingly enough, Danish academics also see students de-selecting peers when these are considered inadequate users of English. One agricultural scientist observes: 'Well, it is difficult to join a group with [people] who cannot write English ... Because if as someone capable in English you accept someone with poor English skills, you have signed up for additional work, right?' (DA) At the same time the Danish data suggest that other languages can serve as an alternative to English, as seen in situations where domestic students attempt to ease internal communications by forming groups composed of Danish speakers only: 'The Danes like to write together with other Danes because it makes it easier. This has probably something to do with language, in part, but also cultural codes' (associate professor, Social Science; DA). A final factor is academic discipline, which is evident in programmes designed to be interdisciplinary. Tange's empirical study (2016) identifies interdisciplinarity as a source of tension within courses recruiting students and staff from a variety of subject areas, causing actors to position themselves in relation to disciplinary in- and out-groups. This adds a new dimension to the notion of 'preferred team members', as some students will cluster according to discipline. An assistant professor (Biology) observes:

> [Students] had selected between three cases, and there we had ensured that nationalities and disciplines were very mixed. And then we could see that once they had formed sub-teams, then there were some who had succeeded … [We] had one group consisting only of biologists and one which only had [Social Science/Humanities]. (DA)

In the light of findings reported in earlier research, it is unsurprising that the international educators interviewed by the author describe a tendency among students to self-select into groups that are homogeneous in terms of nationality, language, and discipline. What is equally clear is that informants consider this a problematic practice in courses labelled 'international', promoting some to adopt an interventionist strategy where the lecturer assumes responsibility for the process of team formation. Building on Huxham and Land (2000), Analoui et al. (2014, 41) identify three assignment methods used at a British business school: 1) students self-select, 2) students grouped randomly, and 3) students grouped to ensure diversity. To these can be added a fourth method described in some of the Danish interviews. Here the formation process combines self-selection with demographic and disciplinary profiling, requesting that all groups meet a set of criteria determined by the lecturer.

The first issue that lecturers have to consider when including group work in an international module is to what extent it is important that students can select their own teams. The literature review showed how a principle of self-selection frequently results in monocultural teams, which is confirmed by the Danish informants, who agree that multiculturalism is best realised when the lecturers intervene. Yet interviewees differ with regard to their willingness to accept the teacher's right to interfere with processes of group formation. Academics from institutional cultures where group work is understood as a student-managed process emphasise that their scope for action is limited, insisting that students should always have the freedom to self-select, even if this comes at the price of intercultural learning and integration. A social scientist reflects:

> [I]t is kind of smart if we can get them to mix. Because then there would also be a learning process in the group. Then some of them, those who come from here, would know how you write a project, and the international students, if they were included in this kind of group, then they could learn from that. That would make it easier for us, right. But this is not something we can do a lot about. And this is not something we try to do a lot about. Because, first and foremost, they should group the way they like. (DA)

In comparison, the lecturers who assume responsibility for group allocation explain that their interference is necessary in order to prevent segregation and facilitate knowledge-sharing between different student groupings. Many international educators claim this position, although there are informants within this group who express discomfort with playing such an active role, insisting that this compromises student rights. Interventionists' key argument is that students, when granted the freedom to choose, inevitably end up working in homogeneous teams, which defies the purpose of internationalisation.

Once they have accepted a responsibility for team formation, academics face a second choice, namely whether to allocate students at random or take into account the demographic characteristics of a cohort. Random allocation is favoured for relatively simple tasks such as those performed in a discussion and presentation group, which involves no joint assignment or grade. For demanding group activities such as project proposals and written reports, many opt for the second method, designing teams that are representative in terms of nationality, language, educational background, and discipline. To motivate their intervention lecturers highlight the need to support international students, stressing that these gain through cooperation with domestic students an enhanced understanding of local academic culture and conventions. However, as this associate professor (Agricultural Science) acknowledges, such an approach can backfire in situations where an ambitious student takes control of the project, reducing peers to the non-participatory role of silent observers:

> [W]e have bad experiences [from situations] where students who are bright, linguistically and academically, are grouped together with less skilled ones. That [bright students] will then control work completely, and the less bright ones become a kind of appendage. Which means they will not speak at all. (DA)

To resolve this dilemma, some lecturers have developed an alternative method of group allocation, which reintroduces a principle of self-selection, but does so in a manner that guarantees diversity. As part of their introduction to group formation, teachers will present a list of criteria that all teams have to meet in order to be approved as a work unit. Selection criteria can be defined on the basis of demography (e.g. nationality, gender, age), or depend on the assignment, ensuring that teams possess the combination of disciplinary, technical, and linguistic skills necessary to solve the task given. In both situations, the allocation method will reduce anxiety considerably because learners are allowed to select peers perceived to be similar in terms of academic ability and ambition. At the same time students are compelled to engage with multiculturalism, actively searching for class members who can help them obtain the diversity profile requested.

Routines, roles, and resources

The categories most frequently used to explain students' groupings are nationality, language, and, occasionally, disciplinary background. Yet a closer reading of lecturers' observations allows for the identification of an additional classification, based on a distinction between learners who are experienced group workers, and those who are not. This testifies to the importance of *routines* to group processes, acknowledging that students can be more or less skilled in the competences required to succeed in collaborative learning processes. Informants mention as routines characteristic of high-achieving teams interpersonal communication, organisational skills, conflict management, and a sense of mutual obligation and commitment. To several Danish lecturers such traits are ascribed to a distinctive, 'Danish' approach to collaborative learning, which confirms Christensen's (2016, 170) assertion that '[i]n Denmark group work is taken for granted'. An agricultural scientist relates:

> Well, our Danish students they will, really from the first year they are here, they will receive instruction focusing on project work, problem-based learning and group work ... And they are also used to this from high school – they kind of bring along this culture themselves. Not all of them think it is fun to work in groups, but they know what is involved and have experience with it. But I find that some of the foreign students, they lack that experience, and I just think that is a [shame]. (DA)

Routines can be divided into *technical requirements* and *tacit knowledge*, which make different demands in terms of experience and engagement. As regards technical skills, these include time management, IT competence, academic writing, formatting a written text, and the facilitation of knowledge-sharing on social media or alternative learning platforms provided by the university. A group may find that the process runs more smoothly if members have developed capabilities in these areas, but even when this is not the case, technical needs are relatively easily to explicate and resolve by actively seeking new knowledge. In comparison, Analoui et al. (2014, 36) characterise tacit knowledge as 'highly personal, hard to formalise, and hard to share with others', and examples are experiential learning, intuition, normative preferences, and system knowledge. In a multicultural team, an important form of tacit knowledge is intercultural competence, which influences individual learners' capacity to contribute to the building of an inclusive group culture, adjust to diverse communication styles, incorporate unfamiliar perspectives, and resolve any conflicts emerging as the result of perceived differences. Arguably, students acquire such insights through participation in collaborative learning processes, which to some extent justifies the lecturers' concern that experienced project workers be included in all multicultural teams.

A second key element is the *roles* that individual learners may claim or assign to peers. In her examination of the 'Danish' group model, Christensen (2016) challenges the myths of equality and inclusion, explaining how students de-legitimise team members by labelling them as 'dominant', 'lazy', 'stupid', and 'anti-social' (176). Learners appear to be engaged in a struggle for power, which is gained either by exhibiting desirable traits such as dedication, intelligence, and sociability, or by pointing to personality traits that challenge peers' claim to membership of the category 'good student'. Applying Christensen's notion of de-legitimate positions to international education, one can identify four types deemed unattractive, namely the *dominant* student, the *inexperienced* student, the *silent* student, and the *freeriding* student. *Dominant* students are avoided as group members because they will attempt to control the process, limiting other members' ability to contribute or have their opinion heard. Empirical studies indicate that male native speakers of English often try to claim such power, but also that such domination is rejected by peers who respond either by ignoring a proposal or overt criticism (Cotton et al. 2013, Day/Kjærbeck 2011). A second example of domination is non-Western students' experience of being marginalised by Europeans:

> One of the students from Ethiopia made the comment that ... [s]he felt like the, even though it was open, because the Westerners are many, they dominate, and they impose on what they want to study. And she did not want to study Edward Snowden and all these things. That we should leave it for students to bundle themselves according to regional, where they come from, to increase the diversity of topics.
>
> (Assistant professor, Media Studies)

Students categorised as *inexperienced* team workers may be included as an acknowledgement of groups' social responsibility, but are positioned as academically deficient and therefore in need of special attention. Accordingly, inexperienced learners could find themselves treated as novices, to be trained by peers seeking a role as experts, which makes it difficult for these students to be allowed to participate as equals. As seen in the previous quotation non-Western students are vulnerable to such positioning, which has caused some to complain: 'This was also coming from last year, we had a problem where some students from India and Malaysia and Kenya and Brazil, or so, they felt that the German students were kind of condescending to them' (assistant professor, Media Studies). Students placed in the role of inexperienced learners are not expected to contribute fully to the project, and over time, this may encourage their adoption of undesirable practices such as communication withdrawal or non-participation. In such situations they risk being stamped as *silent* or *freeriding* members, which may limit their ability to join a strong team in future. A social scientist reflects on the difficult position of students with limited group work experience: 'To sit together and cooperate with others ... to be dependent on the other students. That is a completely new understanding. And they don't know if they need to be more active, or can allow themselves to freeride' (DA).

A final role identified by informants is the team leader. A team leader is distinguished from *dominant* students by the authority vested in this person by group members and the lecturer, and her responsibilities can include tasks such as project coordination, organisation, and conflict management. A biologist reflects on the qualities of a good leader:

> [S]ometimes it is obvious who is going to be the leader. You can tell from just the body language, the personality. And at other times it can be a quieter person who takes the lead simply because they are the most committed, the most diligent. I sometimes, actually, try to avoid automatically taking the one with the strongest personality because you don't want them to dominate the group. So it's a little, it's a bit of human engineering, you know, to get the group dynamics working well.

The function of team leader is particularly important in courses where students' group work imitates project management in business, international organisations, and NGOs. To echo professional practice, one informant explains how he engages his selected team leaders in the process of group formation, requesting that they advertise for group members with specific skills, and then, based on the applications received, appoint peers with the right profiles. Other lecturers consider leaders responsible for group dynamics, allocating to them the role of a mediator who can facilitate intercultural communication and learning.

Once group work is professionalised and team members are recruited on the basis of technical, academic, and personal skills, international educators have adopted what may be characterised as a *capability* approach, organising student teams on the basis of resources rather than demography. Ideally, a concern with identifying and harnessing the diverse skills possessed by individual students underpins the pedagogic principle of collaborative learning, but as revealed in the previous discussion, such an ambition is not always realised in multicultural teamwork. Focusing on the theme of knowledge-sharing Analoui et al. (2014) underline the extent to which students are capable of facilitating skills transfer in diverse groups, providing as examples of knowledge shared 'how to use a software package, help with academic referencing, and one participant described being given help in the construction of a balance sheet' (2014, 38). What this research suggests is that students are able to recognise technical skills and allocate project tasks in accordance with that, but also that groups aim to complete an assignment as effectively as possible, which means that members rarely invest the time necessary to acquire the new insights and techniques offered by peers. As a result, one frequently sees what Analoui et al. (2014, 42) refer to as a 'silo-ing' of workloads, which lecturers should attempt to counter by highlighting member resources, explicating to students what specific skills are represented in their team, and how each of these are necessary to resolve and improve a joint assignment. A historian explains how she forms groups based on learner assessments of their capability in three areas: IT, History, and drawing. Subsequently, she motivates her team allocation by explaining to students how that all competences are necessary to meet the task requirements:

> And then I say, well, I have put you together so that there is someone who likes to draw, there is someone who likes IT, and there is someone who likes History. And the reason I am doing this, is because you will need to make these chronologies and maps, and therefore you need someone who can draw. And you have to upload some things to a First Class conference, so therefore you need someone who can support the others or the group in working out how this will function. And then, of course, since this is a History class, it is good also to have someone who likes the history involved, who can engage you in this. (DA)

The capability approach seems an obvious choice, yet it rarely features among the methods described by informants when prompted about multicultural teamwork. Instead lecturers highlight cultural and linguistic resources, suggesting that students co-construct a shared knowledge pool about European or international affairs. However, as shown previously, the idea of mutual learning may be compromised by distinctions drawn between domestic/international, capable/incapable English users, experienced/inexperienced, and active/silent team members. Such categories frequently emerge from group experiences, but they are confirmed in literature on international education. Academics seeking to employ a capability approach are therefore advised to develop their own strategy, identifying first the resources required for the task given, and then explicating why such competences are relevant to group work.

Teaching multicultural teamwork

Multicultural teamwork has emerged as a popular teaching practice in international education because of the possibilities it offers in terms of integration and intercultural learning. Yet the past examination of group practices has underlined problems associated with such pedagogy, including homophily, ethnocentrism, asymmetrical power relations, and the marginalisation of peers with specific attributes. Academic staff relate such challenges to team formation, learner experience, group dynamics, and routines, which suggests that international educators need to attend to the teaching of multicultural teamwork rather than assume that students can work this out for themselves.

The key to successful teamwork is lecturers' framing of group work. To facilitate collaborative learning in a diverse cohort, informants foregrounded three elements: *task*, *team formation*, and *resources*. First, multicultural teamwork must depart from a concrete assignment, which allows students to benefit from bringing together the various insights found in a multicultural group. In some situations, this requires a curricular adjustment, adding to course descriptions the demand that projects include an intercultural component. Second, academics need to manage team formation in a way that ensures a degree of diversity in all groups. An interesting approach is to focus on capabilities, encouraging students to look for specific resources. To do so, lecturers have to consider what technical and tacit knowledge is useful in a team, and how they can explain to students the importance of such skills. Among the examples cited were History (disciplinary knowledge), IT (technical skills), and drawing (artistic ability), but an international cohort possesses a range of diverse capabilities, and course teachers need to compile their own lists, departing from the specific requirements of their module, programme, and discipline.

11 Exam successes and failure

Assessment and international education

Assessment, in the form of written or oral assignments used by module teachers to test learners' acquisition of particular theoretical and methodological insights, is a crucial element in higher education. Upon their graduation, students' academic success will be manifest in the grades appearing on their degree transcript, which encourages learners to prioritise the tasks and approaches that are most likely to be rewarded in an exam situation. Exams, Krogh (2017, 75) notes, 'have a very governing effect on student study activities', while Brown and Joughin (2007, 57) observe that: 'Assessment is an important basis of esteem and the key measure of success'. Given the stakes involved, it is unsurprising that university students find exam situations emotionally and intellectually demanding (Krogh 2017), and that pressure grows once they transfer into an unfamiliar national, institutional, and disciplinary environment. Educational scholars have therefore insisted that assessment be taken into account when preparing and performing international teaching. One example is Carroll (2015), who lists five challenges that international students face: 1) 'tasks that are impenetrable'; 2) 'test of skills they have not yet been taught or practiced'; 3) 'in contexts they do not understand'; 4) 'requiring artefacts they have never before encountered'; and 5) 'in academic English, which no one speaks at home' (180). Similarly, David Killick identifies problems relating to *performance type*, *assessment criteria*, and *task familiarity* (2017, 147–50), adding the element of *feedback*, which suggests a formative approach to assessment. According to Krogh (2017, 81), *formative diagnostic assessment* is characterised by '[the intention to] qualify sustainable development and learning and an evaluation of ongoing processes … with the purpose of improving efforts and results'. An example is the portfolio format where students submit several papers during term, receive feedback from the instructor, and are given time to improve their writing before handing in the final version, which is subsequently graded. In contrast, a *summative assessment* happens at a particular moment (typically at the end of a module) with the aim to 'determine and "declare" the students' competences at a certain time' (Krogh 2017, 81). In a summative test, students receive a grade based on their performance on the day. If provided, feedback cannot be used to improve the product, although it may effect a change in the approach chosen by students for later exams.

The distinction between formative and summative approaches has not been addressed in relation to international education. Yet it is important when seeking to understand scholars' divergent interpretations of international students' academic achievement. Most researchers agree that learners in transition from different linguistic, socio-cultural, and educational cultures are likely to underachieve compared to local peers. A review of the literature on international student 'failure' brings out a variety of explanations, ranging from scholars ascribing underachievement to individual students' lack of specific skills to those who advocate a formative approach, highlighting how learners need support to acquire new forms of academic literacy.

Five approaches seem common to the discussion of international student achievement. First, there are examples of a *moralist discourse* similar to the one identified by Kaposi and Dell (2012) in relation to plagiarism. Devos (2003) discusses how international students have been constructed as 'poor achievers' in Australian media, which has prompted accusations that internationalisation causes a lowering of academic standards. No similar study has been produced about other destination countries, which might suggest that moral panics of the kind highlighted by Devos are rare. Yet the title of a 2019 article in *Times Higher Education*, 'International students and cheating: How worried should we be?' relies on a discourse that encourages readers to ascribe exam failure to individual learners' moral integrity (McKie 2019).

With regard to theme two, *language*, international students' academic achievement is frequently related to English proficiency, as seen in empirical studies from Britain, Canada, Australia, and New Zealand (Trenkic/Warmington 2019, Neumann et al. 2019, Oliver et al. 2012, Johnson 2008). One may speculate to what extent the high number of articles on the language question causes scholars to overestimate the importance of English proficiency, neglecting alternative explanations such as learners' unfamiliarity with disciplinary conventions or the practice of academic writing (see Lillis/Tuck 2016). The current chapter tests this assumption, drawing on data collected at Danish universities and thus in a context that is traditionally non-English speaking.

Explanation three foregrounds *cultural factors*. Brown and Joughin (2007, 59) suggest that 'approaches to learning and assessment are often deeply embedded within a culture'. They are supported by cross-cultural researchers such as Green (2007), who interprets Asian students' approach to essay-writing as symptomatic of learners' Confucian heritage culture. The cultural interpretation shares with theme one, morality, and two, language, an individualist take on academic achievement, focusing on actors' personal need to adjust their study skills to demands found within their new educational environment.

In contrast, theme four introduces a *developmental* perspective, where responsibility for students' acquisition of academic discourse shifts from the individual learner to teaching staff and the institution. The developmental approach is formative in nature, insisting that students be taught how to write and speak in a manner approved within their present educational context. Such a perspective is visible in literature on plagiarism where scholars have argued in favour of programmes that support students' development of academic writing skills (e.g. Divan et al. 2015, Amsberry 2009).

The final theme of *academic literacy* presents academic writing and speech as socially situated practices that learners need to acquire from actors recognised as disciplinary and institutional experts within a specific educational culture. Accordingly, academic literacy researchers insist that all exam performances be understood in relation to a system with its own set of 'institutional practices, power relations and identities' (Lea/Street 1998, 158–9; as quoted in Lillis/Tuck 2016, 32). Abasi and Graves (2008) provide an example in their study of plagiarism, arguing that international students writing in English rather than their native language are 'vulnerable to accusations of fraud as their inappropriate textual borrowing is a more obvious departure from their own style of writing' (222). This reminds us of the danger of treating international students as a special needs group, which might reinforce stereotypical perceptions of non-natives as 'deviant' learners (Tange/Jensen 2012). The academic literacy approach shares with Bourdieu a concern with power relations within specific disciplinary and institutional environments, accepting that assessment forms may favour students from particular sociocultural and linguistic backgrounds.

The initial discussion has highlighted a number of issues that are important when seeking to obtain a deeper understanding of exam successes and failure in international education. The remaining part of this chapter explores three themes in more depth: 1) *discourses of student failure*; 2) *exam performances as social practice*; and 3) *achieving academic success*.

Discourses of student failure

Abasi and Graves (2008, 222) argued that international students were vulnerable because they are often non-native speakers of English and therefore write in a style that deviates from the norms of standard British and American English. This makes intertextuality, in the form of phrases or passages copied from literature or internet sources, easy to detect for examiners, which could explain the high proportion of non-native English-speaking learners reported for plagiarism at American universities (Bowman 2017). In an interview, Liz Matthews, Michigan State University, warns readers against jumping to conclusions based on such statistics: 'I would caution against the notion that it's only international students who are cheating or that it's students from a particular country. Could faculty have biases that international students cheat more and therefore are looking for it?' (as quoted in Bowman 2017, 59).

Research on academic literacy reveals how learners in transition from different educational contexts struggle to understand the criteria used to assess academic writing and speech when first entering a university department and discipline. According to Bourdieu (1988, Bourdieu/Passeron 1994), academic discourse is acquired through disciplining by subject experts, who use their professorial power to distinguish 'good' student performances from 'deviant'. Bourdieu is supported by Hyland (2000, 2012), who has analysed 'social interaction' between 'experts' and 'apprentice' writers (students, junior researchers) in a variety of disciplines. Students transferring into a new environment encounter disciplining in the form of low marks and critical remarks from the teachers, which can create a sense of failure that is shared by non-native learners, first years, students from non-academic homes, and postgraduates moving into a new discipline (see French 2018, Baker 2017, Graves/White 2016). Yet scholars' concern with plagiarism in the literature on international education leaves the impression that foreign students (typically Chinese) are more prone to academic misconduct than their domestic peers. Arguably, such an understanding reflects a cross-cultural research tradition, which has tended to treat international students as exotic *Others* in need of special attention (see Marginson/Sawir 2011 for further discussion). Because such interpretations are readily available, researchers may be tempted to narrow the range of explanations for student failure down to a question of nationality, attributing any underachievement by non-natives to their deviation from a perceived national norm. According to MacKinnon and Manathunga (2003) this enables the universities receiving international students to maintain an assessment culture built on a 'template of knowledge that only values Western ways of knowing and learning' (132). Such an approach is likely to treat exam failure as an adjustment issue, placing responsibility for managing transition on individual learners instead of acknowledging that assessments are a manifestation of institutional and disciplinary power and likely to consolidate an existing academic order. Within such a system, international students risk ending up in the unfortunate position of a cultural and linguistic *Other* expected to underachieve and therefore treated as divergent from other learners.

Discourses of failure represent a particular way of talking about students in international education. Frequently, these *Sayings* take the form of anecdotes that academic staff use either to highlight issues related to acculturation or single out specific individuals or groups perceived to be 'different'. Across disciplines and institutions, the interviews indicate that students' socio-cultural background and English proficiency are common parameters employed by lecturers when reporting experiences with 'deviation' in an international class. Yet references are also made to learners' educational experiences and disciplinary training, which suggest that one needs to approach the theme of academic failure from a variety of perspectives. Based on observations made by 68 academics working in Danish and British higher education four 'discourses of failure' can be identified: 1) *poor language*; 2) *cultural behaviour*; 3) *previous educational experience*; and 4) *disciplinary boundaries*.

When regarding theme one, *poor language*, there is a consensus among interviewees that this is a common reason for student failure. Lecturers working in Britain tend to associate the question of English deficiency with particular types of international students, noting how Asian learners are challenged by the request to write and speak academic English. A natural scientist observes on his experiences with Chinese students:

> We tell them after every essay: their essays were unsuitable. We tell them after examinations: their way of writing is unsuitable. We tell them they do not write enough. We send them on the English language courses at the university. We *tell* them what they should do and for a week they'll do it. And then they are back to their old ways.

The informant attributes Chinese learners' language difficulties to these students' tendency to seek the company of co-nationals on campus, which is an opinion shared by other lecturers at this British university. This may reflect the relatively high number of Chinese among international students at the institution. In comparison, academics working in Danish higher education are less likely to connect language failure with specific groups of learners. When prompted about students' English skills, academics provide examples of individuals from China, Spain, France, and Nepal, who have failed because of poor written or oral English. Yet many add that Danish students are equally challenged, as seen in this comment from an associate professor (Natural Science):

> I have had an exam where I thought that the person examined was too weak in her explanations, and that she did not use a precise terminology. I lacked precision and this could have turned out really serious. I interrupted her twice and said: Well, are you sure you would not rather be doing this in Danish? (DA)

Moving on to theme two, *failure as cultural behaviour*, there is a consensus that students from specific socio-cultural backgrounds are more likely to underachieve. Common themes in the Danish and British interviews are rote learning, a lack of independent thinking, and plagiarism, which are attributes that lecturers frequently ascribe to students from Asia (China). The concern with 'Chinese learners' seems particularly striking in the Danish interviews, given that the number of Asian students in Denmark is relatively low. One suspects that informants could be reproducing a 'moral panic' discourse picked up from colleagues or Danish media, which have published several stories on 'poor' Asian students in secondary and higher education.

The third discourse of failure ascribes poor exam performance to students' *previous educational experiences*. Informants offering this type of explanation generally present learning and teaching as social practices produced within specific academic cultures and traditions, which opens up the possibility of students underachieving as the result of mismatching expectations. A Humanities lecturer describes the contrast he has observed between exchange students socialised into two different educational environments:

> [T]he Italians are strong because they [come] from a programme similar to ours, right? The Spaniards we get in our supplementary course they come from a discipline which has nothing to do [with our approach]. Which is a very theoretical [approach]. Because this is a contact we for some reason have with a university, [which offers] a very atheoretical course. (DA)

Divergent traditions can also lead to exam failure when learners transfer into universities building on a distinctive learning philosophy such as Problem-Based Learning. Within this type of academic environment, students are taught project-writing skills during their first year of studies so they can use such foundational knowledge for later assignments. This structure presents challenges to learners recruited for exchange or Masters programmes, who have not had the same opportunity to develop these theoretical and methodological insights at previous stages of education and are therefore more likely to fail.

A final discourse relates to the *disciplinary boundaries* that for many academics determine what is 'appropriate' and 'inappropriate' knowledge practices. At postgraduate level, international programmes are often designed as interdisciplinary, which means that course lecturers may have to evaluate performances by learners socialised into alien scientific traditions and methodologies. The experiences conveyed in the interviews suggest that this can result in a lower grade, as seen in the case of students from a Media Studies programme who in Political Science modules encounter examiners dismissive of essays written in a 'journalistic' style. A second issue concerns the appointment of external examiners, which is crucial to ensure a fair treatment of all students. A political scientist observes:

> [These] students do not have 5 or 4½ years of Political Science education and should therefore not be assessed according to the same criteria … And this we will then have to tell our externals, that some are from [the interdisciplinary programme], and they have a different profile and should be assessed accordingly. (DA)

Exam performances as social practice

Academics expressing concerns about external examiners' ability to assess students from interdisciplinary programmes rely on an interpretation of exam performances as social practices, embedded within specific institutional and disciplinary structures. When read within the framework provided by Lea and Street's (1998, 2006) academic literacy model, such an understanding foregrounds the elements of *academic socialisation* and *academic literacies*. The lecturer, who questions the ability of examiners to look beyond their Political Science training, acknowledges that scientific knowledge and discourses have been developed in relation to specific disciplinary communities, whose 'expert' members may mistake their specialised practice for a generic ability to determine what academic conduct is appropriate in an exam situation. This puts at risk students trained in a different discipline, at another university, or in a foreign socio-cultural context, who may receive a lower mark because their interdisciplinary performance is measured against the examiner's mono-disciplinary benchmark. In short, power is at the centre of academic assessment, enabling certain types of students to claim the position of 'good' learners, while others are marked as 'deviant' because their knowledge practices fail to comply with the dominant literacy recognised within their present academic setting.

To establish more precisely how power works in relation to academic assessment, one needs to determine what performance types students have to master in order to solve the various tasks given to them in the course of a BA or MA programme. Drawing on results from a survey among academic staff at an Irish institution, Sheridan (2011, 133) identified 26 varieties of academic discourse that students may encounter in undergraduate and postgraduate courses. Inspired by this research, the author collected all references made to oral and written academic discourse in the three interview studies, and the result confirms Sheridan's argument that exam forms are extremely varied. Table 11.1 summarises the empirical findings, including the number of informants mentioning a particular performance type.

The variation in performance types challenges the perception of academic writing and speech as study skills that are possessed by individual actors and transferable into new disciplinary, institutional, and socio-cultural contexts. Oral and written discourses can be enacted in multiple ways, which suggests that they are competences that students must acquire upon their entry into a specific community of practice. Power is manifest in the disciplining that occurs when learners, in their role as apprentice scholars, receive grades and criticism which either reward or discourage their use of a particular style, vocabulary, reference format, and structure (Coxhead 2016, Hirvela 2016). By giving feedback, lecturers regulate academic speech and writing, inviting students to align their practice with the 'standards' recognised within teachers' discipline and institution. Educational scholars working with academic literacy generally support exam formats that are formative because they enable the students to improve their performance on the basis of feedback received from course instructors. French (2018) proposes a 'fail better' approach, highlighting how the often disappointing exam results achieved by students in transition from secondary education should be treated not as failure but as an important

Table 11.1 Academic literacy types

	DK 1	*DK 2*	*UK*
Theses (MA, BA)	10	4	1
Written exam (closed book, open book)	5	5	2
Home assignment (individual/group; set task/chosen by students; 24 hours/7-day assignment)	10	13	5
Essay (academic; journalistic)	3	3	3
Portfolio (several essays; essays + other written assignments; written/oral; written/creative)	2	4	2
Project (group/individual; set task/students choose; project proposal)	20	9	6
Written assignments (theoretical; case exercise; calculations; statistics; lab. report; literature synopsis)	6	11	2
Multiple choice test	1	3	
Text production (poster; website)			1
Oral exam (individual/group; set task/project-based; performance)	9	6	1
Presentation (individual/group; set task/free/project; Pecha Kucha; discussants; performance)	11	15	6
Discussion (group/class/pairs/workshops)	9	12	
Written paper/oral exam	9	5	
Simulation/role play	1	3	
Quizzes		4	1
Fieldwork		1	
Lab work	4		2

first step in a learning process that eventually allows these learners to become successful writers within their discipline. This involves an engagement with subject-specific practices because, as French (2018, 413) observes: 'disciplinary fields represent a constructed community, characterised by particular forms of writing, which new undergraduates will not always be very familiar with'. Van Heerden et al. (2017, 970) reach a similar conclusion, arguing for feedback as a way to 'induct' students into an unfamiliar disciplinary, institutional, and socio-cultural context. Tian and Lowe (2013) have examined the role of feedback in international students' adaptation processes, highlighting how tutors' criticism plays a key role for Chinese postgraduates seeking to decode what is expected from them within a British academic environment.

A common type of assessment in higher education is the written home assignment. If the argument holds true that exams forms are situated social practices, one should detect divergence in the way local lecturers and students recruited from other academic contexts approach this task. In her examination of 'inclusive and exclusive knowledge practices' (Tange 2016) the present author used the concept *centres of normalcy* to describe how academic staff benchmark the performance of learners in international and interdisciplinary MA education against an implicit national or disciplinary norm. Such a tendency clearly shows in relation to written assignments where the Danish interviews provide examples of national, institutional, and disciplinary criteria used to distinguish 'good' exam performers from those expected to struggle. First, several respondents refer to the 'free' written assignment, which Vinther and Slethaug (2013) characterise as a 'Danish' format, based on the principles of autonomy and dialogue advocated by the 19th-century educator Nikolaj Grundtvig. When used about academic writing, 'free' means that students enjoy a high degree of independence, selecting their own theme, theoretical framework, and methodological tools. If left unexplained, such a performance type challenges international students, as this Humanities lecturer relates:

> There are also our exam forms. Which we take for granted because they are embedded in our curriculum … But this means that there are some of our foreign [students] who for the first time have to complete these 12 times 3 lessons by writing a free, independent home assignment, which we still use quite a lot in [this department]. Where they come, pull themselves together and ask: What is a free assignment? (DA)

A second default culture refers to institutional traditions. This becomes visible in relation to universities founded on pedagogical principles such as Problem-Based Learning. Frequently, institutional approaches are developed with reference to particular academic settings and their localised nature is highlighted through the adoption of names such as the *Odense Model* and *Aalborg approach*. To academic staff this means that all learners new to the university can be treated as apprentices who have yet to learn 'our' way of doing academic writing. A social scientist describes how the PBL-inspired written assignments used in his institution are special because '[w]e do not hand out a title, now you write about this … You can say that they have to define their own topic and make a problem statement etc. … And we pay a lot of attention to method. And it has to be analytical' (DA). Informants who present written assignments as a knowledge practice connected to certain institutional environments tend to be normative about this, insisting that all successful performers acquire such an approach.

A third default culture relates to academics' disciplinary training. Although an example already quoted suggested that some international educators are open to the possibility that transitioning learners may be trained in different disciplines, the interviews reveal that many academics refer to a monodisciplinary benchmark when assessing student performances. An associate professor explains how he introduces his interdisciplinary class to the template used by students specialising in Political Science:

> There are some quite distinctive traditions … We try to follow these without driving our students too hard. So we accept a bit more flexibility, but still the same template which we use for our own students [which means that] that they will get a set task, which is atypical in an MA class,

> but we normally formulate this fairly broadly so they will have to make some choices and engage with the problem statement … They have to make it their own and then to answer it through a consideration of methodology … and drawing on their course reading, including different debates and analytical tools. (DA)

Default cultures provide a reference point that all lecturers within a specific national, institutional, and disciplinary context can use to justify why they reward certain types of writing whilst discouraging others. Yet the three examples reveal common traits such as the insistence that students choose their own topics, work in a problem-driven manner, and engage with course reading in an independent manner. Arguably, the respondents could be exaggerating the distinctive nature of their approaches, which prompts them to single out certain groups of learners as 'deviant' performers. This foregrounds the need to examine to what extent students are prepared for new exam forms and discourses in a manner that is inclusive to all.

Achieving exam success

Across disciplines and institutions there is a shared ambition among the course convenors and lecturers interviewed that all learners partaking in international education should be able to achieve an exam result that reflects their scientific knowledge and skills. What is also evident in the British and Danish interviews is that assessment practices create difficulties for international educators, not least in exam situations where particular types of students are overrepresented among the 'high' or 'low' performers. A natural scientist offers this example of local students overachieving:

> It was striking last year that the Danes scored so highly. And if this was coincidental, that there were some very strong Danes in the module last year, I don't know … It was as if it was those who knew how we value things in Denmark, who scored the highest marks. There were also some of the foreigners who scored high marks, but it was actually rather striking that the Danes, they appeared to know how to manage exams in Denmark, and the others were less confident about that. (DA)

The informant draws attention to three themes that feature regularly in the comments made by lecturers on exam achievement in international programmes. First, there are *grading practices*, which can vary greatly between academic systems and disciplines. This creates noise in situations where students socialised into a culture where examiners are generous in handing out the top grade A, transfer into a system where A is preserved for absolute top performances, and most students are awarded a B or a C. A second topic is the *accessibility of exam forms*. The natural scientist quoted above suggested that local learners could have benefited from previous experiences with the performance types assessed in the programme, thus gaining an advantage compared to the non-natives. This points to a third theme, the *question of fairness*. Divan et al. (2015, 370) reveal in their study of international MA students in the UK how many have not previously submitted a written essay. In consequence, learners face an uphill struggle when in an exam situation they are assessed according to criteria that take for granted practical knowledge that local learners have developed as undergraduates. To even out the imbalance international educators and programme convenors propose two strategies: 1) to adapt the exam formats so one can avoid performance types that favour particular groups; and 2) to train all students in the forms of academic literacy required in their programme.

Academics involved with the design of international education have the option to select the exam formats that they consider most appropriate for their discipline and module. Course lecturers and convenors can use this as an opportunity to reflect on the suitability of specific performance types, taking into account previous experiences they may have with examining students from diverse socio-cultural, disciplinary, and institutional contexts. This can lead to the identification and subsequent deselection of performance types that seem peculiar to a national or institutional educational culture, and which are therefore best avoided in an international course. One example is the oral exam, which is common to Danish higher education, but perceived as stressful by many international students, who find it difficult to manage the intimate situation where learners have to engage in dialogue with two or more examiners. A course convenor (Media Studies) observes:

> First and foremost, we have in this programme deliberately deselected oral exams because we know that this is [a form] that not very many are familiar with, and which would therefore make it easier for some than others. So we have deselected that. So we actually mainly have a kind of seven-day assignments, individual papers, and then we have one so-called sit-down exam. (DA)

A second motive for choosing a specific format is to create conditions that enable all participants to partake as equals. With reference to a module developed for an international MA programme in the Humanities, an associate professor notes how she and a colleague introduced a form of project assignment that had not previously been used at her university. As a result, the lecturers were able to even out any differences in learner experiences and expectations, creating a level playing field for all students sitting the exam.

A second strategy is to rely on a system of formative assessment. The philosophy behind such a teaching practice is that learners need training in the academic literacies deemed relevant within their discipline and course, which means that the lecturer should focus on developing the specific forms of written and oral discourse that students require in order to obtain a satisfactory result in the final exam. A common way to employ formative assessment is to request that students undertake a variety of exercises throughout term, which they collect in a portfolio, which is subsequently graded. Lecturers can comment on the exercises submitted during the course, thereby helping students to improve their performance by enabling them to correct any mistakes or adjust to a new form of academic writing. A historian describes how this works in his module:

> The exam form is a portfolio exam so they need to hand in three exams at the end ... I am not allowed to grade them before. But the essays that they hand in during those weekly [sessions], they are not graded. But they get the feedback, and then they can make them better and then turn them all in again at the end.

The informant ascribes his students' achievement of high grades to the portfolio format, which is an opinion shared by other lecturers. As a teaching practice in international education, portfolios benefit students in several ways. First, teachers receive an early version of exam papers, which they can use to detect any problems related to patchwriting, missing references, and English proficiency, so they can advise any learners needing additional help. Second, students obtain feedback from course teachers on disciplinary and institutional conventions that may be unfamiliar to them, which supports their transition into a new academic culture. Finally, portfolios are an opportunity for learners to 'fail better' (French 2018), inviting them to submit early versions of their work and then revise, based on the feedback received from the teacher. As a result, students' risk of academic failure is reduced considerably, which explains the popularity of the portfolio format among international educators. As regards content, portfolios can contain a variety of formats, including theoretical or methodological exercises, written papers, indvidual or group presentations, multi-modal activities, and creative performances, allowing course teachers to select the tasks that best reflect the learning objectives and traditions within their subject area.

A less formalised variant of formative assessment is the use of mid-term papers or mock exams to train students for the final exam. A political scientist explains how he has tried to prepare an international, interdisciplinary class for a written exam by first offering examples of questions that such an assignment may contain and then giving learners assignments that allow them to practise academic writing:

> I have tried to make some small, voluntary written exercises. This is one of the things that I have introduced. But because this is voluntary, not many choose to do this. But in those one can identify various strengths and weaknesses, which otherwise I would only see when they sit the exam, for we finish with an exam, a seven-day paper, at the end, right? And there you spot some weaknesses and this: Gosh, they really lack some things. (DA)

The informant provides feedback on all papers received, which enables learners new to disciplinary and institutional conventions to obtain advice from the lecturer who will eventually mark their exam papers. Some academics have taken this a step further, using mid-term papers to assess student needs and then arrange workshops dedicated to academic writing, course literature, research methods, and indeed any skill deeemed necessary to successful exam perfomance.

A second form of training involves academic speech, which can be practised through individual or group presentations. Modules assessed through individual or collaborative projects often end with an oral defence, and lecturers train students for this by inviting them to present their case or project proposal in class. This practice serves two purposes. First, it is a useful way to facilitate knowledge-sharing among learners, which may be important in a module where learners spend a considerable amount of time working in project groups. Second, it prepares those with limited experience of oral exams by allowing them to test their presentation skills and receive feedback from peers and teachers. Academics working with project assignments typically use the oral exam to ask students for a reflection on their learning process and teamworking experiences. In addition, the format may help lecturers establish to what extent all learners have partaken equally in designing and writing the project. A biologist observes: 'I ask the students about their teamwork. Was it effective? Did everybody pull their weight? What was this student's individual role? What did they contribute to the group in particular?'

Teaching for exam successes

The discussion has highlighted the importance of attending to assignment and assessment when designing international education. As practices situated within specific disciplinary and institutional environments, academic writing and speech are governed by distinctive rules and routines which will be used by examiners as the benchmark distinguishing successful learners from those who fail. Students in transition from different educational cultures may lack such practical knowledge, which causes them to underachieve unless they receive training in academic literacy.

An *internationalised* assessment practice should incorporate three elements. First, there is a need to *identify and describe* all performance types used in a particular programme. There has been a tendency to treat academic writing and speech as generic skills that work in all academic settings. Yet the discussion of default cultures showed that that there are many ways to approach essay-writing, which means that academic literacy will have to be explained in relation to the specific discipline that students are trying to learn. Second, programme and module conveners must consider the *fairness* of different assessment types. Ideally, one should avoid exam forms that favour particular groups of learners, and one can attempt to do so by either deselecting certain formats or adding elements that reward alternative insights or techniques. Third, international education benefits from *a formative approach* to assessment, which acknowledges transitioning learners' need to receive feedback in order to develop new practices. In a portfolio exam, for instance, all students hand in an early version of their exam assignment, which they can correct afterwards, using the lecturer's comments to improve the product submitted for the final exam. Such a format allows the module teacher to treat everybody as equals, addressing any comments to the specific learner in need instead of singling out for special attention categories of 'deviant' learners defined by language or nationality.

Part IV

Conclusion

12 Constructing a global practice-scape

Quilt-making

The key task of the qualitative researcher is to produce a representation of reality based on knowledge constructed through methods such as interviewing, participant observations, document analysis, and desk research. Denzin and Lincoln (2011, 4) have compared the stage of representation to an act of *quilt-making*, foregrounding the human endeavour involved in assembling a collection of multi-coloured and disconnected pieces into a single model or theory. The discussion in this book has highlighted nine elements that influence individual teachers' experience with and performance of international higher education:

- Four conditions *structuring* the global field of higher education: Globalisation/internationalisation processes, disciplinary communities, mobility as habituated action, and English as the academic lingua franca.
- Five teaching *practices* affected and changed by internationalisation: Programme design, academic roles and routines, curricular contexts, multicultural teamwork, and assessment.

What remains is to construct some kind of order from the bundle of practices identified in the empirical research. The chapter will attempt to accomplish this, guided by two questions: 1) *where and how do practices connect*; and 2) *what kind of change is driving the reconfiguration of higher education that is internationalisation*?

A conceptualisation of 'global teaching practices' requires a deeper understanding of how actors' *Doings*, *Sayings*, and *Relatings* respond to and contribute to the making of international education. To illustrate how this works, the organising practice of *teaching* will serve as the focal point for the discussion. *Teaching* is a nested practice, and, as mentioned in Chapter 2, this means that it incorporates action and interaction performed in a variety of settings and across different scales. To obtain a clearer picture of what the enactment of *teaching* can mean, one may divide activities into the three categories of *Doings*, *Sayings*, and *Relatings*. The *Doings* of teaching involves such practices as designing a module, writing a curriculum, planning classroom activities, making assignments, and evaluating students' achievement. All are multi-layered, as seen in the example of educational design (Chapter 7), which concerned choices relating to the purpose of education, pedagogies supporting students' academic socialisation, and the selection of threshold concepts to ensure learners' progression from novice to expert. The *Sayings* that university teachers rely on when performing higher education include the production of academic writing/speech in class, scaffolding techniques such as visual aids, lecture notes and glossaries, the feedback provided on student assignments, and guidelines explaining to learners how they may approach a particular task. As discussed in Chapter 6, professorial authority is linked to actors' command of the language recognised within a specific disciplinary and institutional environment, which makes a practical mastery of *Sayings* essential to academics' success as educators. The final category of *Relatings* has been defined as 'ways of relating to people and the world' (Kemmis/Mahon 2017, 109). University lecturers engage in relating practices when designing classroom exercises that encourage student participation, selecting cases that connect with learner experiences, choosing discussion topics that invite students to partake in the co-construction of knowledge, and intervening with team formation to ensure that all feel included. Teachers' ability to *relate* depends on their interpretation of the role as lecturer, their ability to communicate in an effective manner, and their perception of students as either net recipients or co-creators of knowledge. Hence, the three categories of *Doings*, *Sayings*, and *Relatings* are interconnected.

Equally important is the understanding of teaching practice as multi-sited and multi-scalar, which means that the concrete acts unfolding within a single location relate to practices situated within other institutional, national, and policy settings. Accordingly, the ordering of international teaching practices requires the development of a theoretical framework that shows how university lecturers simultaneously respond to global, national, and institutional processes and actively internationalise their teaching because of a personal ambition to promote 'the global' through research and education. Even if actions such as participation in international research communities and English-medium publishing have become habituated, it is vital that academic staff be treated as agents contributing to the making of global higher education and not as the passive recipients of processes imposed by institutional policy-makers, national benchmarking schemes, and international conventions. Here the author draws inspiration from Bourdieu's field theory, which suggested that agents are inclined to follow the rules regulating action within a particular environment, but that habits may be modified, or indeed abandoned, in response to changing circumstances.

To develop theory the author will follow three steps. First, international teaching practices are discussed with reference to a single institutional environment, foregrounding the key domains of language, culture, knowledge, and organisational culture. Second, actors' teaching is related to action undertaken in other sites and scales, which highlights the international dimension to higher education and research. Finally, the local and global dimensions are brought together in the form of a model that represents international higher education as a global practice-scape.

Internationalising teaching practices

To *internationalise*, Chapter 3 suggested, describes a process '[transforming] a unit from an inward-looking, national condition to an externally oriented, international focus'. The definition foregrounds the relationship between an organisation and its external environment, which, arguably, is transformed because of demands arising from macro-level processes of globalisation and internationalisation. In comparison, to internationalise teaching practices involves change that happens inside the institution as the result of actors' engagement with developments such as academic migration, Englishisation of scientific knowledge production, international collaboration in research and education, and disciplinary communities' privileging of particular 'global' sites. As discussed in Chapter 3, change can be driven by individual academics' desire to promote an internationalist agenda (Trondal's *bottom-up* process) or implemented through management initiatives such as Hudzik's (2015) strategy for 'comprehensive internationalisation'. Whatever the motive, internationalising has practical implications, necessitating *Learning by Doing* at the organisational as well as individual levels.

To organise the experiences collected in the first interview study a model was created (Figure 12.1) that foregrounded the four key domains of *organisation*, *language*, *culture*, and *knowledge*. The model offers a useful point of departure for the present discussion, providing anchorage points that enable the researcher to pin down where and how internationalising happens.

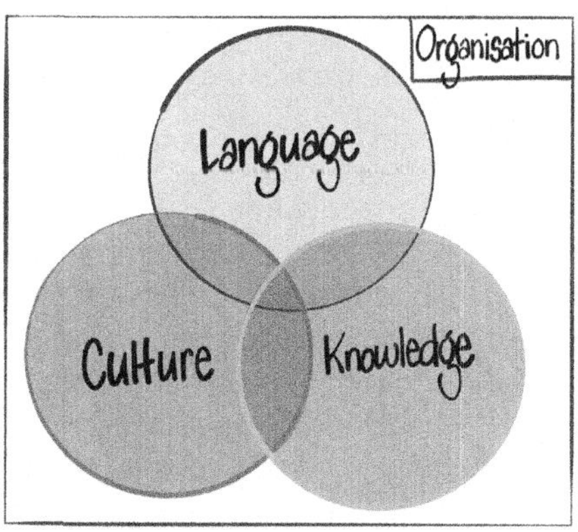

Figure 12.1 Domains

In contexts that are traditionally non-English speaking, an obvious mark of internationalisation is the shift from education in the national language to English. In some institutional settings, this happens as the result of a management wish to recruit more international students and staff, but Englishisation can also occur on the initiative of academics who want to open their modules to exchange students or disseminate research findings to an international audience. Language connects with culture in the sense that a wider use of English often leads to an increase in the number of non-native staff and students, causing a diversification of languages, socio-cultural backgrounds, educational experiences, and disciplinary identities within the organisation. Diversity means that the classroom meeting between lecturer and learners is transformed into an intercultural encounter, which demands that new pedagogies be considered in relation to discussion exercises, multicultural teams, and exam assignments. Inclusive pedagogies are a central part of the third domain, knowledge, which also concerns lecturers' framing of academic disciplines, selection of course literature, academic literacy, and evaluation criteria. Actors' willingness to change teaching practices will depend on the organisational culture, which is presented in Figure 12.1 as the frame incorporating language, culture, and knowledge. At one extreme are universities that recruit foreign students for financial reasons, taking for granted that learners come in order to benefit from an educational system considered superior to the one found in students' home countries. This kind of institutional mind-set fuels deficit discourses of the type discussed in relation to academic norms (Chapter 8) and exam failure (Chapter 11), motivating academic staff to perceive international students as 'empty vessels' to be filled with Western knowledge (Singh 2005). At the other extreme are organisational cultures that accept internationalisation as a process of learning which involves all staff, domestic and international students. Here the predominant ethos is inclusion, which means that no form of action or interaction is rewarded or dismissed automatically. Instead, any dissonance arising from the encounter between staff and students is treated as a learning situation in the Deweyan sense, with actors asking if the episode is unique or symptomatic of a wider problem that should be addressed by the teaching group, department, or institution.

Turning to the practices involved in actors' performance of education, Chapters 7–11 foregrounded examples that show academics engaging with internationalisation in an active, direct manner. From these the three illustrative themes of academic socialisation (*Doing*), participation/silence (*Saying*), and representations of space (*Relating*) have been selected as focal points for the present discussion of why and how lecturers internationalise. The teacher's *Doing* of academic socialisation is vital in higher education as this installs in learners an understanding of the tacit rules governing 'good' academic practice within a discipline or institution. When internationalised, the act of socialising becomes very complex because academics can no longer take a shared knowledge base for granted, but have to start their courses by establishing with students what socio-cultural, educational, linguistic, and institutional experiences are present in the classroom. Subsequently, teachers need to consider if all learners possess the forms of academic literacy rewarded in their class, and if not, what action should be taken to resolve this. In some cases, actors provide explicit guidelines or feedback to support students' adaption to a specific disciplinary and institutional practice. In other programmes, teachers treat internationalisation as their incentive to rethink class exercises and assignments, introducing different formats in an attempt to even out any asymmetries between diverse groups of learners. An adjustment of evaluation criteria involves other actors such as programme convenors, external examiners, and departmental study boards, who will have to approve any new requirements and expectations that arise from the lecturer's act of internationalising. One may add that all *Doings* must be communicated in English, which is not a skill that can be taken granted in all institutional environments.

The significance of *Sayings* was demonstrated in Chapter 8, which offered several examples of lecturers' worrying about silence, which they interpret as symptomatic of education that is somehow flawed because it fails to achieve student–staff interaction. In some situations, learners' quietude can be ascribed to linguistic ability, since many participants in international education are second-language users and possibly challenged by the request that they present an academic argument in English. Yet silence can also be read as a consequence of cultural diversity, with students withdrawing from class debates because these demand from them geographic and socio-cultural knowledge that they do not possess. To further participation in international classes, a variety of pedagogies have been proposed in the previous chapters, including teambuilding exercises, the formation of multicultural teams, linguistic scaffolding, and the selection of themes that can be approached from a variety of learner positions. Finally, students' participation/silence sometimes reflect their previous socialisation into a particular educational and institutional culture, in which case lecturers may want to cooperate with institutional support services such as International Office staff and Learning Lab consultants, who can offer learners guidance in their transition between a teacher-focused and a student-centred culture.

Relatings involve the attempt by teachers to engage with student positions in and experiences of the world. A key concern is the representation of space, which is enacted by teachers when selecting course readings and cases to illustrate a specific concept or model. What can be included in the internationalised syllabi is language-dependent, and lecturers generally accept English as the medium accessible to most. In spite of this, course readings provide an opportunity for lecturers to engage directly with student diversity, enabling them to contextualise knowledge by representing scientific concepts and models through case studies set in a variety of geographical and socio-cultural spaces. Another way to internationalise *Relatings* is through the practice of upscaling where teachers broaden their frames of reference in an attempt to explain scientific knowledge in a way that makes it relevant to learners from different parts of the world. In some cases, this causes lecturers to abandon domestic examples, replacing cases from countries such as Denmark or the Czech Republic with American or British material. Actors justify their privileging of the United States and Britain with reference to labour market expectations, international trends, and the global standards set by academic publishing, which indicates that they relate to students as agents moving in an international rather than a national space. Hence, one could argue that teachers have internationalised their *Relatings* in a way that suggests a perception of higher education as multi-sited and multi-scalar.

Acting and interacting in a global field

The understanding of 'the global' as multi-sited and multi-scalar was introduced in Chapter 3 with reference to the geographic concept of scale. The argument built on Howitt's (2002) distinction between *sites* and *scales*, which is worth revisiting at this point because it foregrounds an important difference between activities that connect sites within a flat, two-dimensional space, and action cutting across scales within a vertical, multi-level system. A perception of global higher education as *multi-sited* relies on a horizontal conceptualisation of space where practices performed in a single location are *extended* through linkages established to similar sites in other parts of the world. Schatzki (2002) uses a network metaphor to represent this form of practice-scape, which is realised in global academia when, for instance, two universities sign a partnership agreement or a scholar travels abroad on a short-term sojourn. In contrast, the interpretation of 'the global' as *multi-scalar* draws on the image of a vertical system where practices are *nested*, which means that activities performed at one level relate to action in other scales. The functioning of global higher education as a multi-scalar system becomes visible in relation to policy-making where structural reforms such as those demanded from signatories of the Bologna Declaration have practical implications for teaching staff who may be requested to align course contents and grading criteria with standards set internationally. Chapter 3 identified six scales relevant to global higher education, which were visualised in the form of concentric circles (Figure 12.2). Yet Figure 12.2 represents a simplified system, the relevance of which will have to be established in relation to the actual *Doings*, *Sayings*, and *Relatings* that constitute actors' performance of international education.

University lecturers' teaching practice is generally associated with activities set within specific locations such as a classroom or laboratory. When observing teachers in action, it is tempting to focus on events unfolding within this bounded space, overlooking the relationships that link the single act performed in class to practices situated in other sites and scales. Chapters 3–6 examined structural conditions in global academia, highlighting how factors such as migration trends, disciplinary communities, and the spread of English

Figure 12.2 A multi-scalar system

have persuaded actors of the need to internationalise education and research. This suggests that internationalisation has become part of the academic *habitus*, in which case one may expect teaching to be realised in a way that reflects its nature as an extended and nested practice.

Teachers' *Doing* of international education begins with the design of a programme. The first decision concerns the form of internationalisation, which can involve different sites and policy scales. If 'the international' is realised through the welcoming of exchange students, actors rely on partnership agreements, which is a multi-sited activity, connecting the institution to universities in other countries. In comparison, international degree and *Erasmus Mundus* programmes are multi-scalar, demanding an engagement with policymakers at the national or supernational/European levels.

A second consideration is the demographic profile of the teaching staff. As the result of increased mobility, many lecturers can be characterised as 'international' because they have found employment outside their home country, travelled abroad as exchange or degree students, or enjoyed sojourns at foreign research institutions. Migration experiences influence actors' perception of the world, encouraging them to compare their present position to any educational, socio-cultural, and institutional settings previously occupied. This multi-sitedness is important for two reasons. First, it provides common ground between international educators and migrant students, who may recognise among the teachers a shared desire to establish linkages between the present location and sites occupied at earlier stages of the educational journey. Second, an understanding of 'the international' as multi-sited impacts the way knowledge is selected and represented, since lecturers exposed to diverse academic traditions are less likely to accept a syllabi dominated by texts produced in power geographies such as the United States and Britain.

The final point relates to the practice of internationalising curricula, which can be done in a way that is *multi-sited*, inviting learners to build on knowledge acquired in other geographical, socio-cultural, and linguistic locations, or *multi-scalar*, which demands that the framing of knowledge is 'global', referring to scales considered accessible to most learners. Ideally, the two practices should work together, although the discussion in Chapter 9 revealed that lecturers' focus on *upscaling* can happen at the expense of multi-sitedness, causing actors to abandon local and national sites altogether.

The *Sayings* of international education relate closely to the question of language. As demonstrated in Chapter 6, there is a shared understanding of English as the lingua franca within higher education and research, which has prompted non-native speakers to accept as natural their need to master this medium for teaching and publishing purposes. English domination may be read as a multi-sited as well as a multi-scalar practice. As regards multi-sitedness, the status attached to the English language derives from the perception of the United States and Britain as world centres of scientific knowledge production, which motivates academics working outside an American or British setting to extend their curricular contexts to include references to these sites. At the same time, Englishisation is symptomatic of a nested system where the English language is associated with a global as well as a national scale. English obtains its privileged status as *the* scientific lingua franca from disciplinary communities of practice, which have accepted that participation in global scholarship includes dissemination of knowledge through English-medium publications and conferences. Related to this is academic literacy, which involves the rules governing scientific writing and speech. Arguably, the routines that teachers encourage students to acquire have been shaped partly by these actors' own socialisation into particular disciplinary and institutional environments, partly by feedback received when seeking to publish conference papers and articles. Academic publishing is structured hierarchically, with scholars competing to publish in a limited number of journals recognised as 'global'. Most 'global' publications are based in North America and Western Europe, and authors are therefore likely to develop a 'Western' style of writing, which they may subsequently adopt as their benchmark when teaching and assessing academic literacy in international education.

Central to the teaching practice of *Relatings* is the intercultural encounter between staff and students socialised into a variety of socio-cultural, educational, disciplinary, and institutional environments. Because of such divergence classroom interaction constitutes an extended practice where actors' present understandings of the roles as teacher and student are influenced by norms and routines internalised in other sites. Many lecturers have a migrant history, which means that they have experienced variation in teaching and learning which enhances their ability to understand student–staff interaction as a multi-sited practice incorporating understandings acquired by learners in diverse institutional settings. More awkward is the situation of the international recruit moving into a new educational culture. As discussed in Chapter 5, the non-native will frequently attempt to perform the role as teacher in the manner internalised within a previous academic environment, which can violate the expectations of local students, causing them to insist that the teacher's practice be localised.

Turning to *Relatings* as a multi-scalar practice, this is realised through forms of interaction that invite actors to connect their individual perspectives or stories to phenomena associated with higher levels in the scalar hierarchy. Often this involves learners' co-construction of a shared meta-narrative or picture of reality. Hence, a lecturer in International Relations may ask her class for opinions on the United Nations in order to build an awareness that intergovernmental institutions are understood differently depending on observers' socio-cultural and geographic positions. The implication is that 'the global' will be constructed in class on the initiative of the lecturer who can prompt students to discuss course theory and cases with reference to multiple scales. This places individual actors' enactment of teaching at the heart of the practice-scape that is international education.

Constructing a global practice-scape

The previous sections presented international education as the outcome of changes occurring inside the organisation as well as the product of actors' external connections with multiple sites and scales. To answer the first guiding question of *where and how practices connect*, two models have been proposed. Figure 12.1 represented internationalisation within the university as a transformation manifest in the three key domains of language, culture,

Figure 12.3 A global practice-scape

and knowledge. Arguably, all domains were internationalised as the consequence of action and interaction performed in other institutional, national, and linguistic settings, which highlights the relevance of practice extension, or multi-sitedness, to intra-organisational change. Figure 12.2 focused on the external environment, visualising this as a three-dimensional system where the contexts of action and interaction were organised in the form of a scalar hierarchy. This representation treats teaching practices as a nested activity, which suggests that performances set within a particular institution simultaneously are shaped by and shaping processes unfolding at the national, supernational, and global levels. Figure 12.3, brings together the intra-organisational and external factors involved in actors' internationalisation of teaching practices

At the core of the model are the three domains of language, culture, and knowledge, because changes affecting any of these will have an immediate effect on the staff and students co-inhabiting the international learning environment. However, a closer examination of the *Doings*, *Sayings*, and *Relatings* that constitute lecturers' enactment of teaching suggests that actors' practices connect with other sites and scales, which justifies the representation of the external environment in the form of a multi-scalar system. What is new in Figure 12.3 are the two arrows, which point outwards, from organisation to global, and inwards, from global to organisation. The arrows have been included to illustrate how the action motivating the transformation that creates global teaching and learning may be initiated in different scales and sites. This relates to the second guiding question: *What kind of change is driving the reconfiguration of higher education that is internationalisation*?

The internationalisation of teaching practice may be interpreted as a change process that emerges from macro-level trends such as the emergence of a global market for higher education, new opportunities offered by cheap technology and travel, a system of knowledge production dominated by the English language, and benchmarking schemes that reward institutions engaging in international education and research. As they become aware of such developments, university managers and planners will seek to raise their institution's stakes in the global competition for talented students and researchers, which could lead to their decision to implement a policy of strategic internationalisation on part of or an entire organisation. At the receiving end of such initiatives are lecturing staff, who may be requested to adjust their language usage, engage with a culturally diverse student cohort, and develop pedagogies suitable for an international learning environment. Figure 12.3 represents this transformation in the form of an arrow pointing inwards from the global to the organisational level, which suggests a rather passive role for academic staff. Yet one could argue that it is only at the point where global trends and institutional policies are transformed into actual teaching practices that international education is realised, which positions lecturers at the centre of change. A second arrow visualises a movement from the individual actor inside the organisation to developments within the global field. This recognises the role of academic staff as agents driving the globalisation of higher education and research. In relation to organisational processes, Chapter 3 revealed how in the pre-Bologna period internationalisation might happen as the result of lecturers' wish to facilitate student exchange, promote an internationalist agenda within their department, or collaborate with partners in transnational networks. There is little empirical evidence that indicates a strong involvement by institutional policy-makers at this early stage, which would support an interpretation of internationalisation as a process driven by enthusiasts among academic staff. Turning to migration, transnational flows of people will always be actor-driven since they involve the decision by individuals to study or work abroad. Although it can be encouraged by support structures implemented at the national and supernational levels (e.g. visa regulations, the Bologna reforms), academic mobility occurs because students or staff consider it to be a desirable option, which relates to the way actors imagine education and research as activities performed within a global rather than national field.

A final example is academics' contribution to the spread of the English language. Even if national and global ranking lists prioritise English-medium publishing, the symbolic power of the language can only be maintained as long as scholars worldwide willingly employ this medium for research dissemination. The discussion in Chapters 5 and 6 revealed that many academics in non-English-speaking contexts accept their need to write and teach in English, which they consider more prestigious, or 'global', than working in the national language. Hence, one could argue that the demand that teaching be internationalised originates with lecturing staff in response to individual experiences with education and research as multi-sited, multi-scalar practices.

The assemblage of university lecturers' *Doings*, *Sayings*, and *Relatings* into a global practice-scape represents a new way to approach international education, foregrounding the importance of actors' practical understandings to classroom action and interaction. The perspective is unique in the way it deals with internationalisation as a process of organisational learning driven by teachers acting in the capacity of reflective practitioners. The author's take on internationalisation contains three important lessons. First, the representation of teaching practices as action and interaction performed both within an organisation and in relation to external developments highlights the complexity of internationalisation as a change process. In the literature, the act of *internationalising* has mainly been addressed with reference to single domains such as language, culture, knowledge, or organisation, but such readings simplify a reality where teaching is shaped simultaneously by the lecturer's personal experience, disciplinary socialisation, linguistic proficiency, intercultural competence, pedagogic philosophy, and organisational status.

A second key lesson concerns the approach taken to internationalisation within institutions of higher education. Increasingly, university managers and planners treat internationalisation as a strategic matter, which has led to an increase in the number of the support staff working in International Offices and Learning Labs. While useful when seeking to address institutional issues such as admission policy, language requirements, and grading criteria, it is important that such professionalisation complements rather than competes with the *Learning by Doing* processes that happen as the result of individual teachers' enactment of international education within a specific programme, discipline, and department. Instead of representing international teaching as a generic skill to be acquired through standardised training sessions, educational consultants will need to engage in a dialogue with academic staff, asking what *Doings*, *Sayings*, and *Relatings* they rely on when internationalising.

A final implication relates to the location of organisational knowledge about international teaching and learning. As reflected in the empirical research, university lecturers engage actively with international education, experimenting in the classroom with new pedagogies that can enhance learners' ability to partake as equals in learning. Of course, teaching practices vary, as will the forms of academic literacy that educators claim as 'natural' to their subject, teaching group, institutional culture, and linguistic environment. Yet all teachers have encountered internationalisation through *Learning by Doing* and can offer reflections that may be harvested by educational researchers seeking deep knowledge about pedagogic action and interaction. Accordingly, the author should like to suggest that experienced lecturers be treated as teachers of practice within their institutions, who should be asked for expert opinions on the change processes that create international education.

References

Aalbers, M. 2004. Creative destruction through the Anglo-American hegemony: A non-Anglo-American view on publications, referees and language. *Area* 36 (3), 319–22.

AAU. 2017. International as-is analyse – Forskning [International analysis – research]. Internal document obtained by author.

Abasi, A., and Graves, B. 2008. Academic literacy and plagiarism: Conversations with international graduate students and disciplinary professors. *Journal of English Academic Purposes* 7, 221–33.

Airey, J., Lauridsen, K., Räsänen, A., Sälö, L., and Schwach, V. 2017. The expansion of English-medium education in the Nordic countries: Can top-down university language policies encourage bottom-up disciplinary literacy goals? *Higher Education* 73, 561–76.

Altbach, P., and de Wit, H. 2015. Internationalization and Global Tension: Lessons from history. *Journal of Studies in International Education* 19 (1), 4–10.

Alvesson, M. 2003. Methodology for close up studies – struggling with closeness and closure. *Higher Education* 46, 167–93.

Ammon, U. 2012. Linguistic inequality and its effects on participation in scientific discourse and on global knowledge accumulation: With a closer look at the problems of the second-rank language communities. *Applied Linguistics Review* 3 (2), 333–55.

Amsberry, D. 2009. Deconstructing plagiarism: International students and textual borrowing practices. *The Reference Librarian* 51 (1), 31–44.

Analoui, B., Sambrook, S., and Doloriert, C. 2014. Engaging students in group work to maximise tacit knowledge sharing and use. *International Journal of Management Education* 12, 35–43.

Andrade, M. 2006. International students in English-speaking universities: Adjustment factors. *Journal of Research in International Education* 5 (2), 131–54.

Appadurai, A. 1996. *Modernity at Large: Cultural Dimensions of Globalisation*. Minneapolis, MN: University of Minnesota Press.

Bain, R., and Mueller, C. 2016. Understanding practice(s) and practising. In K. M. Orr (ed.), *Knowledge and Practice in Business Organizations*, 30–42. London and New York: Routledge.

Baker, S. 2017. Students' writing 'in transition' from A-levels to university: How assessment drives students' understandings, practices and discourses. *Assessment and Evaluation in Higher Education* 42 (1), 18–36.

Bauder, H. 2015. The international migration of academics: A labour market perspective. *International Migration* 53, 83–96.

Bauder, H., Lujan, O., and Hannan, C.-H. 2018. Internationally mobile academics: Hierarchies, hegemony and the geo-scientific imagination. *Geoforum* 89, 52–9.

Bauder, H., Hannan, C.-H., and Lujan, O. 2017. International experience in the academic field: Knowledge production, symbolic capital and mobility fetishism. *Population, Space and Place* 23 (6), 1–13.

Becher, T. 1989. *Academic Tribes and Territories: Intellectual Enquiry and the Cultures of the Disciplines*. Buckingham: Society for Research into Higher Education and Open University Press.

Berg, L. 2004. Scaling knowledge: Towards a *critical geography* of critical geographies. *Geoforum* 35, 553–8.

Bergan, S., and Deca, L. 2018. Twenty years of Bologna and a decade of EHEA: What is next? In A. Curaj, L. Deca, and R. Pricopie (eds), *European Higher Education Area: The Impact of Past and Future Policies*, 295–319. Dordrecht: Springer.

Bernard, H. R. 2006. *Research Methods in Anthropology: Qualitative and Quantitative Approaches* [4th ed.]. Lanham, MD: AltaMira Press.

Berry, J. 1997. Immigration, acculturation and adaptation. *Applied Psychology* 46 (1), 5–34.

Biesta, G. 2009. Good education in an age of measurement: on the need to reconnect with the question of purpose in education. *Education Assessment Evaluation and Accountability* 21, 33–46.

Blasco, M. 2015. Making the tacit explicit: Rethinking culturally inclusive pedagogy in international student academic adaptation. *Pedagogy, Culture and Society* 23 (1), 85–106.

Blommaert, J. 2010. *The Sociolinguistics of Globalization*. Cambridge: Cambridge University Press.

Boden, R., and Epstein, D. 2011. A flat earth society? Imagining academic freedom. *The Sociological Review* 59 (3), 476–95.

Bolton, K., and Kuteeva, M. 2012. English as an academic language at a Swedish university: Parallel language use and the 'threat' of English. *Journal of Multilingual and Multicultural Development* 33 (5), 429–47.

Booth, J. 2006. On the mastery of philosophical concepts: Socratic discourse and the unexpected 'affect'. In J. Meyer and R. Land (eds), *Overcoming Barriers to Student Understanding: Threshold Concepts and Troublesome Knowledge*, 173–81. London and New York: Routledge.

Bothwell, E. 2018. Policy shift forces Danes to close degrees and cut English teaching. *Times Higher Education,* November 27.

Bourdieu, P. 1977. *Outline of a Theory of Practice* [Eng. ed.; 1st ed. 1972]. Cambridge: Cambridge University Press.

Bourdieu, P. 1986a. *Distinction: A Social Critique of the Judgement of Taste* [Eng. ed.; 1st ed. 1979]. London and New York: Routledge.

Bourdieu, P. 1986b. The forms of capital. In J. G. Richardson (ed.), *Handbook of Theory and Research for the Sociology of Education*, 241–58. New York: Greenwood Press,

Bourdieu, P. 1988. *Homo Academicus* [Eng. ed.; 1st ed. 1984]. Cambridge: Polity.

Bourdieu, P. 1990. *The Logic of Practice* [Eng. ed.; 1st ed. 1980]. Cambridge: Polity.

Bourdieu, P. 1991. *Language and Symbolic Power* [Eng. ed.; 1st ed. 1982]. Cambridge: Polity.

Bourdieu, P. 1993. *The Field of Cultural Production*. Cambridge: Polity.

Bourdieu, P. 1996a. *The Rules of Art: Genesis and Structure of the Literary Field* [Eng. ed.; 1st ed. 1992]. Stanford, CA: Stanford University Press.

Bourdieu, P. 1996b. *The State Nobility: Elite Schools in the Field of Power* [Eng. ed.; 1st ed. 1989]. Cambridge: Polity.

Bourdieu, P. 1999. The social conditions of the international circulation of ideas. In R. Shusterman (ed.), *Bourdieu: A Critical Reader*, 220–28. Oxford: Blackwell.

Bourdieu, P., and Passeron, J.-C. 1994. Introduction: Language and the relationship to language in the teaching situation. In P. Bourdieu, J.-C. Passeron, and M. de Saint Martin, *Academic Discourse: Linguistic Misunderstanding and Professorial Power*, 1–34. Cambridge: Polity Press

Bourdieu, P., and Passeron, J.-C. 2000. *Reproduction in Education, Society and Culture* [Eng. ed.; 1st ed. 1970]. London: Sage.

Bourdieu, P., and Wacquant, L. 1992. *An Invitation to Reflexive Sociology*. Cambridge: Polity.

Bourdieu, P., and Wacquant, L. 1999. On the cunning of imperialist reason. *Theory, Culture & Society* 16, 1, 41–58.

Bowman, K. 2017. Educating international students about academic misconduct. *International Student Affairs,* March/April, 56–9.

Bradford, A. 2016. Toward a typology of implementation challenges facing English-medium instruction in higher education: Evidence from Japan. *Journal of Studies in International Education* 20 (4), 339–56.

Brew, A. 2008. Disciplinary and interdisciplinary affiliations of experienced researchers. *Higher Education* 56, 423–38.

Brown, L., and Holloway, I. 2008. The adjustment journey of international post-graduate students at an English university. *Journal of Research in International Education* 7 (2), 232–49.

Brown, S., and Joughin, G. 2007. Assessment and international students: Helping clarify puzzling processes. In E. Jones and S. Brown (eds), *Internationalising Higher Education*, 57–71. London and New York: Routledge.

Buch, A., and Elkjær, B. 2015. Pragmaticism and practice theories: Convergences or collisions. Paper presented at OLKC, Milan.

Bull, T. 2004. Dagens og gårsdagens akademiske lingua franca. Eit historisk tilbakeblikk og eit globalt utsyn [The academic lingua franca of today and yesterday. A historical retrospect and global perspective]. In D. Simonsen (ed.), *Språk i kunnskapssamfunnet: Engelsk – elitenes nye Latin?* [Language in the knowledge society: English – the new Latin of the elites?], 35–45. Oslo: Gyldendal Akademisk.

Burawoy, M. 2016. The promise of sociology: Global challenges for national disciplines. *Sociology* 50 (5), 949–59.

Burnett, S.-A., and Huisman, J. 2010. Universities' responses to globalisation: The influence of organisational culture. *Journal of Studies in International Education* 14 (2), 117–42.

Byram, M. 2018. Internationalisation in higher education – an internationalist perspective. *On the Horizon* 26 (2), 148–56.

Calhoun, C. 2008. Cosmopolitanism in the modern social imaginary. *Dædalus* 127 (3), 105–14.

Canagarajah, S. 2013. *Translingual Practice: Global Englishes and Cosmopolitan Relations*. London and New York: Routledge.

Carmichael, P. 2012. Tribes, territories and threshold concepts: Educational materialisms at work in higher education. *Educational Philosophy and Theory* 44 (1), 31–42.

Carroll, J. 2015. *Tools for Teaching in an Educationally Mobile World*. London and New York: Routledge.

Caruana, V. 2016. Researching the transnational higher education policy landscape: Exploring network power and dissensus in a globalizing system. *London Review of Education* 14 (1), 56–69.

Caruana, V., and Montgomery, C. 2015. Understanding the transnational higher education landscape: Shifting positionality and the complexities of partnership. *Learning and Teaching* 8 (1), 5–29.

Chan, S. 1999. The Chinese learner – a question of style. *Education and Training* 41 (6/7), 294–304.

Chang, J. 2006. A transcultural wisdom bank in the classroom: Making cultural diversity a key resource in teaching and learning. *Journal of Studies in International Education* 10 (4), 369–77.

Charmaz, K. 2006. *Constructing Grounded Theory: A Practical Guide through Qualitative Analysis*. Los Angeles, CA: Sage.

Chapple, J. 2015. Teaching in English is not necessarily the teaching of English. *International Education Studies* 8 (3), 1–13.

Chen, Q., and Koyama, J. 2013. Reconceptualising diasporic networks: Mobile scholars in transnational space. *Globalisation, Societies and Education* 11 (1), 23–38.

Clegg, S. 2012. Conceptualising higher education research and/or academic development as 'fields': A critical analysis. *Higher Education Research and Development* 31 (5), 667–78.

Clegg, S., and Stevenson, J. 2013. The interview reconsidered: Context, genre, reflexivity and interpretation in sociological approaches to interviews in higher education research. *Higher Education Research and Development* 32 (1), 5–16.

Clifford, V. 2009. Engaging the disciplines in internationalising the curriculum. *International Journal for Academic Development* 14 (2), 133–43.

Clifford, V. 2014. Internationalisation: Troublesome knowledge for the disciplines. In P. Trowler, M. Saunders, and V. Bamber (eds), *Tribes and Territories in the 21st Century: Rethinking the Significance of Disciplines in Higher Education*, 197–207. London and New York: Routledge.

Clifford, V., and Henderson, J. 2011. Shifting identities: International staff negotiating new academic identities. In K. Krause, M. Buckridge, C. Grimner, and S. Purbrick-Illek (eds), *Research and Development in Higher Education* 34, 108–17.

Colapietro, V. 2004. Doing – and undoing – the done thing: Dewey and Bourdieu on habituation, agency, and transformation. *Contemporary Pragmaticism* 1 (2), 65–93.

Collins, H. M. 2001. What is tacit knowledge? In T. Schatzki, K. Knorr-Cetina, and E. von Savigny, *The Practice Turn in Contemporary Theory,* 107–19, London and New York. Routledge.

Collyer, F. 2018. Global patterns in the publishing of academic knowledge: Global north, global south. *Current Sociology* 66 (1), 56–73.

Corbin, J., and Strauss, A. 2008. *Basics of Qualitative Research* [3rd ed.]. Los Angeles, CA: Sage.

Cotton, D., George, R., and Joyner, M. 2013. Interaction and influence in culturally mixed groups. *Innovations in Education and Teaching International* 50 (3), 272–83.

Coxhead, A. 2016. Acquiring academic and disciplinary vocabulary. In K. Hyland and P. Shaw (eds), *The Routledge Handbook of English for Academic Purposes*, 177–90. London and New York: Routledge.

Crawford, R. 1992. *Devolving English Literature*. Oxford: Clarendon.

Crawford, R. (ed.). 1998. *The Scottish Invention of English Literature*. Cambridge: Cambridge University Press.

Christensen, G. 2016. A poststructuralist view on students' project groups: Possibilities and limitations. *Psychology Learning and Teaching* 15 (2), 168–79.

Christensen, G. 2013. Gruppearbejde [Group work]. In L. Rienecker, P. Jørgensen, J. Dolin, and G. Holten (eds), *Universitetspædagogik* [University pedagogy], 189–99. Roskilde: Samfundslitteratur.

Crowther, P., Joris, M., Otten, M., Nilsson, B., Teekens, H., and Wächter, B. 2000. *Internationalisation at Home: A Position Paper*. Amsterdam: European Association for International Education.

Cruickshank, K., Chen, H., and Warren, S. 2012. Increasing international and domestic student interaction through group work: A case study from the humanities. *Higher Education Research and Development* 31 (6), 797–810.

Dale, R. 2000. Globalization and education: Demonstrating a 'common world educational culture' or locating a 'globally structured educational agenda'. *Educational Theory* 50 (4), 427–48.

Danish Ministry for Higher Education and Science. 2018a. Bachelor- og kandidatuddannelser [BA and MA education]. www.ufm.dk. Available online at: https://ufm.dk/uddannelse/videregaende-uddannelse/universiteter/OLDuniversiteter/bachelor-og-kandidatuddannelser [accessed September 25 2018].

Danish Ministry for Higher Education and Science. 2018b. *Forskerrekruttering på universiteterne 2015–2017* [Researcher recruitment at the universities 2015–2017]. Analysis available online at https://ufm.dk/forskning-og-innovation/statistik-og-analyser/forskere-ved-universiteterne [accessed June 6 2019].

Danish Ministry for Higher Education and Science. 2019. Statistics on PhD mobility 2014–17. Documentation produced for author.

Day, D., and Kjærbeck, S. 2011. Educational practices in the international university: Language as a resource for distinction in an intercultural project meeting. In B. Preisler, I. Klitgård, and A. Fabricius (ed.), *Language and Learning in the International University*, 99–121. Bristol: Multilingual Matters.

Denzin, N., and Lincoln, Y. 2011. Introduction: The discipline and practice of qualitative research. In N. Denzin and Y. Lincoln (eds), *The Sage Handbook of Qualitative Research* [4th ed.], 1–19. Los Angeles, CA: Sage.

Devos, A. 2003. Academic standards, internationalisation, and the discursive construction of 'The international student'. *Higher Education Research and Development* 22 (2), 155–66.

Dewey, J. 1910. *How we Think*. [reprint; no date or publisher]. Boston, MA: D. C. Heath & Co.

Dewey. J. 1997. *Experience and Education* [Touchstone ed.; 1st ed. 1938]. New York: Touchstone.

Dewey, J. 2011. *Democracy and Education* [Simon & Brown ed.; 1st ed. 1916]. [No place]: Simon & Brown.

Dimova, S. 2017. Life after oral English certification: The consequences of the test for oral English proficiency for academic staff for EMI lecturers. *English for Specific Purposes* 46, 45–58.

Divan. A., Bowman, M., and Seabourne, A. 2015. Reducing unintentional plagiarism amongst international students in the biological sciences: An embedded academic writing development programme. *Journal of Further and Higher Education* 39 (3), 358–78.

Dobbins, M., and Kwiek, M. 2017. Europeanisation and globalisation in higher education in Central and Eastern Europe: 25 years of changes revisited (1990–2015). *European Educational Research Journal* 16 (5), 519–28.

Doherty, C., and Singh, P. 2005. How the West is done: Simulating Western pedagogy in a curriculum for Asian international students. In P. Ninnes and M. Hellstén (eds), *Internationalizing Higher Education: Critical Explorations of Pedagogy and Policy*, 53–73. Dordrecht: Springer.

Doiz, A., Lasagabaster, D., and Sierra, J. 2013. Future challenges for English-medium instruction at the tertiary level. In A. Doiz, D. Lasagabaster, and J. Sierra (eds), *English-Medium Instruction at Universities: Global Challenges*, 213–21. Clevedon: Multilingual Matters.

Doiz, A., Lasagabaster, D., and Sierra, J. 2014. Language friction and multilingual policies in higher education: The stakeholders' view. *Journal of Multilingual and Multicultural Development* 35 (4), 345–60.

Douglas, J. (ed.). 2016. *The New Flagship University: Changing the Paradigm from Global Ranking to National Relevancy*. London: Palgrave Macmillan.

Duong, V. A., and Chua, C. S. K. 2016. English as a symbol of internationalization in higher education: A case study of Vietnam. *Higher Education Research and Development* 35 (4), 669–83.

Eaves, M. 2011. The relevance of learning styles for international pedagogy in higher education. *Teachers and Teaching* 17 (6), 677–91.

Edwards, R., and Usher, R. 2008. *Globalisation and Pedagogy* [2nd ed.; 1st ed. 2000]. London and New York: Routledge.

Egege, S., and Kutileh, S. 2004. Critical thinking: Teaching foreign notions to foreign students. *International Education Journal* 4 (4), 75–85.

Elliot, C., and Reynolds, M. 2014. Participative pedagogies, group work and the international classroom: An account of students' and tutors' experiences. *Studies in Higher Education* 39 (2), 307–20.

Fahey, J., and Kenway, J. 2010. International academic mobility: Problematic and possible paradigms. *Discourse: Studies in the Cultural Politics of Education* 31 (5), 563–75.

Faist, T. 2009. Diversity – a new mode of incorporation? *Ethnic and Racial Studies* 32 (1), 171–90.

Feng, H., Beckett, G., and Huang, D. 2013. From 'import' to 'import-export' oriented internationalization: The impact of national policy on scholarly publication in China. *Language Policy* 12, 251–72.

Fenwick, T., and Edwards, R. 2014. Networks of knowledge, matters of learning and criticality in higher education. *Higher Education* 67 (1), 35–50.

Forstorp, P.-A., and Mellström, U. 2013. Eduscapes: Interpreting transnational flows of higher education. *Globalisation, Societies and Education* 11 (3), 335–58.

French, A. 2018. 'Fail better': Reconsidering the role of struggle and failure in academic writing development in higher education. *Innovations in Education and Teaching International* 55 (4), 408–16.

Friedman, J. 2018. Everyday nationalism and elite research universities in the USA and England. *Higher Education* 76, 247–61.

Galaz-Fontes, J., Arimoto, A., Teichler, U., and Brennan, J. 2016. Demographics, career and academic self-understanding: A comparative view. In J. Galaz-Fontes, A. Arimoto, U. Teichler, and J. Brennan (eds), *Biographies and Careers throughout Academic Life*, 317–40. Dordrecht: Springer.

Galaz-Fontes, J., and Metcalfe, A. 2015. Changing biographies and careers of academics. In U. Teichler and W. K. Cummings (eds), *Forming, Recruiting and Managing the Academic Profession*, 23–50. Dordrecht: Springer.

Gallagher, T. 2018. Promoting the civic and democratic role of higher education: The next challenge for the EHEA? In A. Curaj, L. Deca, and R. Pricopie (eds), *European Higher Education Area: The Impact of Past and Future Policies*, 335–44. Dordrecht: Springer.

Geerlings, L., and Lundberg, A. 2018. Global discourses and power/knowledge: Theoretical reflections on futures of higher education during the rise of Asia. *Asia Pacific Journal of Education* 38 (2), 229–40.

Gerholm, T. 1990. On tacit knowledge in Academia. *European Journal of Education* 25 (3), 263–71.

Giddens, A. 1990. *The Consequences of Modernity*. Cambridge: Polity Press.

Gilbert, N. G., and Mulkay, M. 1984. *Opening Pandora's Box: A Sociological Analysis of Scientists' Discourse*. Cambridge: Cambridge University Press.

Gimenez, J., and Morgan, W. 2014. Academics across borders: Narratives of linguistic capital, language competence and communication strategies. *Globalisation, Societies and Education* 15 (1), 68–95.

Glaser, B., and Strauss, A. 2008. *The Discovery of Grounded Theory: Strategies for Qualitative Research* [Rev. ed.; 1st ed. 1967]. New Brunswick, NJ, and London: Aldline Transaction.

Goastellec, G., and Pekari, N. 2013. The internationalisation of academic markets, careers and professions. In U. Teichler and E. A. Höhle (eds), *The Work Situation of the Academic Profession in Europe: Findings of a Survey in Twelve Countries*, 229–48. Dordrecht: Springer.

Graves, R., and White, S. 2016. Undergraduate assignments and essay exams. In K. Hyland and P. Shaw (eds), *The Routledge Handbook of English for Academic Purposes*, 297–308. London and New York: Routledge.

Green, W. 2007. Write on or write off? An exploration of Asian international students' approaches to essay writing at an Australian university. *Higher Education Research and Development* 26 (3), 329–44.

Gregersen, F., O. Josephson, G. Kristoffersen, J. Östman, A. Holmen, and M. Londen 2017. *More Parallel, Please: Sprogbrug i internationaliseringsprocesser* [Language usage in internationalisation processes]. Report submitted to the Nordic Council of Ministers. Available online at http://sprogkoordinationen.org/media/1461/afslutningsrapport-final-paralellsproglighed.pdf [accessed March 25 2018].

Gregson, N., Simonsen, K., and Vaiou, D. 2003. Writing (across) Europe: On writing spaces and writing practices. *European Urban and Regional Studies* 10, 1, 5–22.

Grenfell, M., and James, D. 2004. Change in the field – changing the field: Bourdieu and the methodological practice of educational research. *British Journal of Sociology of Education* 24 (4), 507–23.

Grootenboer, P., Edwards-Groves, C., and Choy, S. 2017. Practice theory and education: Diversity and contestation. In P. Grootenboer, C. Edwards-Groves, and S. Choy (eds), *Practice Theory Perspectives on Pedagogy and Education*, 1–21. Dordrecht and Singapore: Springer.

Guerin, C., and Green, I. 2016. Cultural diversity and the imagined community of the global academy. *Asia Pacific Journal of Education* 36, 1–12.

Gunter, A., and Raghuram, P. 2018. International study in the global south: Linking institutional staff, student and knowledge mobilities. *Globalisation, Societies and Education* 16 (2), 192–207.

Gutiérrez, K., and Rogoff, B. 2003. Cultural ways of learning: Individual traits or repertoires of practice. *Educational Researcher* 32 (5), 19–25.

Haigh, M. 2002. Internationalisation of the Curriculum: Designing inclusive education for a small world. *Journal of Geography in Higher Education* 26 (1), 49–66.

Haigh, M. 2009. Fostering cross-cultural empathy with non-Western curricular structures. *Journal of Studies in International Education* 13 (2), 271–84.

Halkier, B., and Jensen, I. 2008. Det sociale som perfomativitet – et praktisteoretisk perspektiv på analyse og metode [The social as performativity – a practice theoretical perspective on analysis and method]. *Dansk Sociologi* 19 (3), 50–68.

Halualani, R. 2008. How do multicultural university students define and make sense of intercultural contact? A qualitative study. *International Journal of Intercultural Studies* 32, 1–16.

Halualani, R., Chitgopekar, A, Morrison, J., and Dodge, P. 2004. Who's interacting? And what are they talking about? Intercultural contact and interaction among multicultural university students. *International Journal of Intercultural Relations* 28, 353–72.

Hammerslev, O., and Hansen, J. A. 2009. Indledning: Bourdieus refleksive sociologi i praksis [Introduction: Bourdieu's reflexive sociology in practice]. In O. Hammerslev, J. A. Hansen, and I. Willig (eds), *Refleksiv sociologi i praksis* [Reflexive sociology in practice], 11–33. Copenhagen: Hans Reitzels Forlag.

Hammond, C. 2016. Internationalization, nationalism and global competitiveness: A comparison of approaches to higher education in China and Japan. *Asia Pacific Educational Review* 17, 555–66.

Hardy, C. 2008. Hysteresis. In M. Greenfell (ed.), *Pierre Bourdieu: Key Concepts*, 131–48. Stocksfield: Acumen.

Harrison, N. 2015. Practice, problems and power in 'internationalisation at home': Critical reflections on recent research evidence. *Teaching in Higher Education* 20 (4), 412–30.

Harrison, N., and Peacock, N. 2010. Cultural distance, mindfulness and passive xenophobia: Using integrated threat theory to explore home higher education students' perspectives on 'internationalisation at home'. *British Educational Research Journal* 36 (6), 877–902.

Harvey, D. 1989. *The Conditions of Postmodernity*. Oxford: Basil Blackwell.

Hazelkorn, E. 2018. The accountability and transparency agenda: Emerging issues in the global era. In A. Curaj, L. Deca, and R. Pricopie (eds), *European Higher Education Area: The Impact of Past and Future Policies*, 423–39. Dordrecht: Springer.

Healey, N. 2008. Is higher education *really* 'internationalising'? *Higher Education* 55, 333–55.

Healey, N., and Michael, L. 2015. Towards a new framework for analysing transnational education. *Higher Education Policy* 28, 369–91.

Hébert, C. 2015. Knowing and/or experiencing: A critical examination of the reflective models of John Dewey and Donald Schön. *Reflective Practice* 16 (3), 361–71.

Heng, T. 2017. Voices of Chinese international students in USA colleges: 'I want to tell them that …' *Studies in Higher Education*, 42 (5), 833–50.

Hirvela. A. 2016. Academic reading into writing. In K. Hyland and P. Shaw (eds), *The Routledge Handbook of English for Academic Purposes*, 127–38. London and New York: Routledge.

Hodkinson, P., Biesta, G., and James, D. 2007. Learning cultures and a cultural theory of learning. In D. James and G. Biesta (eds), *Improving Learning Cultures in Further Education*, 21–37. London and New York: Routledge.

Hook, A. 1975. *Scotland and America: A Study of Cultural Relations 1750–1835*. Glasgow and London: Blackie & Son.

Howitt, R. 2002. Scale and the other: Levinas and geography. *Geoforum* 33, 299–313.

Hudzik. J. K. 2015. *Comprehensive Internationalization: Institutional Pathways to Success*. London and New York: Routledge.

Hult, F., and Källkvist, M. 2016. Global flows in local language planning: Articulating parallel language use in Swedish university policies. *Current Issues in Language Planning* 17 (1), 56–71.

Hultgren, A. 2013. *Parallelsproglighed på danske universiteter: En statusrapport* 2013 [Parallel language usage at Danish universities: A status report 2013]. Copenhagen: Centre for Internationalisation and Parallel Language Usage, Copenhagen University.

Hultgren, A. 2014. Whose parallellingualism? Overt and covert ideologies in Danish university language policies. *Multilingua* 33 (1–2), 61–87.

Hultgren. A., and Thøgersen. J. 2014. Englishization of Nordic universities: Policy and practice – a disconnect. *Language Problems and Language Planning* 38 (3), 447–64.

Huxham, R., and Land, R. 2000. Assigning students in group work projects: Can we do better than random? *Innovations in Education and Teaching International* 37 (1), 17–22.

Hyland, K. 2000. *Disciplinary Discourses: Social Interactions in Academic Writing*. Harlow: Pearson Education.

Hyland, K. 2012. *Disciplinary Identities: Individuality and Community in Academic Discourse*. Cambridge: Cambridge University Press.

Inghilleri, M. 2014. Bourdieu's *habitus* and Dewey's *habits:* Complementary views of the social? In G. Vorderobermeier (ed.), *Remapping Habitus in Translation Studies*, 185–201. Amsterdam: Rodopi.

Ippoloti, K. 2007. Promoting intercultural learning in a multicultural university: Ideals and realities. *Teaching in Higher Education* 12 (5/6), 749–63.

Jenkins, J. 2011. Accommodating (to) ELF in the international university. *Journal of Pragmatics* 43, 926–36.

Jenkins, R. 2002. *Pierre Bourdieu* [Rev. ed.; 1st ed. 1992]. London and New York: Routledge.

Johnson, E. 2008. An investigation into pedagogical challenges facing international tertiary-level students in New Zealand. *Higher Education Research and Development* 27 (3), 231–43.

Johnston, R. J. 1996. Academic tribes, disciplinary containers, and the realpolitik of opening up the social sciences. *Environment and Planning* 28, 1943–47.

Jones, E., and Brown, S. (eds). 2007. *Internationalizing Higher Education*. London and New York: Routledge.

Jöns, H. 2011. Transnational academic mobility and gender. *Globalisation, Societies and Education* 9 (2), 183–209.

Jöns, H. 2007. Transnational mobility and the spaces of knowledge production: A comparison of global patterns, motivations and collaborations in different academic fields. *Social Geography* 2, 97–114.

Jöns, H., and Hoyler, M. 2013. Global geographies of higher education: The perspective of the world university rankings. *Geoforum* 46, 45–59.

Jordan, L., Bovill, C., Othman, S., Saleh, A., Shabila, N., and Watters, N. 2014. Is student-centred learning a Western concept? Lessons from an academic

development programme to support student-centred learning in Iraq. *Teaching in Higher Education* 19 (1), 13–25.
Joseph, C. 2008. Difference, subjectivities and power: (De)colonizing practices in internationalizing the curriculum. *International Education* 19 (1), 29–39.
Kahn, H., and Agnew, M. 2017. Global learning through difference: Considerations for teaching, learning, and the internationalization of higher education. *Journal of Studies in International Education* 21 (1), 52–64.
Kane, T. 2014. Whose lingua franca? The politics of language in transnational medical education. *Journal of General Education: A Curricular Commons of the Humanities and Sciences* 63 (2/3), 94–112.
Kaposi, D., and Dell, P. 2012. Discourses of plagiarism: Moralist, proceduralist, development and inter-textual approaches. *British Journal of Sociology of Education* 33 (6), 813–30.
Kastberg, P., and Tange, H. 2014. Discursive constructions of international education: How university lecturers 'talk' about international students. *Hermes* 53, 43–55.
Kauppinen, I. 2015. Towards a theory of transnational capitalism. *British Journal of Sociology of Education* 36 (2), 336–53.
Kemmis, S. 2009. Action research as a practice-based practice. *Educational Action Research* 17 (3), 463–74.
Kemmis, S., and Mahon, K. 2017. Practice architectures of university education. In P. Grootenboer, C. Edwards-Groves, and S. Choy (eds), *Practice Theory Perspectives on Pedagogy and Education*, 107–41. Dordrecht and Singapore: Springer.
Kenway, J., and Fahey, J. 2009. Imagining research otherwise. In J. Kenway and J. Fahey (eds), *Globalizing the Research Imagination*, 1–40. London and New York: Routledge.
Keuk, C. N., and Tith, M. 2013. The enactment of English-medium instruction (EMI) undergraduate program in Cambodia: Students' voices. *International Journal of Innovation in English Language Teaching and Research* 2 (2), 159–75.
Kling, J., and Stæhr, L. 2011. Certificering af universitetsunderviseres engelsksproglige kompetencer [Certification of university teachers' English language competences]. *Sprogforum* 52, 46–53.
Killick, D. 2017. *Internationalization and Diversity in Higher Education: Implications for Teaching, Learning and Assessment.* London and New York: Palgrave Macmillan.
Killick, D. 2015. *Developing the Global Student: Higher Education in an Era of Globalization.* London and New York: Routledge.
Kim, S. 2016. Western faculty 'flight risk' at a Korean university and the complexities of internationalisation in Asian higher education. *Comparative Education* 52 (1), 78–90.
Kim, T. 2010. Transnational academic mobility, knowledge, and identity capital. *Discourse: Studies in the Cultural Politics of Education* 31 (5), 577–91.
Kim, T. 2014. The intellect, mobility and epistemic positioning in doing comparisons and comparative education. *Comparative Education* 50 (1), 58–72.
Kim, T. 2017. Academic mobility, transnational identity capital, and stratification under conditions of academic capitalism. *Higher Education* 73, 981–97.
Kimmel, K., and Volet, S. 2012. Understanding motivation, engagement and experiences of intercultural interactions at university: A person-in-multiple contexts perspective. *European Journal of Psychology Education* 27, 227–45.

Knight, J. 2011. Education hubs: A fad, a brand, an innovation? *Journal of Studies in International Education* 15 (3), 221–40.

Knight, J. 2015. International universities: Misunderstandings and emerging models? *Journal of Studies in International Education* 19 (2), 107–21.

Knight, J. 2017. The changing landscape of higher education internationalisation – for better or worse? In D. Law and M. Hoey (eds), *Perspectives on the Internationalisation of Higher Education*, 13–19. London and New York: Routledge.

Krogh, L. 2017. Assessment of students – a look at validity in emotional situations. In T. Chemi, S. Davy, and B. Lund (eds), *Innovative Pedagogy: A Recognition of Emotion and Creativity in Education*, 71–89. Rotterdam: Brill/Sense.

Land, R. 2014. Crossing tribal boundaries: Interdisciplinarity as a threshold concept. In P. Trowler, M. Saunders, and V. Bamber (eds), *Tribes and Territories in the 21st Century: Rethinking the Significance of Disciplines in Higher Education*, 175–85. London and New York: Routledge.

Larsen, M. 2016. *Internationalization of Higher Education*. New York: Palgrave Macmillan.

Larsen, M., and Beech, J. 2014. Spatial theorizing in comparative and international education research. *Comparative Education Review* 58 (2), 191–214.

Lasagabaster, D. 2015. Language policy and language choice at European universities: Is there really a 'choice'? *European Journal of Applied Linguistics* 3 (2), 255–76.

Lea, M., and Street, B. 2006. The 'academic literacies' model: Theory and applications. *Theory into Practice* 45 (4), 368–77.

Lea, M., and Street, B. 1998. Student writing in higher education: An academic literacies approach. *Studies in Higher Education* 23 (2), 157–72.

Leask, B. 2015. *Internationalizing the Curriculum*. London and New York: Routledge.

Leask, B., and Bridge, C. 2013. Comparing internationalisation of the curriculum in action across disciplines: theoretical and practical perspectives. *Compare: A Journal of Comparative and International Education* 43 (1), 79–101.

Leask, B., Beelen, J., and Kaunda, L. 2013. Internationalisation of the curriculum in action across disciplines: International approaches and perspectives. In H. de Wit, F. Hunter, L. Johnson, and H. van Liempd (eds), *Possible Futures: The Next 25 Years of the Internationalization of Higher Education*, 187–203. Amsterdam: European Association of International Education.

Ledwith, S., and Seymour, D. 2001. Home and away: Preparing students for multicultural management. *International Journal of Human Resource Management* 12 (8), 1292–1312.

Leemann, R. 2010. Gender inequalities in transnational academic mobility and the ideal type of the academic entrepreneur. *Discourse: Studies in the Cultural Politics of Education* 31 (5), 605–25.

Lefebvre, H. 1991. *The Production of Space* [Eng. ed.; 1st ed. 1974]. Oxford and Cambridge, MA: Blackwell.

Leitner, H., and Sheppard, E. 2009. The spatiality of contentious politics: More than a politics of scale. In R. Kiel and R. Mahon (eds), *Leviathan Undone? Towards a Political Economy of Scale*, 231–46. Vancouver: UBC Press.

Levin, M., and Greenwood, D. 2011. Revitalizing universities by inventing the social sciences: Bildung and *Action research*. In N. Denzin and Y. Lincoln (eds), *The Sage Handbook of Qualitative Research* [4th ed.], 27–42. Los Angeles, CA: Sage.

Lewthwaite, M. 1996. A study of international students' perspectives on cross-cultural adaptation. *International Journal for the Advancement of Counselling* 19, 167–85.

Lillis, T., and Tuck, J. 2016. Academic literacies: A critical lens on writing and reading in the academy. In K. Hyland and P. Shaw (eds), *The Routledge Handbook of English for Academic Purposes*, 30–43. London and New York: Routledge.
Ljosland, R. 2004. 'Engelsk, selvfølgelig!' Språklig sosialisering blant doktorgradsstipendiater [English, of course! Linguistic socialisation among doctoral students]. In D. Simonsen (ed.), *Språk i kunnskabssamfunnet. Engelsk – elitenes nye latin?* [Languages in the knowledge society. English – the elite's new Latin?], 137–46. Oslo: Gyldendal Akademisk.
Ljosland, R. 2007. English in Norwegian academia: A step towards disglossia? *World Englishes* 26 (4), 395–410.
Lueg, K., and Lueg, R. 2015. Why do students choose English as a medium of instruction? A Bourdieusian perspective on the study strategies of non-native speakers. *Academy of Management Learning and Education* 14 (1), 5–30.
Ma, J., and Wen, Q. 2018. Understanding international students' in-class learning experiences in Chinese higher education institutions. *Higher Education Research and Development* 37 (6), 1186–1200.
MacKinnon, D., and Manathunga, C. 2003. Going global with assessment: What to do when the dominant culture's legacy drives assessment. *Higher Research Education and Development* 22 (2), 131–44.
MacLellan, E. 2015. Updating understandings of 'teaching': Taking account of learners' and teachers' beliefs. *Teaching in Higher Education* 20 (2), 171–82.
Madge, C., Raghuram, P., and Noxolo, P. 2015. Conceptualizing international education: From international student to international study. *Progress in Human Geography* 39 (6), 681–701.
Mahon, R., and Keil, R. 2009. Introduction. In R. Kiel and R. Mahon (eds), *Leviathan Undone? Towards a Political Economy of Scale*, 3–23. Vancouver: UBC Press.
Manathunga, C., and Brew, A. 2014. Beyond tribes and territories: New metaphors for new times. In P. Trowler, M. Saunders, and V. Bamber (eds), *Tribes and Territories in the 21st Century: Rethinking the Significance of Disciplines in Higher Education*, 44–56. London and New York: Routledge.
Mangan, A., Kelemen, M., and Moffat, S. 2016. Animating the classroom: Pedagogical responses to internationalisation. *Management Learning* 47 (3), 285–304.
Marginson, S. 2008. Global field and global imagining: Bourdieu and worldwide higher education. *British Journal of Sociology of Education* 29 (3), 303–15.
Marginson, S., and Rhoades, G. 2002. Beyond national states, markets, and systems of higher education: A glonacal agency heuristic. *Higher Education* 43, 281–309.
Marginson, S., and Sawir, E. 2005. Interrogating global flows in higher education. *Globalisation, Societies and Education* 3 (3), 281–309.
Marginson, S., and Sawir, E. 2011. *Ideas for Intercultural Education*. New York: Palgrave Macmillan.
Marston, S., Jones, J., and Woodward, K. 2005. Human geography without scale. *Transactions of the Institute of British Geographers* 30 (4), 416–32.
McKie, A. 2019. International students and cheating: How worried should we be? *Times Higher Education,* March 20. Available online at: www.timeshighereducation.com/news/international-students-and-cheating-how-worried-should-we-be [accessed March 2019]
McPherson, M., Smith-Lovin, L., and Cook, J. 2001. Birds of a feather: Homophily in social networks. *Annual Review of Sociology* 27, 415–44.
Meriläinen, S., Tienari, J., Thomas, R., and Davies, A. 2008. Hegemonic academic practices: Experiences of publishing from the periphery. *Organization* 15, 584–97.

Metcalfe, A. 2017. Nomadic political ontology and transnational academic mobility. *Critical Studies in Education* 58 (2), 131–49.

Meyer, J., and Land, R. 2005. Threshold concepts and troublesome knowledge (2): Epistemological considerations and a conceptual framework for teaching and learning. *Higher Education* 49, 373–88.

Meyer, J., and Land, R. 2006a. Threshold concepts and troublesome knowledge: Issues of liminality. In J. Meyer and R. Land (eds), *Overcoming Barriers to Student Understanding: Threshold Concepts and Troublesome Knowledge*, 19–32. London and New York: Routledge.

Meyer, J., and Land, R. 2006b. Threshold concepts and troublesome knowledge: An introduction. In J. Meyer and R. Land (eds.), *Overcoming Barriers to Student Understanding: Threshold Concepts and Troublesome Knowledge*, 3–18. London and New York: Routledge.

Mills, D., and Huber, M. 2005. Anthropology and the educational 'trading zone': Disciplinarity, pedagogy and professionalism. *Arts and Humanities in Higher Education* 4 (1), 9–32.

Mitzi, R. 2017. Bridging borders: Toward a pedagogy of preparedness for visiting faculty. *Journal of Studies in International Education* 21 (3), 246–60.

Moore, P., and Hampton, G. 2015. 'It's a bit of a generalisation, but …': Participant perspectives on intercultural group assessment in higher education. *Assessment and Evaluation in Higher Education* 40 (3), 390–406.

Morley, L., et al. 2018. Internationalisation and migrant academics: The hidden narratives of mobility. *Higher Education* 76, 537–54.

Mortensen, J., and Haberland, H. 2012. English – the new Latin of academia? Danish universities as a case. *International Journal for the Sociology of Language* 216, 175–97.

Munk, M. 2009. Transnational investments in informational capital: A comparative study of Denmark, France and Sweden. *Acta Sociologica* 52 (1), 5–23.

Murray, N., and McConachy, T. 2018. 'Participation' in the internationalized higher education classroom: An academic staff perspective. *Journal of International and Intercultural Communication* 11 (3), 254–70.

Nicolini, D. 2012. *Practice Theory, Work, and Organization*. Oxford: Oxford University Press.

Nikunen, M., and Lempiäinen, K. 2020. Gendered strategies for mobility and academic career. *Gender and Education* 32 (4), 554–71.

Nilsson, B. 2003. Internationalisation at home from a Swedish perspective: The case of Malmö. *Journal of Studies in International Education* 7 (1), 27–40.

Neumann, H., Padden, N., and McDonough, K. 2019. Beyond English proficiency scores: Understanding the academic performance of international undergraduate students during the first year of study. *Higher Education Research and Development* 38 (2), 324–38.

Oberg, K. 1960. Culture shock: Adjustment to new cultural environments. *Practical Anthropology* 7, 177–82.

Okech, J., Pimpleton-Gray, A., Vannatta, R., and Champe, J. 2016. Intercultural conflict in groups. *Journal for Specialists in Group Work* 41 (4), 350–69.

Oliver, R., Vanderford, S., and Grote, E. 2012. Evidence of English language proficiency and academic achievement of non-English speaking background students. *Higher Education Research and Development* 31 (4), 541–55.

Otten, M. 2009. *Academicus interculturalis?* Negotiating interculturality in academic communities of practice. *Intercultural Education* 20 (5), 407–17.

Pedersen, A. 2015. Sådan konstruerer man et Massive Open Online Course (MOOC) på Coursera. [How to design a Massive Open Online Course (MOOC) on Coursera]. In L. Rienecker and P. Jørgensen (eds), *Universitetspædagogiske praksisser* [University pedagogy practices], 177–93. Frederiksberg: Samfundslitteratur.

Peelo, M., and Luzon, T. 2007. Designing embedded courses to support international cultural and academic adjustment in the UK. *Journal of Further and Higher Education* 31 (1), 65–76.

Pennycook, A. 2017. *The Cultural Politics of English as an International Language* [2nd ed.; 1st ed. 1994]. London and New York: Routledge.

Perkins, D. 1999. The many faces of constructivism. *Educational Leadership* 57 (39), 6–11.

Phillipson, R. 2006. English, a cuckoo in the European higher education nest of languages? *European Journal of English Studies* 10 (1), 13–32.

Popov, V., Brinkman, D., Biemans, H., Mulder, M., Kuznetsov, A., and Noroozi, O. 2012 Multicultural student group work in higher education: An explorative case study on challenges as perceived by students. *International Journal of Intercultural Relations* 36, 302–17.

Preisler, B. 2014. Lecturing in one's first language or in English as a lingua franca: The communication of authenticity. *Acta Linguistica Hafniensia* 46 (2), 218–42.

Primeri, E., and Reale, E. 2012. How Europe shapes academic research: Insights from participation in European Union framework programmes. *European Journal of Education*, 47 (1), 104–21.

Qiang, Z. 2003. Internationalization of higher education: Towards a conceptual framework. *Policy Futures in Education* 1 (2), 248–70.

Rata, E. 2012. The politics of knowledge in education. *British Educational Research Journal* 38 (1), 103–24.

Reckwitz, A. 2002. Towards a theory of social practices: A development in culturalist theorizing. *European Journal of Social Theory* 5, 243–63.

Redden, E. 2017. Survey of international students asks what they'd like their professors to improve. *Inside Higher Ed.* Downloaded from www.insidehighered.com/news/2017/02/24/survey-international-students-asks-what-theyd-their-professors-improve [accessed March 2017].

Reid, R., and Garson, K. 2017. Rethinking multicultural group work as intercultural learning. *Journal of Studies in International Education* 21 (3), 195–212.

Richards, C. 2019. Higher education privatisation, internationalisation and marketization: Singaporean versus Malaysian models of Asian education hub policy. *Compare: A Journal of Comparative and International Education* 49 (3), 375–92.

Richardson, J. 2009. Geographic flexibility in academia: A cautionary note. *British Journal of Management* 20, 160–70.

Risager, K. 2006. *Language and Culture: Global Flows and Local Complexity*. Clevedon: Multilingual Matters.

Rizvi, F. 2007. Postcolonialism and globalization in education. *Cultural Studies: Critical Methodologies* 7 (3), 256–63.

Robertson, S. 2010. Critical response to Special Section: International academic mobility. *Discourse: Studies in the Cultural Politics of Education* 31 (5), 641–7.

Robertson, S., and Dale, R. 2015. Towards a 'critical cultural political economy' account of the globalising of education. *Globalisation, Societies and Education* 13 (1), 149–70.

Rose, H., and McKinley, J. 2018. Japan's English-medium instruction initiatives and the globalization of higher education. *Higher Education* 75, 111–29.

Ross, J. 2019. Universities 'complicit' in tarnishing of internationalisation. *Times Higher Education,* November 1.

Rostan, M. 2015. International aspects of academic work and career at the beginning of the twenty-first century. In U. Teichler and W. K. Cummings (eds), *Forming, Recruiting and Managing the Academic Profession*, 241–58. Dordrecht: Springer.

Rostan, M., and Ceravolo, F. 2015. The internationalisation of the academy: Convergence and divergence across disciplines. *European Review* 23 (1), 338–54.

Ryan, J. 2011. Teaching and learning for international students: Towards a transcultural approach. *Teachers and Teaching* 17 (6), 631–48.

Ryan, J., and Viete, R. 2009. Respectful interactions: Learning with international students in the English-speaking academy. *Teaching in Higher Education* 14 (3), 303–14.

Saarinen, T. 2012. Internationalization of Finnish higher education – is language an issue? *International Journal for the Sociology of Language* 216, 157–73.

Sälo, L. 2017. *The Sociolinguistics of Academic Publishing: Language and the Practices of Homo Academicus.* Cham: Palgrave Macmillan.

Saltmarsh, S., and Swirski, T. 2010. 'Pawns and prawns': International academics' observations on their transition to working in an Australian University. *Journal of Higher Education Policy and Management* 32 (3), 291–301.

Samuelowicz, K., and Bain, J. 2001. Revisiting academics' beliefs about teaching and learning. *Higher Education* 41, 299–325.

Sanderson, G. 2008. A foundation for the internationalization of the academic self. *Journal of Studies in International Education* 12 (3), 276–307.

Sandström, A., and Neghina, C. 2017. *English-Taught Bachelor's Programmes: Internationalising European Higher Education*. Amsterdam: European Association for International Education.

Saunders, M. 2014. Imperatives for academic practices: Catalysts for sustained change. In P. Trowler, M. Saunders, and V. Bamber (eds), *Tribes and Territories in the 21st century: Rethinking the Significance of Disciplines in Higher Education*, 169–74. London and New York: Routledge.

Savin-Baden, M. 2006. Disjunction as a form of troublesome knowledge in problem-based learning. In J. Meyer and R. Land (eds), *Overcoming Barriers to Student Understanding: Threshold Concepts and Troublesome Knowledge*, 160–72. London and New York: Routledge.

Schapper, J., and Mayson, S. 2005. Managerialism, internationalization, Taylorization and the deskilling of academic work: Evidence from an Australian university. In P. Ninnes and M. Hellstén (eds), *Internationalizing Higher Education: Critical Explorations of Pedagogy and Policy*, 181–97. Dordrecht: Springer.

Schatzki, T. 1996. *Social Practices: A Wittgensteinian Approach to Human Activity and the Social*. Cambridge: Cambridge University Press.

Schatzki, T. 2001. Practice-minded orders. In T. Schatzki, K. Knorr Cetina, and E. von Savigny, *The Practice Turn in Contemporary Theory,* 42–55. London and New York. Routledge.

Schatzki, T. 2002. *The Site of the Social: A Philosophical Account of the Constitution of Social Life and Change*. University Park, PA: Pennsylvania University Press.

Schatzki, T. 2005. The sites of organizations. *Organization Studies* 26 (3), 465–84.

Schatzki, T. 2017. Practices and learning. In P. Grootenboer, C. Edwards-Groves, and S. Choy (eds), *Practice Theory Perspectives on Pedagogy and Education*, 23–43. Dordrecht and Singapore: Springer.

Schatzki, T., Knorr Cetina, K., and von Savigny, E. (eds). 2001. *The Practice Turn in Contemporary Theory*. London and New York: Routledge.

Shaheen, N. 2016. International students' critical thinking-related problem areas: UK university teachers' perspectives. *Journal of Research in International Education* 15 (1), 18–31.

Sheridan, V. 2011. A holistic approach to international students, institutional habitus and academic literacies in an Irish third level institution. *Higher Education* 62, 129–40.

Shohamy, E. 2013. A critical perspective on the use of English as a medium at universities. In A. Doiz, D. Lasagabaster, and J. Sierra (eds), *English-Medium Instruction: Global Challenges*, 196–210. Bristol: Multilingual Matters.

Siiner, M. 2016. University administrators as forced language policy agents. An institutional ethnography of parallel language strategy and practices at the University of Copenhagen. *Current Issues in Language Planning* 17 (3/4), 441–58.

Simpson, B. 2009. Pragmaticism, Mead and the practice turn. *Organization Studies* 30 (12), 1329–47.

Singh. M. 2005. Enabling transnational learning communities: Policies, pedagogies and politics of educational power. In P. Ninnes and M. Hellstén (eds), *Internationalizing Higher Education: Critical Explorations of Pedagogy and Policy*, 9–36. Dordrecht: Springer.

Singh, M., and Meng, H. 2013. Democratising western research using non-western theories: Rancière and mute Chinese theoretical tools. *Studies in Higher Education* 38 (6), 907–20.

Singh, M., and Shrestha, M. 2008. International pedagogical structures: Admittance into the community of scholars via a strategy of double knowing. In M. Hellstén and A. Reid (eds), *Researching International Pedagogies,* 65–82. Dordrecht: Springer.

Song, X., and McCarthy, G. 2018. Governing Asian international students: The policy and practice of essentialising 'critical thinking'. *Globalisation, Societies and Education* 16 (3), 353–65.

Spencer-Oatey, H., and Dauber, D. 2017. The gains and pains of mixed national group work at university. *Journal of Multilingual and Multicultural Development* 38 (3), 219–36.

Spiro, J. 2014. Learning interconnectedness: Internationalisation through engagement with one another. *Higher Education Quarterly* 68 (1), 65–84.

Spradley, J. 1979. *The Ethnographic Interview*. Fort Worth, TX: Harcourt Brace Jovanovich College Publishers.

Stephan, W., and Stephan, C. 2000. An integrated threat theory of prejudice. In S. Oskamp (ed.), *Reducing Prejudice and Discrimination,* 23–46. Mahwah, NJ: Lawrence Erlbaum Associates.

Stott, P., and Sullivan, S. (eds). 2000. *Political Ecology: Science, Myth and Power*. London: Edward Arnold.

Straker, J. 2016. International student participation in higher education: Changing the focus from 'international students' to 'participation'. *Journal of Studies in International Education* 20 (4), 299–318.

Strauss, P., U-Mackey, A., and Young, S. 2011. 'I know the type of people I work well with': Student anxiety in multicultural group projects. *Studies in Higher Education* 36 (7), 815–29.

Strauss, P., U-Mackey, A., and Crothers, C. 2014. 'They drag my marks down!' – challenges faced by lecturers in the allocation of marks for multicultural group projects. *Intercultural Education* 25 (3), 229–41.

Swartz, D. 1997. *Culture and Power: The Sociology of Pierre Bourdieu*. Chicago, IL, and London: University of Chicago Press.

Sweeney, A., Weaven, S., and Herington, C.2008. Multicultural influences on group learning: A qualitative higher education study. *Assessment and Evaluation in Higher Education* 33 (2), 119–32.

Tange, H. 2008. Intercultural education as intercultural learning. In M. Hellstén and A. Reid (eds), *Research International Pedagogies,* 99–114.Dordrech: Springer.

Tange, H. 2010. Caught in the Tower of Babel: University lecturers' experiences with internationalisation. *Language and Intercultural Communication* 10 (2), 137–49.

Tange, H. 2012a. Organising language at the international university: Three principles of linguistic organisation. *Journal of Multilingual and Multicultural Development* 33 (3), 287–300.

Tange, H. 2012b. Wars of words: Management policy and employee practice at the international university. *Tamara: Journal of Critical Organizational Inquiry* 10 (4), 5–15.

Tange, H. 2016. Inclusive and exclusive knowledge practices in interdisciplinary, international education. *International Journal of Inclusive Education* 20 (10), 1097–1108.

Tange, H. 2019. Academic staff as 'transition managers' in interdisciplinary, international MA education: A Danish case study. *Learning and Teaching* 12 (2), 44–67.

Tange, H., and Jensen, I. 2012. Good teachers and deviant learners? The meeting of practices in university level international education. *Journal of Research in International Education* 11 (2), 181–93.

Tange, H., and Kastberg, P. 2013. Coming to terms with 'double knowing': An inclusive approach to international education. *International Journal of Inclusive Education* 17 (1), 1–14.

Tange, H., and Millar, S. 2016. Opening the mind? Geographies of knowledge and curricular practices. *Higher Education* 72, 573–87.

Tange, H., and Millar, S. [forthcoming]. Telling texts: Constructing the 'international' in course syllabi in Danish higher education. Book chapter prepared for anthology.

Tange, H., and Wilken, L. [forthcoming]. Grounding global academics? Lecturer positions and dispositions within international research and education. Book chapter prepared for anthology.

Tannock, S. 2018. *Educational Equality and International Students*. London: Palgrave Macmillan.

Taylor, C. 2006. Threshold concepts in Biology: Do they fit the definition? In J. Meyer and R. Land (eds), *Overcoming Barriers to Student Understanding: Threshold Concepts and Troublesome Knowledge*, 89–99. London and New York: Routledge.

Teichler, U. 2017. Internationally mobile academics: Concepts and findings in Europe. *European Journal of Higher Education* 7 (1), 15–28.

Teichler, U. 2016. Mobility and internationality of academics in the Humanities and Social Sciences. *European Review* 24 (2), 253–63.

Thomson, P. 2008. Field. In M. Greenfell (ed.), *Pierre Bourdieu: Key Concepts*, 67–81. Stocksfield: Acumen.

The Australian. 2019. Editorial: Time for unis to cut the cringe. October 14.

Tian, M., and Lowe, J. 2013. The role of feedback in cross-cultural learning: A case study of Chinese taught postgraduate students in a UK university. *Assessment and Evaluation in Higher Education* 38 (5), 580–98.

Tight, M. 2008. Higher education research as tribe, territory and/or community: A co-citation analysis. *Higher Education* 55, 593–605.

Tight, M. 2013. Discipline and methodology in higher education research. *Higher Education Research and Development* 32 (1), 136–51.

Tight, M. 2019. Globalization and internationalization as frameworks for higher education research. *Research Papers in Education* [pre-print online version], 1–23.

Tran, L. 2016. Students' academic, intercultural and personal development in globalised education mobility. In C. Ng and P. Renshaw (eds), *Reforming Learning and Teaching in Asia-Pacific Universities*, 95–113. Dordrecht: Springer.

Tran, L., and Pasura, R. 2019. Teacher interactive and reflexive positionings in accommodating international students: Implications for teacher professional development. *Professional Development in Education* 45 (4), 539–50.

Trenkic, D., and Warmington, M. 2019. Language and literacy skills of home and international university students: How different are they, and does it matter? *Bilingualism: Language and Cognition* 22 (2), 349–65.

Trice, A. 2005. Navigating in a multinational learning community: Academic departments' responses to graduate international students. *Journal of Studies in International Education* 9 (1), 62–89.

Trondal, J. 2010. Two worlds of change: On the internationalisation of universities. *Globalisation, Societies and Education* 8 (3), 351–68.

Trowler, P. 2014a. Disciplines and academic practices. In P. Trowler, M. Saunders, and V. Bamber (eds), *Tribes and Territories in the 21st Century: Rethinking the Significance of Disciplines in Higher Education*, 30–8. London and New York: Routledge.

Trowler, P. 2014b. Disciplines and interdisciplinarity: Conceptual groundwork. In P. Trowler, M. Saunders, and V. Bamber (eds), *Tribes and Territories in the 21st Century: Rethinking the Significance of Disciplines in Higher Education*, 5–29. London and New York: Routledge.

Turner, Y. 2009. 'Knowing me, Knowing you,' Is there nothing we can do? Pedagogic challenges in using group work to create an intercultural learning space. *Journal of Studies in International Education* 13 (2), 240–55.

UNESCO 2018. *UIS Stat*. Online database available at http://data.uis.unesco.org/ [accessed June 2 2019].

Valiente, C. 2008. Are students using the 'wrong' style of learning? *Active Learning in Higher Education* 9 (1), 73–91.

Vandermensbrugghe, J. 2004. The unbearable vagueness of critical thinking in the context of the Anglo-Saxonisation of education. *International Education Journal* 5 (3), 417–22.

Van der Walt, C., and Kidd, M. 2013. Acknowledging academic biliteracy in higher education assessment strategies: A tale of two trials. In A. Doiz, D. Lasagabaster, and J. Sierra (eds), *English-Medium Instruction at Universities: Global Challenges*, 27–43. Clevedon: Multilingual Matters.

Van der Wende, M. 2015. International academic mobility: Towards a concentration of minds in Europe. *European Review* 23 (1), 70–80.

Van der Wende, M. 2017. Opening up: Higher education systems in a global perspective. *Centre for Global Higher Education Working Papers* 22 (June).

Van Heerden, M., Clarence, S., and Bharuthram, S. 2017. What lies beneath: Exploring the deeper purposes of feedback on student writing through considering disciplinary knowledge and knowers. *Assessment and Evaluation in Higher Education* 42 (6), 967–77.

Van Manen, M. 1995. On the epistemology of reflective practice. *Teachers and Teaching: Theory and Practice* 1 (1), 33–50.

Vertovec, S. 2001. Transnationalism and identity. *Journal of Ethnic and Migration Studies* 27 (4), 573–82.

Vinther, J., and Slethaug, G. 2013. The influence of internationalisation and national identity on teaching and assessments in higher education. *Teaching in Higher Education* 18 (7), 797–808.

Volet, S., and Ang, G. 1998. Culturally mixed groups on international campuses: An opportunity for inter-cultural learning. *Higher Education Research and Development* 17 (1), 5–23.

Volet, S., and Jones, C. 2012. Cultural transitions in higher education: Individual adaptation, transformation and engagement. In S. Karabenick and T. Urdan (eds.), *Transitions across Schools and Cultures*, 241–84. Bingley: Emerald Group.

Wächter, B., and Maiworm, F. (eds). 2014. *English-Taught Programmes in European Higher Education: The State of Play in 2014.* Lemmens: ACA Papers on International Cooperation in Education.

Waters, J. 2018. International education is political! Exploring the politics of international student mobilities. *Journal of International Students* 3, 1459–78.

Waters, J. 2007. 'Roundabout routes and sanctuary schools': The role of situated educational practices and habitus in the creation of transnational professionals. *Global Networks* 7 (4), 477–97.

Welch, A. 1997. The peripatetic professor: The internationalisation of the academic profession. *Higher Education* 34, 323–45.

Wenger, E. 1998. *Communities of Practice: Learning, Meaning and Identity.* Cambridge: Cambridge University Press.

White, R., and Jerome, L. 2013. Self-segregating social groups in a super-diverse university. In P. Cunningham (ed.), *Identities and Citizenship Education: Controversy, Crisis and Challenges*, 538–51. London: Institute for Policy Studies in Education.

Wilken, L. 2011. *Bourdieu for begyndere* [Bourdieu for beginners; 2nd ed.]. Frederiksberg: Samfundslitteratur.

Wilken, L., and Dahlberg, M. 2016. Navigating global space of tertiary education and ending up in Denmark: Educational strategies of mobile students. *COMCAD Working Papers* 146.

Wilken, L., and Tange, H. 2011. *Internationalisation and social practice within the field of Danish higher education.* Project application submitted to the Danish Independent Research Council (Humanities).

Wilken, L., and Tange, H. 2014. Internationalisering og progression [Internationalisation and progression]. *Dansk Universitetspædagogisk Tidsskrift* 9 (17), 20–29.

Wong, J. 2004. Are the learning styles of Asian international students culturally or contextually based? *International Education Journal* 4 (4), 154–66.

Woods, P., Barker, M., and Hibbins, R. 2011. Tapping the benefits of multicultural group work: An exploratory study of postgraduate management students. *International Journal of Management Education* 9 (2), 59–70.

Wu, S. 2002. Filling the pot or lighting the fire? Cultural variations in conceptions of pedagogy. *Teaching in Higher Education* 7 (4), 387–95.

Yates, L., and Trang, N. 2012. Beyond a discourse of deficit: The meaning of silence in the international classroom. *International Education Journal: Comparative Perspectives* 11 (1), 22–34.

Yershova, Y., DeJaeghere, J., and Mestenhauser, J. 2000. Thinking not as usual: Adding the intercultural perspective. *Journal of Studies in International Education* 4 (1), 39–78.

Zhou, Y., Jindal-Snape, D., Topping, K., and Todman, J. 2008. Theoretical models of culture shock and adaptation in international students in higher education. *Studies in Higher Education* 33 (1), 63–75.

Zhou, Y., Knoke, D., and Sakamoto, I. 2005. Rethinking silence in the classroom: Chinese students' experiences of sharing indigenous knowledge. *International Journal of Inclusive Education* 9 (3), 287–311.

Ziguras, C. 2016. The five stages of Brexit grief for universities. *University World News*, October 14.

Index

Note: Page numbers in **bold** refer to tables and *italics* refer to figures.

Printed in Great Britain
by Amazon

45642678R00117